# Theories of Visual Perception

IAN E. GORDON
*University of Exeter*

## JOHN WILEY & SONS

Chichester · New York · Brisbane · Toronto · Singapore

Copyright © 1989 by John Wiley & Sons Ltd.

Reprinted October 1989
Reprinted August 1990
Reprinted December 1991
Reprinted May 1993

*British Library Cataloguing in Publication Data*

Gordon, Ian E.
  Theories of visual perception
  1. Visual perception
  I. Title
  152.1'4

ISBN 0 471 92195 5 (cloth)
ISBN 0 471 92196 3 (paper)

Printed and bound in Great Britain by
Antony Rowe Ltd, Chippenham, Wiltshire

Theories of Visual
Perception

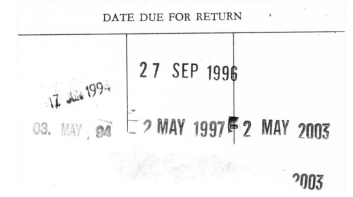

*For*
*Jenny and Charles*
*Tessa, Harry and Malcolm*

# Acknowledgements

I thank my third-year students of the past few years for their enthusiasm, helpfulness and good-humoured tolerance.

Alan Staniland, my former teacher, introduced me to the pleasures of studying perception: I am permanently in his debt.

Bob Brown and Michael Howe of the Exeter department have been generous with their advice.

My main thanks go to my friend and colleague, Dave Earle. He and I have shared a large portion of the perception teaching at Exeter for several years. This has been an enduring pleasure and I thank him for all his many kindnesses, not the least of which has been the care and patience with which he has read and commented upon most of the main sections of this book. Chapter 10 was entirely his idea, but his influence extends far beyond this.

# Contents

# Preface

This book is about theorizing in perception, with particular reference to vision. It is aimed at advanced undergraduate psychology students, but has been written in such a manner that it should be of interest to students in related disciplines such as philosophy and physiology. It is hoped that it will also be of use to others who are interested in the phenomena of seeing, but who lack formal training in experimental science.

Perception is a rewarding subject to teach. It would be a dull person who did not respond with wonder when shown some of the remarkable things which the senses can do. And to be trained to observe perception at work in daily life can have a permanent effect on one's awareness. The formal study of perception brings one into contact with some of the best scientific minds of the past and present: this book describes three pieces of research which have won the Nobel Prize.

Perceptual effects tend to be highly reliable. A demonstration which has worked in the laboratory will not fail in front of an audience. As the subject matter of perception seems to be inherently interesting, the phenomena highly reliable and easy to demonstrate, the teacher is in a most fortunate position. Perceptual experiments tend not to be very complicated (although the equipment may be) and students can quickly learn to appreciate even the most advanced pieces of research.

It is also true to say that although modern perceptual research is basically scientific and experimental, a background in the arts is not a major disadvantage to the student. Provided he or she can acquire some basic knowlege of the physics of stimuli, the biology of the nervous system, and the essentials of experimental design, the world of perceptual research and theory is there to be explored. What is more, whilst knowledge of art and literature is not itself a qualification for entrance to academic perception courses, such knowledge can be invaluable later. Scientists have never had a monopoly of interest in, for example, colour vision. Knowing what the Impressionists were trying to do can yield insights into this aspect of vision which are as interesting as any gained from formal experiments.

Once a visual phenomenon has been discovered it is customary to publish it together with a tentative hypothesis as to its causes. Here too first- and second-year undergraduate students usually cope quite well; most explanations at this level are quite lucid and convincing—journal editors see to that.

Students' difficulties commonly begin when they attempt to learn about the more general theories of perception. For example, any moderately diligent student can come to terms with the differences between Three-Factor and Opponent-Process theories of colour vision (dealt with in Chapter 5). Equally, it is not hard to master the explanation of the perception of contours in terms of neural processes in the retina. But it may be very hard to accept that general theories of visual perception (the main subject of this book) can differ as markedly as do, for example, the Gestalt Theory, Ecological Optics, and the Computational Theory of Vision. These major theories, to be discussed later, approach the same cluster of phenomena in very different ways and seek to explain them using very different concepts. Why should this be so? Why do we find major differences in the style of exposition, the terminology, and the level of explanation—which can vary from mathematical to neural to philosophical? Which is the best general theory? Is it possible to create an amalgam of the successful parts of different theories?

Questions of this sort, which seem perfectly fair, eventually encouraged me to organize a new third-year seminar at Exeter. This had the title, 'Theories of Perception', and during the next few years I and some able undergraduates wrestled with a variety of general theories, particularly those relating to visual perception. Things went quite well until the time came to introduce Marr's book *Vision* as a topic for discussion. This struck most students (and me) as a difficult work, something which stretched us considerably. I therefore began to circulate some notes of my own on the Computational approach to vision. Student feedback led to the refinement of these until it seemed worth expanding them into a chapter-length exposition. But in order to arrive at a balanced evaluation of Marr's work it became necessary to revise my thoughts on some of the rival approaches to visual perception. *Theories of Visual Perception* grew from there.

Preliminary versions of all the main parts of this book have been commented upon by three generations of students. It is hoped that the resulting account of seven major theoretical approaches will be sufficiently clear to help any student studying perception at university level. The choice of theories will display the sheer variety of attacks on the problem of how we see the world, and the inclusion of work from the past should do something to explain the origins of this variety.

Those who study visual perception in a modern psychology department are in the fortunate position of being able to get their hands on the apparatus necessary to generate most of the interesting phenomena of vision. But not all readers will be as fortunate as this. For them, I have gone to some pains to try to describe the key phenomena as clearly as possible, so that they will appreciate the theoretical explanations which follow. Many procedural details are also made quite explicit and I have not hesitated to introduce additional basic material where this might help. Thus what is basically a fairly advanced undergraduate text will, I hope, contain enough clear descriptions to permit lay readers to appreciate some of what is going on in the study of visual perception. Some technical work is very hard to describe briefly and lucidly; this will become apparent in the descriptions of certain crucial experimental tests of some of the theories. However, I have done my best. The references listed at the end of each chapter will be helpful as they commonly contain fuller descriptions than there is space for in this book.

In these ways I hope to have opened up the fascinating problem of explanation in visual perception to a wider audience than is usual. More experienced readers will always know when to skip particular sections.

Regrettably, I have had no formal training in philosophy: the emphasis in this book is always upon experimental psychology. But the problem of explaining vision leads inevitably in the direction of philosophy. After all, the key questions any perceptionist should have in mind are: What can we know about the external world; How do we come by this knowledge? So whilst this is not a philosophical text, many of the questions raised are of a philosophical nature. But the thing about philosophical questions is that they are hard to answer. My goal is to interest the reader in some of the deeper problems of perception, but I do not offer any easy solutions: there are none.

# Chapter 1

# Introduction to the various theories of visual perception

There are many theories of visual perception. Few psychologists know them all; no teaching department includes more than a small subset in its perception courses. And the theories are often very different from each other—a fact which can prove perplexing to students. In this short introductory chapter an attempt will be made to explain why theories concerned with a single sense—vision— should differ so markedly in their style and content. The bias towards visual in general theories of perception is also explained. The chapter is intended to provide a general orientation, particularly for those who are new to the study of visual perception and whose knowledge is grounded in areas other than psychology, such as philosophy, physiology, or the visual arts.

We shall begin with a few general remarks about theories, particularly as they have developed in psychology and related disciplines. Note that the remarks represent a very great oversimplification of the continuing debate about the nature of scientific theories. Further, some of the work to be described later in the book does not strictly qualify for the label 'theory': we shall include some very general approaches to perception, such as psychophysics and artificial intelligence, which are of great intellectual and technical importance, but which could be adopted by workers approaching the problems of visual perception from different theoretical starting points. Nevertheless, these general approaches are used in attempts to explain the phenomena of vision; for this reason they are appropriate subjects for discussion.

The following account aims merely to form an appropriate framework for subsequent evaluations of perceptual theories. Readers who wish to learn more about current thinking in the philosophy of science should consult the references given at the end of the chapter.

## SCIENTIFIC THEORIES AND THE STUDY OF PERCEPTION

The majority of those who have worked on perceptual problems have adopted the standards and assumptions of experimental science. That is to say, whenever they have theorized about phenomena they have attempted to meet certain accepted scientific criteria. These may be briefly summarized.

(1) Theories should offer economical accounts of a range of facts. A theory is not much use if a description of it is as long as that required to describe the relevant phenomena.

(2) Theories should attempt to explain phenomena, or at least suggest causal links between them.

(3) Theories should be testable. They should be stated in such a manner that deductions can be derived and tested empirically.

These points may be illustrated by reference to a perceptual theory, the Young–Helmholtz theory of colour vision.

Humans can see several million different colours. And our colour vision is *trichromatic* in that all the colours we can see can be generated by suitable mixtures of three primary lights. One of the first scientific theories of colour vision, the Young–Helmholtz theory, used the remarkable fact of trichromacy as its starting point. The theory (which will be described more fully in Chapter 5) clearly satisfies the first of the above criteria. Colour vision is described in terms of three mathematical curves, each representing the absorption properties of a hypothetical receptor in the eye. The curves are, in effect, an elegant way of summarizing human colour sensitivity.

But the Young–Helmholtz theory also attempts to *explain* colour vision. It holds that there are three types of receptor in the eye, each sensitive to a portion of the spectrum, and it is the combined activity of these receptors which underlies colour sensitivity and explains why this is trichromatic. The theory meets the second of the listed criteria.

The Young–Helmoltz theory is no longer accepted as a completely adequate theory of colour vision. It cannot account for changes in the appearance of coloured lights when their intensity changes; it does not explain why yellow appears always as a unitary, primary, colour even when it has been formed by mixing red and green light; it has difficulty in accounting for certain forms of human colour deficiency. The theory is obviously testable and therefore meets the last of the above criteria.

Most theories of perception have this in common: like the Young–Helmholtz theory they attempt to satisfy the basic criteria listed above. For this reason they merit the label 'scientific'. But it is important to state here that theories of perception are in other ways very different from each other. This will become very apparent in subsequent chapters.

## THE ORIGINS OF THEORIES

In the history of experimental psychology one can see very different approaches to the activity of theorizing. In one tradition the curiosity of researchers is triggered by the discovery of a new phenomenon. As more is learned about the phenomenon it becomes possible to offer explanatory hypotheses. These become broader, stimulating the search for related phenomena and tying them together. Eventually a theory emerges. This Baconian approach to science was endorsed by one of the founders of experimental psychology, Gustave Fechner (1801–1887), who recommended that in the study of aesthetics one should start 'from below'; in other words, do simple, analytic studies from which general patterns may emerge. Many examples of this continuing tradition will be seen in subsequent chapters; it will be very noticeable in the accounts to be given of psychophysics and neurophysiological theories.

There is, however, a diametrically opposed tradition of theorizing in experimental psychology, one in which the starting point may be a philosophical belief that something must be the case; that the fundamental nature of human perception or thought is such that certain experimental outcomes are only to be expected: they are merely confirmations of a theory which depends upon some reasoned analysis of human capacities or behaviour.

A good example of such theorizing 'from above' is the work by Piaget (e.g. 1967) into children's reasoning. Many readers will have some familiarity with the famous demonstrations in which, for example, it can be shown that children of a certain age think that if a lump of clay is rolled out into a long shape, this shape contains more clay. Or that liquid poured from a squat vessel into a tall thin one increases in volume. But Piaget's theory of intellectual development (including the development of perception) did not *arise from* such simple experiments. It was his views on the nature of logic and thought that prompted his demonstrations. It is as if (to use a hypothetical and non-Piagetian example) an analyis of arithmetic in logical terms showed that addition is more basic than, and prior to, multiplication; that the one must exist before the other is possible. Then if this is true about the logic, must it not also be true of the users of the logic? So, one would expect children to be able to master these mathematical skills only in the right order. It is in this sense that Piaget's demonstrations are *confirmations*: they represent an extrapolation of an epistemological theory to the intellectual development of the child.

In Chapter 3 we shall see something of this approach when considering the work of the Gestalt theorists. To some extent it can be said that these workers arrived at a conception of what perceivers are really like, that the functioning of the nervous system is such that the world is seen in the only way possible. Then in Chapter 7 it will be shown how a major challenge to accepted views of perception stemmed from a critical analysis of these views and a desire to replace them with what seemed like a truer account of perception. In both these cases the thinking is really more important than the experimental research; the experiments are really demonstrations rather than sources of new hypotheses.

A third source of theory is one which is stressed less frequently in formal treatments of the philosophy of science or the history of psychology. This is the influence upon research and theory of new techniques and methods of analysis. Techniques do not exert a direct influence upon theorizing, rather they open up new possibilities for the exploration of phenomena which in turn can provoke new explanations.

In the early 1950s the first twin-track tape recorders became available. This now seems like a fairly small technical advance. But it was such a machine that allowed Cherry (1953) to conduct his famous experiments on dichotic listening in which he showed, for example, that a person who is shadowing a message in one ear may learn very little about a message delivered simultaneously to the other: although the sex of the speaker can be identified, the language they are speaking, for example English or German, will not be noticed. This single demonstration stimulated a host of similar studies, and these led eventually to Broadbent's widely influential Filter Theory of attention (Broadbent, 1958).

Research on personality and intelligence has made intensive use of the technique of Factor Analyis. Without this statistical method it is very doubtful whether it would have been possible to detect the underlying regularities to be found in batteries of test scores. Now there are theories both of intelligence and personality which are couched in the technical language of factor analyis: the factors which are a basic part of the technique have been adopted as psychological explanatory constructs within major theories.

Good examples of the influence of technique will appear in later chapters, particularly in discussions of psychophysics, neurophysiological theories, and the computational approach to visual perception.

A final stimulus to theorizing is the availability of models. This will be dealt with more fully below. For now it suffices to note that models have had a very important influence on perceptual theories. In the next chapter we shall describe the impact on psychophysical research of the Theory of Signal Detection. Not only did this provide psychologists with a valuable new technique for the exploration of sensory thresholds, it suggested a new model for the observer, a model which was rapidly adopted in several different areas of enquiry.

## DIFFERENCES BETWEEN THEORIES OF VISUAL PERCEPTION

At this point we will attempt to explain why theories of perception are commonly so different from one another. There are many theories within the area of visual perception which can be described as specific or local. These include, for example, theories concerned with certain aspects of colour, movement, acuity and depth perception. As these areas of perception are very different from one another, it is hardly surprising that they require very different explanations: the theories differ because the phenomena they seek to explain are themselves very different. But there are also several general theories of perception, and here too one finds great variety of style and content. This is perhaps more surprising. At least three different reasons can be given for this variety.

First there is the influence which the past exerts upon the present. It will be shown later how, for example, the recognition of serious flaws in knowledge-based models of perception led some theorists to concentrate upon the environment in an attempt to show that it provides stimulation of such richness that objects and events may be perceived directly, without the involvement of reasoning and inference. The recoil from a theory which seems to be basically wrong in its assumptions may encourage theorists to produce something very different.

A second reason concerns the availability of models. Much scientific thought has been shaped, directly or indirectly, by the models or metaphors currently available to theorists. For example, in the 1640s Descartes was developing what were to become very influential views on the mind–body problem. The essence of Cartesian Dualism is that the human body is a physical machine controlled by the mind. This control is exercised by 'animal spirits' flowing through channels in the body, with the pineal gland in the brain forming the point where the body interacts with the mind or soul. It is interesting to ask what physical models would have been known to Descartes at the time he was writing his *Discourse on Method*. The answer is that in the Royal Parks of France were a number of remarkable automata. These were mechanical human figures driven by water pressure and connected to hidden pipes in such a manner that the weight of people crossing adjacent flagstones caused them to move. Familiarity with these ingenious machines (which are mentioned in his writings) contributed significantly to Descartes' thoughts on dualism.

The nineteenth century was a period of great social change. The full impact of the new technology had created the large industrial cities of the western world. Pockets of discontent throughout Europe convinced many that social revolution was imminent. Indeed, a new stereotype emerged: the bomb-throwing anarchist. During this same period the most widely admired and influential model of brain function—that proposed by the neurologist Hughlings Jackson (1835–1911)—stated that the function of the most recently evolved, 'higher' centres of the brain was to exert control over the older and more primitive functions of the remainder.

> 'When the highest centres were damaged there was a release of the lower functions. In normal functioning the highest centres were 'protected' and partially insulated from the lower; in cases of brain damage they were the first to suffer dissolution.'
>
> (Hearnshaw 1964)

Substitute 'revolution' for 'damage' and 'social classes' for 'centres', then it seems quite possible that this model of the brain is more than a neutral account of clinical and anatomical data. It may be revealing some of the hidden anxieties of an upper-class British scholar.

The early behaviourists formulated a model of learning in which the results of experience changed connections between stimuli and responses. This new approach to learning was undoubtedly influenced by a new invention: the telephone exchange.

For the past twenty years psychological theorists in a variety of areas have based their models upon the modern digital computer. The result is that much contemporary description within psychology is peppered with terms such as *stages, retrieval, control, content-addressable memory, buffer memory, information*, and so on. For some, the computer has become an intriguing and indispensable model of the human brain.

No wonder that, with such very different models available to influence thinking, psychologists and others should have produced such a variety of theories. Nowhere is this effect more noticeable than in theories of visual perception.

A third reason why general theories of perception should show such great variation in style and language needs a slightly fuller discussion. We need to consider what it is that a general theory of visual perception is trying to do. Figure 1.1 is a simple diagram of a perceiver in an environment. The diagram shows various regions which are commonly delineated by researchers. Each region may be described quite briefly.

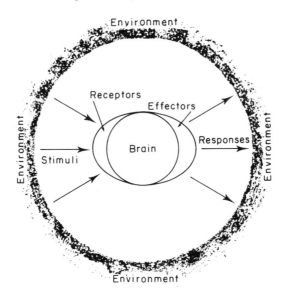

Figure 1.1   The regions of interest to perceptual theorists. (1) the environment, (2) incoming stimulation, (3) receptor surfaces and the peripheral sensory nervous system, (4) the brain, (5) peripheral effector processes, (6) motor responses by the perceiver

1. The environment. This is the physical world of surfaces and objects which we assume to have an existence independent of the perceiver. When this region is studied, it is typically described as the organism's *ecology*. To date, the study of ecologies has been the province of geologists, geographers and biologists, but this is an area of increasing relevance to the psychologist.

2. Incoming stimuli. Objects in the world give rise to events, some of which can be detected by perceivers. Knowledge of the important properties of stimuli has come mainly from physics (light, sound, heat, pressure) and chemistry (volatile substances).

3. Sensory surfaces and peripheral neurons. Before a perceiver can respond to stimuli there must be a change whereby stimulus energy becomes converted into a neural code. It is important to know the nature of this transduction: how light is absorbed by the eye, how changes in frequency affect the ear, how substances are absorbed by the nasal membranes. Important questions concern the pathways taken by neural messages, the codes which are used to represent differences in quality, intensity and duration, and the interactions which take place between neurons. Anatomists and physiologists have sought answers to these questions for more than a century, and are still doing so.

4. The brain. The problems here are almost too obvious to list. Most behaviour depends upon brain processes, but these are commonly not available to direct study and must be explored indirectly—by making inferences from behaviour. Indeed, the whole of the activity labelled Psychology can be viewed as an attempt to gain insights into how brains perform their functions. Very often, and for good reasons, the term Mind has been preferred to Brain. We shall not become enmeshed in the notorious Mind/Brain problem; rather we shall bypass it in subsequent expositions, noting simply that mind and its relation to brain has been the subject of lengthy debate by psychologists and philosophers, whilst the direct study of the brain has been the province of neurophysiologists and neuroanatomists, some of whose work will be described later in this book.

5. Effector systems. Organisms make explicit responses. Stimuli trigger numerous kinds of events in the body. For example, the pupil constricts in response to light; careful study of this response has enabled researchers to detect which wavelengths of light animals are or are not sensitive to. And in Chapter 6 reference will be made to the effects of very brief visual exposures of taboo words on the sweat rate of the palm. This can be used as a sign that the words have been detected and that they have induced emotional responses in the subject.

6. Motor responses. Perceivers are not passive, they move around in the world and in this way partially determine the stimulation they receive. The quickest action any human is capable of is an eye movement. What triggers and guides these movements and what role do they play in perceiving? It has been discovered, for example, that the eye takes in much less information during an eye movement than when it is stationary. We make eye movements which are abrupt and ballistic (in that once started they cannot be stopped) and also

movements which are smoothly graded: what guides the selection of appropriate movements? This area of research has been dominated by psychologists and physiologists.

At a more general level, the study of motor activity is simply the study of the behaviour: what organisms actually do. And this is, of course, the major concern of experimental psychology.

Finally, the environment. The behaviour of organisms does not take place in a vacuum, but in the world. And so this classification ends where it began: with the physical world in which living things dwell and which they act upon in so many different ways.

The foregoing is merely a sketch, an oversimplification, and as such it must not be taken too seriously. Indeed, as schemes such as Figure 1.1 cannot be arrived at in a theoretically neutral manner, they are doubly dangerous. For example, it will be stated in later chapters that there are those who hold that movement of the observer is a vital component of perceiving and that to delineate the motor aspect of perception as a separate 'region' does violence to the truth. Nevertheless, although our classificatory scheme begs some important theoretical questions, we shall use it as a way of highlighting important characteristics of particular theories. One thing the scheme does is to help explain the variety to be found among those theories of perception to have emerged during the first 100 years of experimental psychology.

For a theory to have any psychological relevance it will refer directly or indirectly to region 4, the brain. It must, for the brain is the seat of all psychological functions. But there is something else which can be noted about general perceptual theories and how these differ from theories which are of psychological interest but belong mainly to physics, chemistry, physiology or anatomy. This point will be defended in subsequent chapters; for now we shall simply assert that, commonly, the greater the number of regions of Figure 1.1 to be included in a theory, the more that theory tends to be general in form. This is almost a tautology. But, as will be shown, *the particular subset of possible regions among which underlying relationships are sought differs from theory to theory*. It is this fact which makes general perceptual theories so confusingly varied, as a few examples will show.

Consider first theories which are somewhat restricted in focus. Three-factor theories of colour vision (which will be described more fully in a later chapter) state that there are three pigments in the cone cells of the eye, each maximally sensitive to a particular region of the visible spectrum. Each theory clearly attempts to link two parts of Figure 1.1: incoming stimuli and activity at the receptor surface. The brain is also involved, of course, because the theory is attempting to explain part of our general response to light. But three-factor theories are not general theories, even of colour vision. They explain the appearance only of what are described as 'film colours': the colours we see when looking at surfaces through narrow apertures. Three-factor theories cannot predict the appearance of coloured textured surfaces, nor can they explain how we see objects as having stable colours under different illuminants. The theories cannot do these things because, in their present form, they do not embrace enough regions of Figure 1.1 to enable them to do so.

The same generalization applies to theories in senses other than vision. For example, an advance in our understanding of pain has come from a theory which attempts to explain some important pain phenomena in terms of possible interactions among sensory neurons in the spine. Of course, the theory arose from thinking about a very important psychological experience: pain itself. And the fully developed theory has an important cognitive component. But the central, novel, part of the theory is about how neurons in the spine inhibit or amplify each other's behaviour in a manner which psychological and neurological evidence seems to demand. The theory does ultimately address the question of remedial pain procedures, thus relating neural function to experience. But this is not its main job, which is to give a plausible account of how certain interactions between neurons could achieve certain outcomes, given what is known about their individual functions. Not surprisingly, the theory is couched in the language of neural function, rather than subjective experience. And it is clearly not a general perceptual theory. It cannot, for example, explain individual or cultural differences in pain responsiveness, nor does it deal with the important problem of what initiates the neural pain response in the first place.

Now consider another group of related phenomena and the different ways in which they can be approached theoretically. As an object recedes from a perceiver the angle it subtends at the eye diminishes in a lawful manner. This simple fact is known from the application of geometry to aspects of the physical world (regions 1 and 2). The same geometry (using the theorem of similar triangles) permits the calculation of corresponding changes in the size of retinal images (region 3). These are different regions of course, but in this case the manner in which the effects of distance on stimulation are described is not really important. Descriptions of things and events in regions 1, 2 and 3 can be rendered essentially equivalent.

We can now ask about the size of the smallest stimulus which a person can detect: how far can the object recede (or shrink) before it becomes invisible? This obviously involves the sizes of visual angles and their corresponding retinal images (regions 2 and 3). Either description will do for most purposes, unless we wish to relate detection to the number of cells per unit area of the retina, in which case image size may be the more convenient. Note that we cannot use object size alone as an adequate description: a tree at 100 metres subtends roughly the same angle as one's thumb. And whilst the brain (region 4) clearly plays a vital part in threshold performance, this performance is commonly described only in terms of visual angles or retinal image sizes.

However, when someone is asked to estimate or match the apparent size of a receding object, it is usually found that, within wide limits, *perceived size is not affected by distance*. This phenomenon is known as Size Constancy and will be cited frequently in later chapters for it raises interesting theoretical issues. But note that any perceptual theory which attempts to explain size constancy (and other phenomena of perceptual stability) cannot do so if analyis is limited solely to one or two regions of Figure 1.1. This is because at least four regions are involved: the world, in which objects approach and recede from the eye and which forms the context in which they are seen (region 1), accompanying changes in stimulation (regions 2 and 3) and central factors (region 4) which are needed to explain (a) how perceivers manage to compensate for the shrinking visual image and (b) how artists who wish to depict the three-dimensional world are able to overcome constancy and respond to the true visual angles of things. And as size constancy is stronger when the observer is free to move his or her head and eyes, a complete account of the phenomenon will also have to include the contribution made by the motor system (regions 5 and 6).

Although general theories of perception never attempt to relate *all* the regions defined in Figure 1.1, most are concerned with more than two. Which regions are focused upon depends upon the attitude and assumptions of the theorist. These differ, and it is this possibility of choice which is largely responsible for the great variety amongst perceptual theories generally and theories of vision in particular.

## THEORIES OF VISUAL PERCEPTION

The title of this book requires a little explanation. A fairer title might be 'Some theories ...', for it has been possible to describe only seven major theoretical approaches. And of these only one is exclusively visual in its domain—the computational approach to vision. The remainder all include some discussion of perception in other modalities. But the title 'Theories of Visual Perception' was chosen deliberately. All the general theoretical approaches to be described focus much more closely on vision than any other sense. In fact, removal of the visual content from any of the theories would reduce each to a very short statement. Why should this be so?

One answer is that we are a species in whom the visual sense is strikingly dominant. Touch is important, particularly in establishing our earliest emotional ties, and few would wish to live without hearing—not to be able to converse or listen to music would be a tragic loss for all of us. But our waking experience is largely visual. In fact, 'waking up' is mainly opening our eyes and noticing things. To lose consciousness is essentially to stop seeing (we stop hearing also, but this isn't what we remember about it). All this is mirrored in our language: for example, the ensemble of adjectives available to describe the visual appearance of things far exceeds that available for describing their sounds or smells. The bias among theories of perception is merely a natural reflection of the dominance of vision in those perceivers about whom we are most curious: ourselves.

There is a second, rather more trivial reason why visual phenomena dominate work in perception: the stimuli are easier to produce. In later chapters numerous examples will be given of important discoveries which have been made using remarkably simple visual stimuli. These are often no more complicated than carefully drawn lines, narrow beams of pure light, or simple clusters of dots. Provided these can be displayed under carefully controlled conditions, major explorations of visual function become possible. In fact, in the remainder of this book probably the most complicated single stimulus to be referred to is a picture of a human face.

The situation in other modalities is not as fortunate. Substances for quantitative research into the sense of smell must be blasted up into the nasal passages. Controlled pain induction requires quite elaborate procedures. Production of sound stimuli with precisely controlled duration, frequency, intensity and phase requires expensive equipment. Suppose, for example, one wished to deliver two words to a subject, one to each ear, and that it was important that the words arrived exactly simultaneously, it could take several days (and some fancy electronics) to set up the experiment. Contrast this with the ease with which pairs of words can be displayed visually.

The theories to be discussed are mainly concerned with visual aspects of perception because this is the sense which has received the most research attention in the past 100 years. In showing which phenomena each theory handles well or badly it is inevitable that this long-standing bias towards vision will reappear.

## THE ORGANIZATION OF THE FOLLOWING CHAPTERS

Chapter 2 gives an account of psychophysical research and theory, with particular emphasis on theories of the threshold. Of the seven theoretical approaches to be described, this is the narrowest in focus. However, many of the data used in current thinking on vision have been discovered by psychophysical measurement. Equally importantly, the true nature of sensory thresholds is not yet known with certainty. It is interesting that this should still be subject to research and debate, for it was the measurement of a sensory threshold which launched the new discipline of experimental psychology: Chapter 2 covers a century of research into sensory thresholds.

Chapters 3 and 4 describe two older theories, Gestalt Theory and Egon Brunswik's Probabilistic Functionalism. The Gestalt approach to perception is justly famous and although the original form of the theory does not now have many adherents, many of the phenomena which Gestaltists highlighted still attract research and debate. Probabilistic functionalism, however, did not achieve widespread popularity. But it was the first theory to stress the probabilistic nature of perceiving, the importance of the perceiver's ecology and the role of evolution in the development of perception. Probabilistic functionalism foreshadowed several important contemporary developments in perception.

Chapter 5 describes the neurophysiological approach to visual perception. Replacing hypothetical constructs by possible neural mechanisms has always appealed to some theorists. And there has long been a two-way traffic between psychology and neurophysiology, in that discoveries about the nervous system cannot fail to exert some influence upon psychologists; at the same time, the work of neurophysiologists commonly represents an attempt to explain phenomena discovered in psychological research. Some of the most recent theorizing about vision, for example the computational approach to be discussed in Chapter 8, relies heavily on recent neurophysiological discoveries, some of which will be described.

Chapter 6 presents a summary of what has been the most popular and successful approach to perception: the Empiricist or Constructivist paradigm. This maintains that perception resembles thinking. The perceiver is considered to act as an intuitive scientist, making and testing hypotheses about the world on the basis of inadequate or distorted sensory evidence. The adoption of the computer as a model of the brain (or mind) was a very natural step in the history of empiricism: the value of this model is discussed in this chapter and in Chapter 8.

Chapter 7 describes a new paradigm for perception: Direct Perception or Ecological Optics. J. J. Gibson's work, and its subsequent extensions, challenges many of the assumptions of empiricism and argues that stimulation is sufficiently rich in information about the world to permit that world to be perceived directly, without the need for intervening constructional stages.

Chapter 8 is an account of the computational approach to vision, as exemplified by the work of David Marr. Marr's theory of vision derives from Artificial Intelligence and is considered by some to be the most important theoretical development of recent years. Marr develops a framework for the analysis of any process, including vision. His work helps us to appreciate some of the strengths and weaknesses of previous approaches to the study of vision.

Chapter 9 offers some general comments on theorizing in visual perception. An attempt is made to show how knowledge of the successes and failures of the various general theories of visual perception might be used to guide subsequent theorizing. The question of what a theory of visual perception should attempt to achieve is discussed and certain fundamental difficulties are highlighted. Chapter 10 should be read as a coda to the main book. It contains some puzzles for the reader to ponder.

## NOTES ON CHAPTER 1

The following references may be helpful introductions to theory in science generally and psychology in particular.

Chalmers (1982). This is a very good introduction to scientific explanation generally, with some reference to problems within psychology.

Churchland (1984). This is a short but useful paperback outlining modern thinking on the philosophy of mind.

Quine and Ullian (1970). This describes the ways in which science is based upon belief. It is a very good book.

# Chapter 2

# Psychophysics and the concept of the threshold

Psychophysics is not a theory of perception; rather it is a set of techniques which experimental psychologists have developed over many years in order to measure sensory and perceptual thresholds (the distinction between these will become clear later). In essence, a psychophysical procedure requires (a) a set of stimuli, displayed under carefully controlled conditions and (b) a subject or observer (a more common term in this area), who is instructed to make one of a restricted number of responses; it could hardly be more simple. And yet, much of what is known about the workings of the various perceptual systems in humans and animals has been discovered by applying psychophysical techniques. Indeed, most of the data to be described in the remainder of this book have come from experiments using techniques drawn from the psychophysical repertoire. This has been a very impressive achievement: to have made important discoveries about the workings of the nervous system without entering or tampering with that system has been one of the most notable contributions of experimental psychology. It is more than a century since the results of the first psychophysical experiment were published, and yet this method of investigation is still in use in laboratories throughout the world.

There are four reasons why it is appropriate to start the main part of this book with a review of psychophysics. First, the review will reveal the source of much of the data which theories of perception must explain. Second, the historical treatment of psychophysics will be a useful background for the later treatments of general theories. Third, psychophysics has done more than simply provide techniques for the exploration of the senses: it has given rise to theories of the threshold. Examining theoretical successes and failures where the phenomena are relatively straightfoward will be a useful preparation for discussions of theories in more complex areas of perception. A final reason for beginning with psychophysics is that it is in this area that theories are closest to data. The limited range of psychophysical theories will be explained later, but for now it can be said that it is in this chapter that those readers who have never carried out a psychological experiment will get the best idea of the flavour of experimental work—how psychologists actually go about the task of discovering new phenomena and forming hypotheses about them.

The main aim of this chapter is to examine the concept of the sensory threshold. To provide orientation in terms of our original classificatory scheme, to measure and explain a threshold is to focus upon the relationship between properties of a stimulus and the sensation or response arising from that stimulus. Thus in terms of the scheme the relevant arc is one connecting physical stimuli arising from the external world with psychological events occurring inside the perceiver, by-passing if necessary the problem of intervening peripheral sensory mechanisms.

It is demonstrably true that there are sounds we cannot hear, objects we cannot see, and odours we cannot smell. We know that these stimuli are present, for we have instruments which can tell us so. And when the strengths of these stimuli are increased we may then be able to detect them. We also know that other species can often detect stimuli which we cannot. Now the question is: What happens as the intensity of a stimulus is raised from a value at which we cannot detect it to one when we can? Is there a value such that the stimulus makes an impact which is simply insufficient to send a message is to the brain, and another, just greater, when the message is transmitted? Is there, in other words, a sensory *threshold*? This is the theoretical problem to be dealt with in this chapter. We shall review the historical development of the concept of the threshold and then try to show why this once dominant idea in perception has been challenged in the past few years.

Perceptual thresholds are related phenomena, although the questions asked may differ. For example an experiment may be designed to discover the minimum time needed to read a word, to assess the number of elements in a pattern or to decide whether two faces are the same or different. The techniques of measurement here are very similar to those used in the estimation of sensory thresholds, but the underlying theory may be very different.

Two main types of sensory threshold have been defined. *Absolute Thresholds* represent the smallest amounts of energy required for stimulus detection and are therefore concerned with the observer's sensitivity. *Relative* or *Difference Thresholds* require discriminations, for example by how much must the intensity of a stimulus be raised in order for the change to be detectable; they are measures of the observer's acuity or resolving power.

The remaining contents of this chapter are organized around five related topics:

(1) Number and measurement.
(2) The creation of psychophysics and the Weber–Fechner law.
(3) The Neural Quantum Theory.
(4) Direct Scaling and the perception of supra-threshold stimuli.
(5) The Theory of Signal Detection.

## NUMBER AND MEASUREMENT

Numbers and measurement play so large a part in twentieth-century life that we tend to take them for granted. Following a little education we are all expected to know the distance to the sun, the atomic weight of hydrogen, the value of the gravitational constant. Children are now routinely taught to count to base 2 as well as to base 10. Many families, probably the majority, are familiar with electronic calculators; a high proportion own computers. No one expresses surprise or admiration when a space vehicle arrives back on earth within minutes of its estimated time of arrival. Our society depends upon a lot of measurement and calculation and we accept this as quite normal.

But imagine the excitement which the discovery of number and measurement must have caused. The ancient Greeks, who had a deep interest in aesthetics, found that if a vibrating string is divided into two equal lengths, each will sound the octave of the original. Dividing the string 3:2 produces the interval of a perfect fifth; 3:4 yields a perfect fourth. How uncanny: simple ratios between small integers produce perfect harmonic intervals. What a strange relationship to have discovered between mathematics and music.

When Greek mathematicians divided the circumference of a circle by the diameter they found the answer to be an irrational number: $\pi = 3.141592654\ldots\ldots$ which never ends and never repeats and is yielded by all circles. The Greeks then discovered that if a line is divided into two portions $a$ and $b$ such that the ratio of $a$ to $b$ equals that of $b$ to the whole (i.e. $a:b = b:a + b$) then this proportion has remarkable properties. A rectangle constructed from such a Golden Section is pleasing; it also has the property that it can be subdivided into other rectangles, the sides of which are all Golden Section (see Figure 2.1). And the formula for the Golden Section can be converted into a simple expression: $(-1 + \sqrt{5})/2$. The solution of this expression to nine decimal places is 0.618033989, the Golden Ratio. Note however that this too is an irrational number (because 5 has no simple integer solution), and now imagine the initial impact of these discoveries: at the heart of a strange and seemingly powerful aesthetic rule—used in the construction of the Parthenon (and the basis of Le Corbusier's Modular 2000 years later)—is another number which is not an integer. Small wonder that the properties of $\sqrt{5}$ became a guarded secret known only to small religious sects.

The interest in measurement and the fascination with numbers persisted over the centuries. From the eighteenth century onwards successful measurement was increasingly the mark of a mature science. Many gains in understanding stemmed from the ability to measure things. Engineers learned how to quantify important properties of materials in terms of the concepts of stress, strain and elasticity. Chemists produced estimates of the atomic weights of elements. Many of the main physical constants, such as gravity, received numerical values. And much important scientific work during the eighteenth and

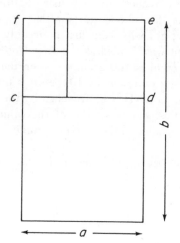

Figure 2.1 The Golden Rectangle. $a : b = 0.618$. If the shorter side ($a$) is projected onto the longer ($b$) a new Golden Rectangle is formed ($c\ d\ e\ f$). This process may be repeated indefinitely

nineteenth centuries made use of a marvellous mathematical tool: the calculus.

So far, however, we have made no reference to the measurement of any *human* attribute. True, certain pioneers had collected data on skull shape and size and attempted to relate these to the cultural and evolutionary development of different peoples (providing a pseudo-scientific basis for future racism), but there had been little or no measurement of what people could do. Then, in 1846, a German physiologist published the results of a simple experiment which was to become the catalyst for the new science of experimental psychology. The experiment had succeeded in measuring a human sensory threshold.

## CLASSICAL PSYCHOPHYSICS AND THE WEBER–FECHNER LAW

E. H. Weber was professor of physiology at Leipzig when he published an account of some experiments on the sense of touch: *Der Tatsinn und das Gemeingefühl*. During these experiments Weber had observers make judgements between pairs of lifted weights. His concern was with the smallest difference which could be detected and how this varied with the absolute magnitude of the weights.

German physiology at that time used some unusual units of weight. We shall therefore illustrate Weber's findings using fictitious data. Basically, what Weber discovered was that if one starts with a standard weight of, say, 10 grammes, a second weight will seem just noticeably heavier if it is raised to 11 grammes; this point was defined as the *Just Noticeable Difference* (JND). But if the standard weight is 100 grammes, then the second weight will need to be raised not by 1 gramme, but by 10, before a difference can be detected. In other words, this other JND is not reached by the addition of a fixed value to the standard stimulus, but is a *ratio* of the value to the standard. These researches were then repeated in the visual and auditory modalities, with similar results.

Weber's finding later became elevated to the status of a law, which is defined as:

$$\frac{\Delta S}{S} = K$$

Where $\Delta S$ is the change in stimulation, $S$ is the magnitude of the standard stimulus and $K$ is a constant for that particular modality. Other *Weber Fractions*, as they became known, included 1 : 50 for the judged lengths of lines, and 1 : 160 for musical tones.

The significance of Weber's research is three-fold. First, he offered a rule which is in use to this day. For example, should a lighting engineer wish to increase the perceived brightness of illumination in part of a room or hall, the relevant Weber fraction is a good guide to what change will be noticeable. Second, Weber had shown how a fundamental property of a sense modality could be discovered by the systematic use of a non-destructive, simple procedure. Third, the extension of Weber's work by Fechner created a new subject, Psychophysics, which was to be of great importance in launching the new science of experimental psychology.

The true nature of the relationship between Weber's data and Fechner's subsequent use of them has been disputed (see Boring, 1950 for a detailed account of the history of psychophysics); this need not concern us here. What is important is the way in which Weber's main finding was interpreted by Gustav Fechner.

Fechner (1801–1887), a successful and established physicist by the age of thirty-three, had an abiding interest in philosophy. It is known (Boring, 1950) that he suffered a breakdown in mid-life and resigned his Chair. Fechner describes how, following his illness, he had an insight which was to change the direction of his career. We shall describe this insight as clearly as possible, again using fictitious data to simplify the account. It is important to remember (a) that actual threshold data are never as clear-cut as the hypothetical ones below, and (b) a constant Weber fraction for weight is assumed: in fact the fraction changes somewhat with absolute stimulus magnitude. These facts do not invalidate the demonstration.

Imagine a determination of a difference threshold for lifted weight. Let the standard be 100 grammes and assume that the Weber fraction in this case is 1 : 10, or 10 per cent. If we follow Weber's simple procedure we shall find that the JND is 10 grammes (10 per cent of the standard). At this point the observer will just be able to feel (reliably) that the two weights differ. Now let us take as the standard a weight of 200 grammes and determine a new difference threshold. With a Weber fraction of 10 per cent the JND should occur at around 220 grammes. We continue with an increasing range of standard stimuli. Weber's Law implies that the following results will be recorded (all units are grammes and have been rounded off):

| Standard stimulus: | 100 | 200 | 300 | 400 | 500 | 600 | 700 |
|---|---|---|---|---|---|---|---|
| JND at : | 110 | 220 | 330 | 440 | 550 | 660 | 770 |

These results can be displayed in an alternative form:

| Stimulus increase to produce JND: | 10 | 20 | 30 | 40 | 50 | 60 | 70 |
|---|---|---|---|---|---|---|---|
| JND step: | 1 | 1 | 1 | 1 | 1 | 1 | 1 |

The key to Fechner's insight is contained in the bottom line of this table. Note that as the change in the standard necessary to produce the JND is growing rapidly, the JND is simply incrementing. As we have said, real experiments never turn out as cleanly as this hypothetical one, but the implications of Weber's Law are unambiguous.

Fechner's insight was this: *JNDs might be sensations*. At one moment the standard and comparison weights cannot be discriminated, they feel the same. But with a slight increase in the weight of the comparison a difference becomes just perceptible. But is not this felt difference a *sensation* of heaviness?

It takes but a little imagination to understand Fechner's excitement so many years ago. Was this the beginning of an answer to one of the age-old problems of philosophy, namely the relation between mind and body, the mental and the physical? To produce incremental, *arithmetic* steps in sensation, the physical stimulus must grow *geometrically*. Measurement had revealed a link between the laws of physics and the laws of the mind; the external and internal worlds could be linked via a simple mathematical equation.

Fechner was the first to write Weber's Law in the form given above. He himself produced new expressions with which to describe the relationship between physical stimulation and subjective response, the best known of which is:

$$\text{Sensation} = C \log \text{Stimulus intensity}$$

In this formula C represents a weighting constant for each modality (including the relevant Weber fraction), and the logarithmic multiplier represents the exponential or geometric growth in stimulus intensity required to yield successive JNDs.

During the remainder of his career Fechner worked on the development of other techniques for the exploration of sensation and perception. Below is a brief description of the main classical psychophysical methods which have evolved and which have proved so valuable in the exploration of the human senses.

## The psychophysical methods

The essence of all methods is that stimuli are presented in a systematic manner and that the observer's task is simplified by requiring of him/her one of only two or three responses. We shall illustrate the three main classical methods with reference to the measurement of a difference threshold, an index of the acuity or resolving power within a sense. It will be easy to see how the techniques could be applied equally well to the measurement of absolute thresholds.

### *The method of limits or minimal changes*

A standard stimulus is selected and the difference threshold assessed by systematically changing the value of a comparison stimulus. For example, suppose we wish to measure the difference threshold for brightness. One way to do this is to select a particular intensity of light for the standard and display this as a lit rectangle. A second rectangle is presented which is noticeably more intense than the first; the observer will be able to say, effortlessly, that this comparison stimulus is brighter. Then the intensity of the comparison stimulus is reduced by a fixed amount and it and the standard are presented again. As this procedure is repeated there will come a time when the observer says that the two stimuli appear the same or equal. Further changes are made to the comparison stimulus until eventually the observer responds by saying that it now looks darker. At this point the trial is stopped and a note made of the points at which the response 'brighter' changed to 'equal', and then to 'darker'. The threshold on this trial is estimated as lying halfway between the two changeover values. On the next trial the variable comparison stimulus is set to a markedly darker value and moved in the other direction towards the standard. These upward and downward trials alternate, with the starting points randomized somewhat to prevent anticipation or counting on the part of the observer. A typical threshold determination will require about twenty trials, which should yield a good estimate of the observer's brightness discrimination in this region of the intensity range.

This procedure is pleasant to use and observers find it simple and sensible. Provided care is taken to control variables such as stimulus duration (observers tend to take much longer to make decisions close to threshold), the method usually yields clean data. Incidentally, a similar procedure, involving only up-ward trials, was once used to test the threshold of detonation of explosives. The variable stimulus in this case being the height from which a detonating weight was dropped (presumably by testers nickamed Lefty).

## The constant method

The essence of the constant method is that the standard stimulus is presented with a particular comparison stimulus for several trials. On each trial the ob-server must say which of the two stimuli is greater (or smaller, louder etc.) The proportion of correct guesses is recorded and then another comparison stimu-lus is chosen and the procedure repeated. The spatial or temporal positions of the standard and comparison stimuli are randomized on each presentation. The threshold is calculated from a plot of comparison stimulus magnitude against the proportion of correct guesses (sometimes using transformed or 'normalized' data for statistical reasons).

## The adjustment method

This is the most straightfoward of all methods. It is very close to the common-sense view of what a threshold should be and is something many of us do in our daily lives when we tune a radio or television receiver.

The adjustment method involves fixing the value of the standard whilst set-ting the comparison stimulus to a value where it is obviously different. Then the observer is instructed to alter the setting of the comparison stimulus until the two stimuli appear equal and the setting is recorded. (Alternatively, the two stimuli may be identical at the start, the observer's task being to adjust the variable comparison stimulus until it appears to be just different.) The observer is not required to make any verbal response: he or she simply keeps altering one of the two stimuli. Several trials are run and average settings used to calcu-late the difference threshold. Averages of the observer's settings form the data from which the difference threshold is calculated. Observers find the adjustment method pleasant and easy.

The classical psychophysical techniques have been refined and added to over the years. *Tracking procedures* vary stimulus values continuously whilst the ob-server attempts to maintain them just around threshold. *Staircase procedures* are based on the Method of Limits, but include decision rules for the selection of stimuli which are based on the observer's immediately preceding perfomance. Under these conditions performance slowly converges upon the threshold value of the stimulus. *Animal psychophysics* involves the use of training procedures which enable the animal to communicate whether or not it is capable of making the required discriminations. In *infant research*, responses that the observer is capable of making, such as sucking, eye-tracking and head turning are used to indicate the presence or absence of discriminations. In several modern applications psychophysical measurement is placed under the control of computers.

The reader who has persisted through all this detail is now almost ready to measure a sensory threshold. Almost, but not quite. In all sensory research it is necessary to take certain precautions. In most visual studies it is necessary to control and measure the room illumination, for that will affect the visual threshold. And one needs to keep the observer under that illumination for a period before the threshold determination in order to adjust his or her light adaptation. And changing the intensity of a visual stimulus is not always completely straightfoward: for example, one cannot just use resistors to dim lights without making sure that the change in temperature of the light source has not produced a corresponding change in colour—tungsten lights get redder as they get dimmer. And the whole question of motivating an observer to endure such prolonged measurement is not without its problems. Nevertheless, the methods described do work and any intelligent person can be taught to use them to produce good scientific data.

Many of the valuable even extraordinary things which we know about perception generally and the senses in particular have stemmed from the application of these basic psychophysical methods. For example, the absolute threshold for light in a dark-adapted human observer is equivalent to detecting a lit candle at a distance of 30 miles. This means that some rod cells of the retina must fire when they have absorbed only one or two quanta of light. As one cannot have less light than one quantum, *the rod cells of the retina must have reached an evolutionary limit*. And psychophysics has also proved that the sensitive hair cells of the inner ear, which are responsible for transducing sound-induced movement into neural impulses, must respond when they move through a distance *less than the diameter of a hydrogen atom*. These are remarkable findings. It would be difficult to overestimate the importance of Weber's and Fechner's contribution to psychology and physiology.

These then are some of the ideas and techniques which launched the new discipline of pychophysics, together with some of the areas which they have illuminated. But although we have described Fechner's aim of finding measurable links between the physical and mental worlds, we have as yet said nothing about his theory of the threshold. It was, after all, a consideration of threshold phenomena which inspired the whole enterprise of classical psychophysics.

## The classical theory of the threshold

As developed by Fechner (and other nineteenth-century workers) the basic concept of the threshold was quite simple. One value of the stimulus produces just insufficient neural energy to trigger a critical event in the nervous system and detection or discrimination does not occur. The next increment of stimulation does trigger the event. Stated so baldly, this is not very different from how we might describe the weight dropping onto the explosive: it is a commonsense interpretation which could be true. And the basic plausibility of the idea is reinforced by a phenomenon many readers will have observed. Following a dental injection only one half of the mouth may be affected. Touching one side of a lip produces no sensation, but moving across the body mid-line suddenly reveals the presence of normal sensitivity in the other half. It is as if a step or threshold has been crossed between these adjacent regions which finer and finer measurement should be able to locate.

Were this simple picture to be true, certain outcomes should follow. For example, suppose that a difference threshold has been measured by gradually increasing the intensity of the comparison stimulus. If the probability of the response 'greater' is plotted as a function of stimulus intensity, then the result should be that displayed in Figure 2.2: the probability will suddenly change from zero to 1.0, yielding the rectilinear plot shown in the figure. Once the threshold has been crossed further increases in the value of the comparison stimulus cannot increase response probabilty; changes below threshold are also without effect.

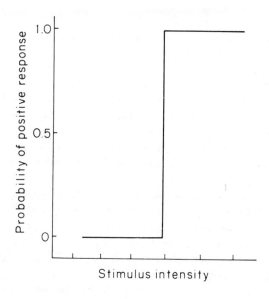

Figure 2.2 The psychophysical function implied by the definition of a threshold as simply a step between two states of sensitivity

Early psychophysicists soon discovered that actual threshold data do not typically match the rectilinear function shown in Figure 2.2. It is much more common to find that they are better fitted by a *sigmoid* or *ogival* function of the form displayed in Figure 2.3. What does this mean? In order to explain

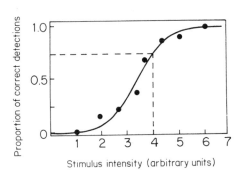

Figure 2.3  Typical threshold results (illustrative data) fitted by an ogive. In this case the threshold is defined as that stimulus value (4) associated with a detection rate of 75 per cent. Compare this function with Figure 2.2

the answer to this question it is necessary to introduce some basic statistical notions. Readers who have some knowledge of simple probability theory and statistics should skip the next short section.

The curve shown in Figure 2.4 is known as the *Normal* or *Gaussian Probability Distribution*. The horizontal axis represents values of a random variable, x, and the vertical axis is the probability density value associated with each value of x. For the present purpose it is necessary to appreciate only two things: (a) as illustrated, the curve in Figure 2.4 is a mathematical abstraction, it does not necessarily represent anything to do with the real world, (b) the curve is designed so that its total area represents a probability of 1.0, and as the curve is symmetrical about a mean value, the areas to the left and right of the mean are equivalent to probabilities of 0.5.

The interest and usefulness of the normal distribution lies in the fact that if we sample from populations in the real world and measure some aspect of the sample which is affected by many random factors, then the resulting frequency distributions commonly have a shape similar to that shown in Figure 2.4. For example, measuring the lengths of leaves from a tree, or heights of persons, or the weights of babies, gives rise to distributions very similar to the normal curve (there are few very large or very small babies, and weights tend to cluster around the average). In such cases, of course, the horizontal axis will represent the values of the measure (length, height, weight, etc.) and the vertical axis will be relative frequency. This relationship, between how things are and a theoretical probability distribution, is at the heart of many statistical techniques for it permits powerful predictions to be made concerning the nature of populations which we know only through samples.

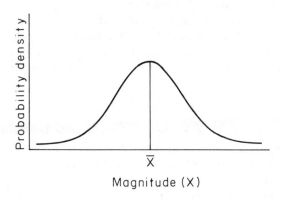

Figure 2.4   The Normal or Gaussian Probability distribution

Suppose now that we select a value to the left of the distribution in Figure 2.4 and record the area of the curve to the left of that value: the result will clearly be zero or thereabouts. Moving along the horizontal axis and recording successive area values yields a plot known as the Integral of the distribution, or the *Cumulative Probability Function*, and its sigmoid or ogival shape is *very similar to that shown in Figure 2.3*.

This resemblance, between actual psychophysical data and a theoretical probability distribution, was all that was needed to form the first theory of threshold performance. Fechner and others claimed that the threshold ogival plot was evidence of random, uncontrolled, factors 'smearing' a rectilinear function and changing its form from that of Figure 2.2 to that of Figure 2.3. The random factors include variation in the actual stimulus due to physical fluctuations, momentary changes in the observer's attention, and other forms of random activity in the receptor or the nervous system. For a correct detection to be possible the stimulus must induce neural activity greater than that arising from all this random activity.

Formally, this essentially statistical interpretation of the threshold is known as the *Phi-Gamma* hypothesis. Various refinements were made to the model outlined above, but the essence of the classical theory is captured by this idea of a real threshold obscured by random uncontrolled events. This interpretation has persisted until modern times; as a result, modern psychophysical data are often plotted in the form shown in Figure 2.3, with the threshold typically defined as that value of the stimulus associated with a response probability of 0.75, which is midway between the levels of pure guessing (0.5) and perfect detection or discrimination (1.0). And there are now statistical techniques, such as Probit Analysis, which assume that the true form of threshold data is the ogive and fit actual results to this function.

Thus the classical view of the threshold, embodied in the phi-gamma hypothesis, has proved doubly valuable, for it suggests how to handle empirical threshold data by curve-fitting analysis, whilst at the same time explaining their origins. The theory's long and successful history is not surprising.

## THE NEURAL QUANTUM THEORY

The classical interpretation of the threshold is plausible and leads to successful ways of handling data which, it must be stressed, are among the most reliable and reproducible in experimental psychology. Why then should this interpretation be challenged?

There is no doubt that some of those whose work will be outlined in this section were influenced by their knowledge of the behaviour of neurons. The all-or-none principle of neural impulse generation is clearly describing a discontinuous process (a neuron either fires or it does not; it never fires 'weakly'). Why then assume that the sensitivity which neurons mediate is a continuous dimension?

It is universally accepted that observers in threshold determinations cannot maintain perfect attention, that they are likely to change over time, and that physical stimuli will vary slightly from trial to trial. But what if these extraneous 'nuisance' variables could be eliminated? Would the true nature of human sensitivity remain essentially continuous, or would the underlying nervous system reveal its abrupt, discontinuous nature? It was thoughts such as these which led some to challenge the classical concept of the threshold.

The theory of the neural quantum was first formalized by Stevens, Morgan and Volkmannn (1941). The theory assumes that sensitivity in the nervous system is discontinuous and is mediated by neural 'quanta'. For the purpose of exposition we shall treat these hypothetical neural quanta as boxes, each triggered when it is filled by a certain fixed amount of stimulus energy.

We may now re-examine the difference threshold situation in terms of the neural quantum theory. Presentation of the standard stimulus excites a number of quanta. Then the comparison stimulus is presented. On the simplest possible quantum model the observer responds 'different' only when this new stimulation excites one additional quantum. (This is rather like a pair of scales in which containers of liquid form the weights, but a new weight can be added only when full.) It follows that the resulting psychophysical function will be a linear one; in fact it will take the form shown in Figure 2.2, in which the probability of the response, 'different', rises abruptly from zero to one. As we have seen, actual threshold data never take this form, so this basic neural quantum model must be refined.

Two additions to the model are necessary in order that it can generate sensible psychophysical functions. The first is an obvious one: there is no reason to suppose that stimulus energy will be delivered in amounts exactly matching neural quanta—why should it? It seems much more likely that the most common effect of stimulation will be to trigger a certain whole number of quanta, with some surplus energy left over. This surplus cannot, by definition, exceed one quantum's worth. The second additional assumption is that the observer's sensitivity varies from moment to moment in a Gaussian manner (refer to Figure 2.4 if this is not clear). These assumptions lead to a very interesting deduction: the various possible amounts of surplus energy, from just greater than zero to just less than one quantum's worth, will be distributed according to a *rectangular* distribution. This is because all amounts are equiprobable. And the integral of a rectangular distribution (its cumulative area) is a linear, not an ogival, function. (Readers who dislike mathematical concepts should not be discouraged, the essence of this result can be captured in diagrams, as will be shown.)

Thus the neural quantum theory states that when a standard stimulus is presented its energy excites a number of discrete quanta plus a variable amount of surplus. Under certain conditions of testing this surplus energy could still be available when the comparison stimulus is delivered. During all this time the observer's sensitivity is varying in a Gaussian manner, so that stimulus energy is having a varied impact, as it were. Threshold task demands are such that the observer will wish to avoid responding 'different' when in fact there is no physical difference between standard and comparison stimuli: observers are usually instructed to 'take care', to 'concentrate', etc. But such an erroneous response must be a risk whenever a momentary increase in the observer's sensitivity coincides with an unusually large surplus from the standard to excite one extra quantum. A conscientious observer is therefore assumed to play safe by adopting a two-quantum criterion, responding 'different' only when the comparison stimulus energizes two additional quanta.

These various assumptions and deductions predict a novel psychophysical function: that shown in Figure 2.5, which is linear but with a definite slope. It is now possible to redefine the threshold in quantum terms. The smallest increment in stimulation which will always produce a 'different' response is assumed to excite two quanta; the largest increment which just never elicits a 'different' response indicates the size of one quantum. The threshold is then calculated by interpolation from the psychophysical function of Figure 2.5 and is defined as the stimulus value associated with 1.5 quanta. Thus the neural quantum theory generates very precise quantitative predictions relating stimulus change and response probability.

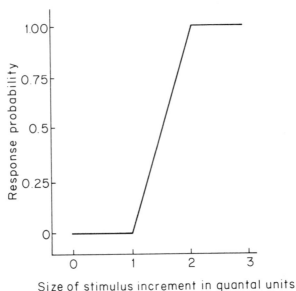

Size of stimulus increment in quantal units

Figure 2.5   The psychophysical function predicted by the modified neural quantum theory

One of the first technical innovations designed to examine the quantum alternative to the classical theory was in fact published before the formal statement of the theory by Stevens *et al*. This was a report by Békèsy (1930), who measured the difference threshold for hearing in the following manner. The observer was presented with a standard tone for 0.3 seconds immediately followed by a comparison tone of different intensity. By minimizing the delay between presentations it was hoped to eliminate the random variations associated with changing attention, sensitivity, and so on. The results of this study are highly interesting. When the percentages of different judgements were plotted as a function of the ratio of change of the comparison stimuli ($\frac{\Delta S}{S}$) *linear* functions were obtained. These were very different from the classical ogives typically obtained in psychophysical experiments, and they raised the possibility that the hearing system responds to intensity changes in a series of discontinuous steps.

Stevens, Morgan and Volkmann (1941) presented continuous tones to their observers, together with brief increments in frequency which occurred every three seconds. The observer's task was to indicate whenever a change of pitch was heard. When percentage detections were plotted against amount of stimulus change, the result was a set of linear functions. Similar linear data were obtained by DeCillis (1944) for the detection of moving stimuli on the skin, and Jerome (1942) for the olfactory detection of a certain smell. In several other published studies it was found that many (although not all) observers generated data which were essentially rectilinear rather than ogival in shape. The neural quantum theory seemed to be receiving a significant amount of empirical support.

## An evaluation of the neural quantum theory

One does not now find many modern references to the neural quantum theory, which came under attack very shortly after it was first published. The criticisms of the theory have taken three forms: methodological, statistical, and theoretical.

### Methodological criticisms

There have been several criticisms of the way in which data favourable to the neural quantum theory have been obtained. First, the attempt to minimize sources of extraneous variation requires that all data from a particular observer be gathered in a single continuous session involving many trials. The incremented stimulus, which the observer is attempting to detect, is often presented repeatedly at the same value over blocks of trials. These are obvious sources of possible bias. Unfortunately, the quantum theory can be tested only by quantum procedures, so that some obvious validation procedures are simply not possible. Finally, it must be stated that attempts to replicate the best-known findings in this area have not always met with success (see Corso, 1970, for an invaluable review).

### Statistical criticisms

These have concentrated upon the curve fitting procedures used in neural quantum research. Commonly, the test as to whether a particular function is best fitted by an ogive or a straight line is a goodness of fit test based upon the chi-square statistic. There have been many instances over the years where psychologists have inadvertently misused the chi-square statistic. More careful curve fitting (described in Corso, 1970) of data gathered in a manner identical with that employed by Stevens *et al.* revealed only a small percentage of cases in which linear functions could be said to provide unique best fits to the data. Similar criticisms have been made of the DeCillis data referred to earlier (Corso, 1970). A long evaluative review by Blackwell (1953) is equally critical of data from quantum experiments. Generally, then, there is some doubt over the status of the empirical support claimed for this theory.

*Theoretical criticisms*

If, as we have stated, the inspiration for the quantum approach to thresholds was the known behaviour of neurons, then this may have been misguided. It is true that the propagation of a nerve impulse down an axon fibre obeys the all-or-none law. But the synaptic and dendritic processes which precede and follow the generation of impulses are essentially graded in nature. Indeed, the all-or-none behaviour of the axon can be interpreted simply as a means of conveying graded messages from one part of the nervous system to another, using a frequency code. Thus the behaviour of neurons does not necessarily imply that the sensitivity they mediate should also be discontinuous.

Finally, there is an alternative explanation of observers' behaviour in a threshold situation which can account for the linear psychophysical functions obtained under special conditions of testing. Barlow (1961) has shown that if the nervous system does in fact exhibit random activity or 'noise', then an observer who adopts the tactic of maintaining a low rate of false detections of the comparison stimulus will generate data which are essentially linear. Thus we need not adopt something as novel as the neural quantum theory to explain the unusual psychophysical functions which have been reported.

The neural quantum interpretation of the threshold has been presented here because it is so different from traditional thinking. As we have shown, the theory has been criticized on various grounds, and at the time of writing it does not appear to have many active supporters. But the neural quantum theory is an impressive illustration of how simple but very clearly stated assumptions, combined with rigorous deductive reasoning, can lead to a novel and empirically testable theory.

It may happen that future technical developments in neurophysiology, for example direct recording from brain centres, will make it possible to measure the impact of stimuli upon the nervous system under conditions where observer variables such as attention, set and response strategies have been effectively bypassed. Who knows but that under such powerful and direct methods of testing some aspects of sensory sensitivity may, after all, turn out to be essentially quantal in nature?

## DIRECT SCALING TECHNIQUES

These are associated with the work of S. S. Stevens and his colleagues (Stevens, 1957, 1959, 1961,1962; Galanter, 1962; Stevens and Galanter, 1957). They have been applied mainly in situations where stimuli are clearly supra-threshold. The starting point for Stevens' work was a doubt as to whether Fechner and other pioneers were really correct in assuming that the JND is a unit of sensation. For example, if one stimulus is 10 JNDs and another 20 JNDs above the auditory threshold, should not the second stimulus seem twice as loud as the first in a direct comparison? It won't: the second sound will be judged as much more than twice as loud—as several empirical studies have shown. Fechner's Law appears to break down when extrapolated to supra-threshold stimuli.

A second doubt concerning assumptions made in classical psychophysics concerns the constancy of the JND. It is now known that difference thresholds (and, therefore, JNDs) for loudness are not subjectively equal: the more intense the standard, the greater the apparent loudness of the JND when sounded alone. However, with other stimulus dimensions—for example, pitch—the JND does remain subjectively equal. Thus we may need to maintain a distinction between two aspects of sensation (and stimulation): first, the quantitative—for example weight, loudness, brightness; second, the qualitative—for example hue, spatial position, pitch. In the first case changes in subjective intensity probably represent additional responses in the nervous system; in the second changes in the quality of the stimulus probably engage different regions of the nervous system (red receptors rather than blue receptors, for example). Stevens incorporates these distinctions into his work and refers to the quantitative and qualitative dimensions of stimulation and their accompanying sensations as, respectively, *Prothetic* and *Metathetic* continua.

The research for which Stevens is best known concerns the relation between changes in the intensity of supra-threshold stimuli and the accompanying growth of sensation. This is pertinent: our usual transactions with the environment are not limited to very weak stimuli. Stevens developed a set of new psychophysical procedures the three best known of which are Fractionation, Cross-Modal Matching and Direct Scaling. In *Fractionation* the observer is presented with a stimulus of a certain intensity. The observer's task is to manipulate this intensity until it appears halved or doubled. The question is, What physical setting is chosen to produce this fraction of the starting sensation? In *Cross-Modal Matching* the observer attempts to communicate the subjective intensity of a stimulus via another modality. For example, the perceived brightness of a light may be matched by adjusting the loudness of a tone or the force exerted on a lever. Perhaps surprisingly, observers find this novel cross-modal matching quite easy to do. In *Direct Scaling* the observer is presented with two extremes of the stimulus range and asked to assign a number to each of them. Then the entire range of stimuli is presented in random order and the observer assigns a number to each to match the resulting sensation.

With these techniques Stevens introduced a new type of psychophysics. His main findings and theoretical conclusions will now be described. Stevens' investigations of the growth of sensation above threshold led him to propose a modification to the Weber–Fechner law. Remember that the implication of

Fechner's equation is that arithmetic (equal step) changes in sensation require equal *ratios* of stimulation. This is why Fechner's basic equation is written as Sensation = k log Stimulus. Stevens argues that, particularly with supra-threshold stimuli, the relationship between sensation and stimulation is better expressed as, *equal* ratios of sensation correlate with equal ratios of stimulation. This is not to imply that the stimulus and response ratios are the same. Rather that each time the intensity of a particular stimulus is multiplied or divided by, for example, ten, the sensation may double or halve. The relationship will not always be this clear-cut of course, but the essence is that it will always be between two ratios.

This claim implies that if observers' ratings in, for example, a direct scaling experiment, are plotted in logarithmic form on one axis of a graph, and stimulus intensities are represented in logarithmic form along the other axis, then straight line functions should emerge. The steepness of each line will indicate the rate at which sensation grows as a result of stimulation. And in many cases this is exactly what Stevens discovered. Now the log-log relationship can be equally well expressed in an equivalent form: $S = aX^b$, where $S$ = the subjective response, $X$ is stimulus intensity, $a$ is a weighting function which allows for different units of measurement, and $b$ is the exponent indicating the rate of growth of sensation. This form of equation is known as a Power Function, and is the way in which most direct scaling data are presented. For example, the exponent in the power function for brightness has been reported as 0.33; that for electric shock is more than 3.0. To show what these mean we simply take the antilog of the numbers. For brightness, antilog 0.33 = 2.14, which means that when we raise the stimulus intensity by a ratio of ten, the sensation of brightness approximately doubles. For electric shock, antilog 3.0 = 1000; in this example a ten-fold increase in stimulation produces a thousand-fold increase in judged sensation. Readers may wish to satisfy themselves that if the intensity of the electric shock was doubled, then sensation would increase by a factor of eight. These results are typical of quantitative or prothetic continua. Functions for qualitative or metathetic continua are different: on these continua exponents of the power functions are frequently around 1.0; that is to say, a certain ratio change in stimulation causes the same proportionate change in sensation. When we consider metathetic continua such as spatial position, this linearity simply reflects the accuracy of our perception; in this case our mode of responding is clearly adaptive. Some typical power functions are shown in Figure 2.6.

The last of Stevens' findings to be reported here is implicit in some of the earlier sections. It is simply that this form of scaling seems to be consistent across situations. For example, one could scale brightness by having the observer adjust the intensity of a vibrating stimulus. Then vibration can be scaled against loudness. Finally, one can scale loudness against brightness. The claim is that power functions derived from these different procedures agree, and thus the procedure appears to be coherent.

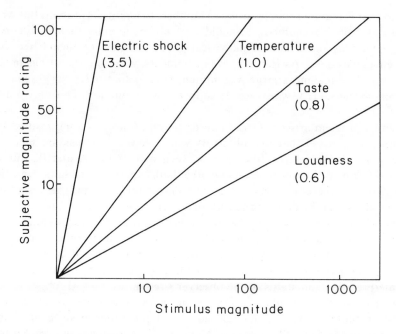

Figure 2.6   Power functions for four sensory modalities (logarithmic scales). The exponents (in brackets) indicate how rapidly sensation grows with increased stimulus intensity. (Data from Stevens, 1961)

## An evaluation of direct scaling

Direct scaling has been criticized on both empirical and theoretical grounds. The first empirical criticism is that departures are frequently observed from power functions when low stimulus intensities are presented for scaling. The form these departures take is that at very low levels sensation magnitude falls off more rapidly than predicted from the power function. Second, it has been found that whilst the power function may adequately represent the average performance of a group of observers, individual results commonly depart from this form (Pradham and Hoffman, 1963). And whilst it has been claimed that scaling techniques are free from context effects (see for example, Stevens and Galanter, 1957; Galanter, 1962) this has been shown to be simply not true (Poulton, 1968; Helson and Kozaki, 1968). There are then some difficulties associated with the application of direct scaling procedures.

The emphasis of this account is, of course, upon theory, and it is in terms of its theoretical assumptions that direct scaling has been most severely criticized. Doubts arise over direct scaling when we analyse what is happening in the measurement situation. In the frequently used method of magnitude estimation, the observer is required simply to assign numbers to a range of stimuli. But what is the status of these numbers? Should we feel free to enter them into curve-fitting equations and then base numerical power functions on them? Are they good enough as data? As Engen (1971) comments, when we use ratings in this manner we are making a large assumption, namely that observers respond to numbers in the same way as they do to forms of stimulation. This may not be true.

Another problem arises over the interpretation of direct scaling results. For example, we can say that two observers whose power functions are identical agree about the subjective difference between two stimuli A and B. But we cannot tell from the power functions whether both experience the same sensation arising from A; there is simply no way of knowing this and thus there is a limit to what direct scaling data can tell us about sensations.

Then there is the possibility, which direct scaling procedures cannot rule out, that a particular observer may elect to use the same range of numbers whatever range of stimuli, weak or intense, is presented. The data will still be fitted by power functions, but once again there will be considerable doubt over the interpretation and status of the observer's responses.

There is also some doubt concerning the mathematical nature of Stevens' power functions. Stevens' claims that equal stimulus ratios produce equal sensation ratios, that sensation intensity grows as stimulus intensity is raised to a power. In a careful mathematical analysis Treisman (1964) demonstrates that the power function does not provide a unique fit to direct scaling data. Any suitable logarithmic equation, such as Response $= n$ log Stimulus Intensity, will give just as good an account of the data. Thus the interpretation of what is happening during direct scaling cannot be sought in the properties of the power function *per se*.

As a final criticism, it must be pointed out that there has, as yet, been no external validation of the direct scaling methods. Moving across modalities or from direct estimation to fractionation techniques cannot do this job: the system remains a closed one and as such cannot give rise to an adequate theory of the growth of sensation.

Despite these criticisms it is clear that Stevens' direct scaling studies gave an important fresh impetus to psychophysics. His writings remind us that psychophysics was designed to illuminate the relationship between mind and body, in particular the relation between stimulation and sensation, and it seems foolish therefore to restrict our interest to threshold situations. Sensations are interesting, particularly when they are strong ones, and Stevens attempted to discover more about them. In doing so, he revived interest in one of the classical problems in psychology. And whatever the eventual fate of the power function and the ideas behind it, the many demonstrations which Stevens has given of the logarithmic nature of the link between sensation and stimulation remain convincing. The range of intensities to which the human eye can respond is 1 : 10,000,000,000. The range of intensities we can hear is 1 : 1000,000,000,000,000. Responding logarithmically (that is to ratios rather than arithmetic values) is an obviously adaptive economy for the visual and auditory systems: how else could a system that can respond to a few quanta of light also respond to intensities millions of times greater—it would be impossible to assign neural mechanisms so as to cover all the arithmetic steps across this huge range. It follows that the ultimate laws connecting sensation and stimulation will probably include a logarithmic component. Whether this will appear in a power function remains to be seen.

## THE THEORY OF SIGNAL DETECTION (TSD)

This approach to psychophysics is of great interest because it offers a fundamental challenge to the classical concept of the threshold. As an introduction to TSD, one of the classical psychophysical procedures, the Constant Method, may be briefly re-examined. Suppose that one wishes to measure the absolute threshold for light. The observer is initially dark-adapted for about an hour. Then a warning signal sounds and the observer is presented with either a very faint light or a blank screen. The stimulus present/stimulus absent conditions are in random order. On each trial the observer's task is to indicate whether or not a stimulus has occurred. Then a new intensity of light is selected and the next set of trials is run. The threshold is calculated on the basis of the number of stimuli detected at each intensity, but with a correction for guesssing. This is because an observer responding positively on every trial will gain a 50 per cent score, given the way the trials are organized. For this reason, the traditional method of calculating the threshold involves subtracting the observer's errors from his or her correct responses. There are of course refinements in the ways in which this is done, but the essence of the procedure has been described.

With very faint stimuli (stimuli around the threshold value, in traditional terms) it is obvious that even conscientious observers will be wrong on a proportion of trials. But note how their errors are treated: *they are weighed in exactly the same way as correct responses.* That is, make ten errors and the 'correct' score is reduced by ten. It is assumed that errors reveal nothing about the observer's sensitivity, and that they are directly (inversely) related to correct scores. It is for this reason that the observers used in the determinations of the main sensory thresholds have always been given intensive practice and detailed instructions to be as careful as possible: errors are a nuisance.

But think for a moment about what it would be like to be tested in the absolute threshold determination described above. All readers have been in complete darkness. Many will have noticed this interesting phenomenon: the darkness isn't really black. After a short time small patches of light can be seen in the visual field, and the total experience is of pinky-grey rather than jet black. This phenomenon, once termed the 'self-light of the retina', is due to random firing of cells in the eye and optic nerve. Similar effects can be noticed in touch and hearing.

It follows that during the determination of the absolute threshold for light, some of the weaker stimuli presented will not be subjectively brighter than the 'light' which the observer can see in the darkness. When this happens the observer will surely have to guess whether the experience he or she is having is due to internal or external causes.

The Theory of Signal Detection and its associated techniques originated in Statistical Decision Theory (Wald, 1950), which is a set of formal rules for choosing between statistical decisions. Initially, TSD was associated with ideal detectors, but was quickly applied to problems arising in electronics. Any electrical circuit (and any communication channel) will contain *noise*. The molecules in transistors, resistors, electrical cables and so on are never at rest. Turn on a television set in the small hours of the morning and one sees, not a blank screen, but a dancing array of dots. Radios and telephones 'hiss'. Even digital players, if set to maximum gain, will emit a slight additional sound—the irreducible random activity of the amplifier circuit.

In the context of electronics it is obviously of great interest to know what effect such 'noise' will have upon the efficiency with which signals can be processed. Noise sets a limit upon the sensitivity of any channel, *for it shares some of the properties of signals*, just as spontaneous retinal activity can occasionally be mistaken for faint lights. Thus in any radar system, to use a real-life example, there must be a target size such that its representation on the display is no larger than the random noise of the equipment. At what point must we abandon attempts to detect small (or distant) signals? How can the probability of successfully detecting faint targets be optimized? What is the best strategy for maximizing the detection of real targets whilst mimimizing the (erroneous) detection of spurious targets (or noise)? And if technical refinements permit us to improve a particular detection circuit, reducing the noise by some known amount, what will be the corresponding gain in the detection of signals? TSD raised the exciting possibility of solving these applied problems.

In 1954 Tanner and Swets published an extremely influential paper in which they claimed that certain psychological problems, including the detection of weak stimuli, might yield to the application of TSD techniques. We shall now outline their new approach to psychophysics.

Consider again the absolute threshold task. It is obvious that on each trial or presentation the observer has two choices to make: he or she can decide that the stimulus (or signal, in TSD terminology) is present or that it is absent. And the signal may indeed be present or absent. This situation can be represented in the form of a matrix into which we shall insert the usual TSD terminology:

|   | | Response | |
|---|---|---|---|
|   | | Yes | No |
| s | | | |
| i | present | hit | miss |
| g | | | |
| n | | false | correct |
| a | absent | alarm | rejection |
| l | | | |

Thus there are two ways of being right and two of being wrong in this situation. In classical psychophysics the errors would be interpreted as either failure of sensitivity (the miss) or carelessness or response bias (the false alarm). In practice, entries in the table take the form of relative frequencies or probabilities.

In Tanner and Swets' application of TSD to psychological phenomena a new model of the human perceiver is proposed. When applied to vision the model assumes the presence in the visual system of a physiological process the value of which varies randomly over time. We need not define value too carefully, nor do we need to know exactly what the process is—it could be the closeness of a group of neurons to their threshold of firing, or it could be fluctuations at a synapse, or something else—it is necessary to assume only that (a) the process is involved in detecting light and (b) its fluctuations form a random, Gaussian distribution.

Consider the left-hand curve of Figure 2.7. This represents the random process and is known as the *Noise Distribution* (N); it represents the activity of the system in the absence of stimulation. We now make the reasonable assumption that when the system receives external stimulation, energy from this is added to the momentary value of the noise distribution. This creates a second distribution (on the right in Figure 2.7) which is known as the *Signal Plus Noise Distribution* (S+N). (The two curves are also known as Probability Density Functions.) If the incoming stimulation is strong, or if the system is basically very sensitive (which amounts to the same thing) then there will be a correspondingly greater separation between the N and S+N distributions.

This is the model of signal detection. Viewed in this way, the task of the observer in any detection situation is to select a criterion value and when the 'value' of the system (plotted on the horizontal axis in Figures 2.7 and 2.8) exceeds this give a positive response. The criterion (usually designated Beta) is also known as the Likelihood Ratio. Above any point on the horizontal axis are two values, that of the N distribution and that of the S+N distribution. The criterion is defined as the ratio of the two distributions' values at that point. In any detection situation there will be one best position for the criterion. This criterion value is that formally chosen by an Ideal Observer.

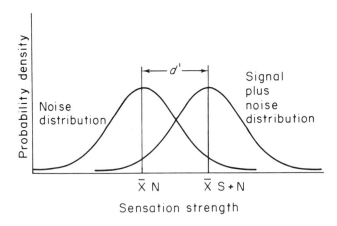

Figure 2.7    The two distributions of Signal Detection Theory (TSD). The left-hand curve is the noise distribution arising from spontaneous random activity within the observer. The right-hand signal plus noise distribution results when the effects of signals are added to the noise distribution

But how does an actual observer decide upon the position of the criterion? The answer, in TSD terms, is according to the task demands of the experiment. More formally, this is described in terms of a Payoff Matrix which defines the rewards and penalties associated with the four cells of the matrix printed above. That is to say, the observer can be urged to be very careful (and rewarded accordingly), or quite reckless. This in turn will decide the relative frequencies of hits, misses, false alarms and correct rejections.

One of the strengths of TSD is that it is able to predict the effects of choosing different criteria. For example, the observer may adopt a very risky criterion, as indicated by the left-hand vertical line in Figure 2.8. Then all values which exceed this criterion will produce a positive response. The observer will then detect a high proportion of signals—the area of the S+N distribution to the right of the criterion in Figure 2.8—the Hit Rate will be high. But note that an inevitable consequence will be that a large number of events which are part of the N distribution will also trigger responses—the False Alarm Rate will also be high.

Alternatively, the observer can adopt a more cautious criterion, indicated by the right-hand vertical line in Figure 2.8. In this case, only high values will produce responses. The result will be a very low false alarm rate but many fewer hits, as is shown by the large area of the signal distribution lying to the left of the criterion in Figure 2.8.

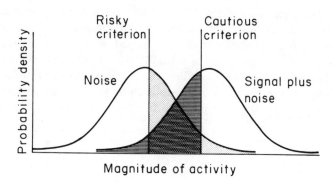

Figure 2.8 The effects of a shift in the observer's criterion predicted by the Signal Detection model. Note that although the risky criterion will ensure a high hit rate (the large area of the signal plus noise distribution lying to the right of the criterion), there will be a large number of False Positive responses (the area of the noise distribution lying to the right of the criterion). The cautious criterion will produce fewer False Positives (the small area of the Noise distribution lying on the right of the criterion) but many misses (note the large area of the signal plus noise distribution lying to the left of the criterion)

Referring again to Figure 2.7 it is obvious that another variable is the separation between the two distributions. As stated earlier, the stronger the incoming signal the greater will be the separation of the N and S+N distributions. Equally however, an estimate of this distance can be used as an index of the sensitivity of a hypothetical (or actual) observer. The index of sensitivity is known as $d'$ ($d$ prime) and is defined as the difference between the means of the two distributions divided by their variances. Later, we will show how $d'$ is calculated from actual data.

The attractiveness of this new model when it first appeared was partly due to the distinction it made between two aspects of an observer's performance. The criterion is clearly a subjective *response* effect, and as such may be affected by attentional set and instructions, including the payoff matrix. And this is clearly independent of the observer's sensitivity, which is clearly not under the influence of the payoff matrix. Thus TSD promised a 'purer' measure of sensitivity than was possible in traditional psychophysics, and this was a very exciting possibility.

Further interest stemmed from the fact that, in terms of the TSD model, shifting the criterion will not generally result in linear changes in hit and false alarm rates, as classical psychophysics would predict. In Figure 2.9 the probability of hits is plotted against that of false alarms for a given separation of the two distributions, that is for a given $d'$. To appreciate the origin of the curve, suppose that a criterion had been moved smoothly across the horizontal axis in Figure 2.7 and pairs of hit and false alarm rates recorded at each position. The resulting figure describes the *Receiver Operating Characteristic* (ROC). Note that initial small rightwards shifts in the criterion lead to a disproportionate gain in hits as opposed to false alarms. This is a very important result.

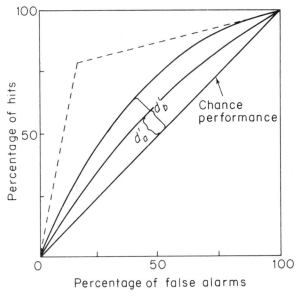

Figure 2.9   Receiver Operating Characteristic (ROC) curves. $d'_a$ would result from an insensitive observer or (equivalently) from weak signals. $d'_b$ is the performance expected from a sensitive observer or from the use of stronger signals. The dotted function represents the relationship between hits and false alarms predicted by the classical model of the threshold

Using methods which are basically simple, but tedious to describe, it is also possible to plot on the ROC curve the relationship between hits and false alarms which can be deduced from the traditional psychophysical model of the observer. Here it is assumed that stimuli below a given threshold value simply cannot be detected, that the observer can only guess (leading to the traditional correction for guessing), and that above the threshold there is a smooth increase in the probability that signals will be detected. Note that this function starts somewhere on the vertical hit axis and is linear and segmented: it looks very different from the ROC curve and is shown as the dotted line in Figure 2.9. It ought then to be possible to test between the classical and the TSD models by actual experiment.

Detailed accounts of the statistical basis of TSD are given in the references at the end of this chapter. The present attempt to describe the Theory of Signal Detection without using any equations is rather like trying to swim with one hand tied behind the back: it can be done, but it takes longer. The preceding paragraphs are necessarily rather simplified; nevertheless, the reader who has persisted so far should now have a good idea of the thinking behind TSD and will be able to appreciate how different this is from the classical threshold approach.

## TSD in practice

Running a TSD detection task is very similar to the orthodox psychophysical method of threshold measurement. In some applications signals of different intensities are presented alone, in others they are presented together with noise, and these trials are randomly mixed with blank trials or with trials presenting noise alone. The first thing to establish is the observer's criterion or likelihood ratio (Beta). This is done either by manipulating the observer's behaviour with instructions to be more or less risky, or by recording confidence judgements after each decision. Then separate analyses are made of hit and false alarms rates for decisions grouped as 'very confident', 'confident', 'less confident', and so on. Each run through a TSD procedure yields pairs of values of hits and false alarms from which the ROC curve may be plotted.

The sensitivity index $d'$ can be estimated from the ROC curve by measuring the distance from its peak to the ascending left-right diagonal (as shown in Figure 2.9). Or $d'$ can be calculated from published tables of ordinates of the normal distribution. Other techniques employ special graphical solutions and there are even published tables from which $d'$ values can be obtained directly, provided certain experimental procedures have been followed. In practice it is all much easier than it sounds.

## Applications of TSD

The Theory of Signal Detection was a major shift in thinking about psychophysics. It was a new paradigm from which to consider threshold phenomena. Here at last was a way of assessing and allowing for response effects, affording what seemed to be much cleaner estimates of sensitivity. The years following Tanner and Swets' seminal paper saw a rush of publications revealing a new interest in psychophysical phenomena. One hundred years after Fechner there was suddenly a new model of human sensitivity which rejected the classical concept of the threshold.

And the impact of TSD was not restricted to sensory research. It seemed likely that the model would throw light on other psychological phenomena. For example when trying to remember something we often find that we cannot recall the particular word required but have a strange feeling that we are just about to. Our intuitions are correct: people experiencing the 'tip of the tongue' phenomenon can in fact make very good guesses about the word they cannot recall: they often guess correctly its approximate length, even its syllabic structure (Brown and McNeil, 1966). But as scored in traditional memory experiments such failures to recall, even the production of similar words, would be penalized as errors. By encouraging the use of payoff matrix methods of scoring, manipulating observers' criteria and then calculating indices akin to $d'$, a new impetus was given to research in traditional areas such as recognition and recall. TSD became a very stimulating addition to the psychologist's technical and theoretical repertoire.

TSD was successful. In many detection experiments the results generated ROC curves of the form displayed in Figure 2.9 rather than that predicted from classical threshold theory (the dotted line in Figure 2.9). The sheer range of successful applications of TSD is impressive. It includes the study of brightness discrimination (Tanner and Swets, 1953); the detection of tones against noise (Tanner, Swets and Green, 1956); touch and warmth discrimination (Eijkman and Vendrik, 1963); time discrimination (Creelman, 1962); intelligibility of speech (Clarke, 1960); memory (Swets, 1973); anxiety (Grossberg and Grant, 1978); eyewitness testimony (Wells, Lindsay and Ferguson, 1979); and even studies of the efficacy of acupuncture (Clark and Yang, 1974; Chapman, Chen and Bonica, 1977). What began as a formal application of statistical decision theory to the problems of the ideal observer became a widespread research technique in numerous areas of psychology and physiology.

### An evaluation of the theory of signal detection

It seems likely that TSD techniques will have a lasting place in the sensory psychologist's technical repertoire. As promised, they do seem to offer a genuine way out of the problem of disentangling response and sensitivity effects in detection and other situations. The theoretical background to TSD is a rigorous one, and the concept of an ideal observer against which to measure actual human performance is appealing. However, some doubts have been expressed concerning the appropriateness of TSD to psychology. Some of these will now be outlined.

First, there has been debate as to whether the ROC curve always provides a best fit to detection task data. Remember that in Figure 2.9 results predicted on the basis of the classical theory of a sensory threshold led to a plot which was very different from the ROC curve predicted by TSD and obtained in many TSD experiments. However, high-threshold theory (Blackwell, 1953), low-threshold theory (Luce, 1960), and two-threshold theory (Green, in Swets 1964), are all attempts to preserve some notion of a classical threshold but with the observer seeking to maximize payoffs for detections of signals against noise above this point. The most elaborate of these, two-threshold theory, uses a three-segment plot on the ROC graph; it is clear that such a plot must be able to provide a fairly good fit to TSD data and thus the model represents a rival to TSD. However, claims concerning these particular alternatives to TSD do not appear to have attracted much subsequent support, as judged by published literature.

A second doubt concerns the plausibility of the TSD model in an actual setting. Familiarity with the concepts of signal detection theory can be claimed when one can think in terms of the two-distribution model shown in Figures 2.7 and 2.8. But this very familiarity can cause one to accept too uncritically one of the main assumptions of TSD: that the observer has a model of the S+N distribution available for decison-making during an experiment. This second Gaussian or normal distribution is a key assumption in arriving at ROC calculations, but how does the distribution form? There can be no objection to the assumption that noise is present in the nervous system and that its random character is modelled by the Gaussian curve. But in typical applications of TSD data are collected from very early trials. We must therefore ask how a sufficient sample of events could have been sampled for the S+N distribution to have been formed; what evidence is available to the observer to permit him or her to optimize the setting of the maximum likelihood criterion during these early trials? In any statistical situation, Gaussian distributions do not take on their characteristic shape until hundreds, even thousands of samples have been added. We cannot find any acceptable treatment of what seems to be an important theoretical flaw in the application of TSD to human experiments.

Psychophysics is a practical as well as a theoretical part of psychology. The adequacy of any theory is measured in part by how useful its predictions turn out to be. It is fair to point out that during the past ten years there has been a marked reduction in the number of publications in psychophysics (and other areas) which have employed TSD techniques. This conclusion is reinforced by an examination of the dates of key papers listed in this chapter. Threshold data continue to be reported, but many workers (the present author is one) seem to have reverted to using classical procedures. It seems as though the classical concept of the threshold is simply too useful to be lightly abandoned.

Whatever the eventual place of TSD in psychophysics it can be asserted that it has been a stimulating alternative to the old concept of the threshold and it has afforded a valuable method of separating response and sensitivity effects.

This may well be a permanent contribution and one which will influence future models of the human observer.

## FINAL REMARKS ON PSCHOPHYSICS

At the start of this chapter it was claimed that psychophysics was one of the undoubted successes of experimental psychology. We repeat this claim. To have discovered so much about the workings of the nervous system without penetrating that system is quite remarkable. In a later chapter on the neurophysiological approach to perception it will be possible to show how psychophysical data make sense in terms of what we now know about the neurophysiology of the nervous system and how elegantly these two different approaches have been combined.

The basic method of psychophysics, which, as we have shown, involves the careful presentation of calibrated stimuli and the recording of controlled responses has been extended to other areas. It has been possible to record many important data from human infants and animals using clever combinations of psychophysical methods and training techniques. And the basic methodology of psychophysics has been widely adopted in other areas of experimental psychology, often with profitable results.

Generally then the invention of psychophysics has been of great importance in experimental psychology generally and the study of perception in particular. However, it cannot be said that the theories which have emerged from psychophysical research have had a particularly wide impact, with the possible exception of signal detection theory. Why should this be so?

One answer, of course, is that psychophysics has contributed more on the technical than the theoretical side. Another is that this is an area which is theoretically restricted. In terms of the general model shown in Figure 1.1 it is clear that the regions linked by psychophysics are few in number: theories of the threshold attempt to find links between stimuli (usually defined as events in either Region 2 or Region 3 of the model) and responses (detections or sensations in Region 4, the brain). This is obviously one reason for the success of the entire enterprise: 100 years of technical research have been focused upon a restricted range of problems, typically those concerning sensory sensitivity and acuity and the relationships between them and properties of stimuli.

But this success has been gained only at a price. Artificial stimuli are impoverished in their lack of meaning, and they are not ecologically representative of the world we inhabit—how often are we exposed to narrow bands of spectral light or pure tones? When we perceive objects, as opposed to artificially simple arrays in the laboratory, it is usually in a context of other objects. We shall see in the chapter on the Gestalt theory that interactions between stimuli generate novel effects which no theory based on thresholds and sensations can account for. And it will be shown in the chapter on empiricism in psychology that words heavy in meaning, such as taboo words and those associated with death and illness have different recognition thresholds from control words. That is to say, once one moves from a psychophysics dealing with, say, the detection of straight lines to the study of rather more complex arrays—words—the influence of the observer's familiarity with language and all its associations becomes a very important variable, one which classical psychophysics cannot adequately deal with. A rigorous, scientific attack on the remaining problems of perception must include more regions of Figure 1.1. It must give more weight to the ecology from which stimuli arise and it must take more account of what observers bring with them to the act of perceiving.

We end where we began, with the problem of the threshold. It is a fact that any lay person entering a modern psychological laboratory is likely to be dazzled by the array of modern scientific apparatus. Computer-driven experiments, precise timing and control devices and accurately calibrated stimulus generators abound. These are all available to those who would make new discoveries about the senses. Even Fechner, a visionary, could hardly fail to be impressed. But it cannot be said that his dream of linking the mental and the physical has been fully realized. Fechner's methods have allowed us to learn more about human processes, particularly sensory processes, than he could have imagined. But the theoretical concept of the threshold is still under debate 130 years after Fechner's pioneering work, and the true nature of sensation still eludes us. How strange that one of the first theoretical problems to be tackled by psychologists continues to provoke and perplex.

## NOTES ON CHAPTER 2

An account of the classical psychophysical methods is given in Woodworth and Schlosberg (1955). See Chapters 8 and 9.

Details of some modern psychophysical methods can be found in the Engen (1971) reference. This also contains a good introduction to Direct Scaling techniques. Corso (1970, Chapter 11) provides a valuable discussion of the theory of the neural quantum and the present account owes much to Corso's exegesis. Swets (1954) is a good technical introduction to the theory of signal detection (referred to as 'Sensory Decision Theory' by some authors)

For an account of the historical origins of psychophysics see Boring (1950), particularly Chapter 14. It will be obvious from this account that our treatment of Fechner's concept of the threshold is somewhat oversimplified: he did speculate to some extent about observers' subthreshold performances, using the concept of *negative sensations*; a description of this would have deflected us from the main account.

# Chapter 3

# The Gestalt theory

The first general theory to be described, Gestalt theory, is important and un-usual: important because the discoveries of the Gestalt psychologists are now part of our permanent knowledge of perception; unusual, because, as we shall show, the emphasis in the explanatory parts of the theory is very much on the brain. What needs to be explained, Gestalt theorists believed, is the relationship between the world and everyday experience: the world of meaningful objects and events. Their explanation was in terms of brain processes. From the point of view of our simple classificatory model, the relevant arc is that connecting the physical world to the central nervous system, and hence to mental experience.

Gestalt theory is closely associated with the work of three men: Wertheimer (1880–1943), Köhler (1887–1964 ), and Koffka (1886–1941). There were (and are) other Gestaltists but these psychologists developed the Gestalt approach which was to exert an important influence on the psychology of perception. We shall begin by tracing some of the historical origins of this important movement.

## HISTORICAL BACKGROUND

The benefit of hindsight allows us to discern the patterns of influence which made the development of the Gestalt theory almost inevitable. The publication of Kant's *Critique of Pure Reason* in 1781 had a major impact on subsequent European philosophy. Nobody could do justice to this influential and difficult work in a few lines, but it is possible to take a single Kantian idea as an example of his thinking and show its potential importance for psychology. Imagine an object moving from left to right across one's field of vision. The movement takes time and occurs through space. That we perceive the object's motion is something we take for granted; we can even guess about mechanisms which enable us to do this. But what about the framework within which the object moves? We cannot perceive space itself, there is literally nothing *to* perceive. Space is what the object moves through. Similarly, we cannot perceive time as such: it too is simply a framework within which events are ordered. But the perception we have had would clearly be impossible without our awareness of these frameworks. Where does this awareness come from? Kant's answer (stated here with some crudity) is that space and time are *a priori* intuitions. That is, they are 'givens', superimposed upon reality by our minds. Much of Kant's life

46

was spent in justifying this claim and examining the consequences. For now we can say simply that there is one consequence which is of great psychological as well as philosophical importance if Kant's claim is true: perception must be innately determined. Mind imposes a structure on the perceived world and this world is the only one we are capable of perceiving. This leads to *Nativism*, which, as will be shown, became a central tenet of the Gestalt approach. Gestalt psychology did not appear until 100 years after Kant's death, but it was clearly influenced by his philosophical investigations.

But there were other influences at work in nineteenth-century Europe. Many people, as a result of Darwinism, had abandoned their religious beliefs. If God was no longer to be seen at the centre of things, who was? The answer was, Man. It is significant that the nineteenth century witnessed the great flowering of the Romantic movement in literature and the arts. Common to much of the creative work associated with this movement is the battle of the individual—a hero or heroine—against fate. Think for a moment about the great romantic poems of the period, the operas, the emotions induced in us by the music of Beethoven (for example, The Eroica), Brahms and Tchaikovsky. The themes which emerge again and again are those associated with the heroic struggles of individuals. This was part of the Zeitgeist at the time of the emergence of the Gestalt movement and its emphasis on the dynamic role of the perceiver in making sense of the world.

That was the historical background to Gestalt psychology. But the movement's beginnings were also a reaction against two contemporary approaches to psychology, *Structuralism* and *Behaviourism*.

Structuralism, which reached its peak between 1870 and 1910 with the work of Wundt in Germany and Titchener in America, was an attempt to explore the mind in a manner analogous to the chemical analysis of complex substances. Just as the chemist can consider compounds in terms of their basic chemical elements, Wundt, Titchener and others believed that the laws of the mind would be revealed by careful study of its elements and their relationships. In this case the 'mental elements' of the analysis were *sensations*. On this view, any rich subjective experience is essentially a blend of simpler, more basic experiences or sensations, and the job of the psychologist is to list these. But this reduction to sensations is not easy. There is a constant tendency to commit the 'stimulus error' in which the source of a sensation is confused with the sensation itself. For example, one frequently says that one hears *something*, say an engine. But the engine is not itself a sensation. One should say that one has certain sensations *like* those normally arising when one is near an engine. The technique for avoiding the stimulus error and for correctly identifying the sensations one is having is a difficult one which must be learned and practised, usually by the investigator who is the subject in the research. This technique, known as trained *introspection*, was the basic source of data in the experiments of Wundt, Titchener and others.

Reduced to its simplest level, structuralism leads to a view of perception in which the perceived world is a *mosaic*. Each stimulus element in a scene yields its own sensation and the totality of these sensations forms the percept. Stated baldly, it is obvious that such a scheme could not work. How to explain, for example, why things remain the same size as we move away from them if our perception is tied to particular sensations, in this case those arising from the shrinking retinal image? To avoid this trap, the major theorist Helmholtz (who was Wundt's contemporary and whose career overlapped with Titchener's) had been driven to an empiricism which asserted that experience and memory must correct and enhance the momentary effects of stimulation. This in turn suggests that much of perceiving must be learned. Whilst not denying the role of experience, the Gestalt theorists rejected both the mosaic view of perception and the emphasis on learning, both of which came under attack in their own writings.

Structuralist introspection as a method of studying perceptual phenomena is long dead and must strike the reader as somewhat unusual. It may help to include an example of the sort of thing which the Gestalt theorists attacked. Here is Titchener introspecting on the taste of two fairly familiar substances.

> ' Thus the "taste" of lemonade is made up of a sweet taste, an acid taste, a scent (the fragrance of lemon), a sensation of temperature and a pricking (cutaneous) sensation. The "taste" of limewater is made up of a weakly sweet taste, a sensation of nausea (organic sensation), a sensation of temperature and a biting (cutaneous) sensation'.
>
> (Titchener, 1901, p.62)

Note that the phrase 'fragrance of lemon' implies that Titchener may not have fully succeeded in reducing the taste into its basic sensations: an analysis of the lemon fragrance is now required. The reader who would like to try this sort of thing is directed to the limewater problem; Titchener's use of the word 'nausea' is curiously apt.

The structuralists knew most of what there was to know about the experimental psychology of perception at the turn of the century. Their writings reveal total familiarity with the works of Helmholtz, for example. It is their philosophical approach to perception and their use of introspection which is unusual. Introspection failed (and with it, this type of structuralism) for a number of reasons: trained observers frequently disagreed in their introspections; introspective data cannot be easily quantified; most importantly, many mental processes are simply not available to self-observation. In fact, the influence of structuralism was probably at an end by the time the first Gestalt discoveries were announced. However, as we shall see, the approach made a useful man of straw for the Gestalt theorists, all of whom were gifted polemicists.

The second focus of the Gestaltists' attacks was behaviourism. Once again, it could be said that the Gestaltists exaggerated the influence of this movement, at least on contemporary work in perception (and it must be pointed out that the behaviourists were also hostile to structuralism). Nevertheless, it was true that behaviourists did attempt to explain behaviour in terms of a model derived from classical conditioning. This concentrated upon simple stimulus-response relationships, and tended to treat stimuli as essentially simple events confronting organisms. Further, the behaviourists had stated that the subject matter for psychology was objective behaviour, and only objective behaviour. Mental events, subjective experiences, had no place in this new, tough-minded scientific approach.

Gestalt theorists published lengthy rebuttals of the behaviourist case (see for example Köhler, 1947, Chapter 1). One of the most telling criticisms is that which Köhler advanced against the objectivity which behaviourists aspired to. Köhler argued that this was a chimera, and that even in physics—which claims to deal with the objective world—the concepts and observations are never objective in the sense the behaviourists had assumed:

> 'How do I define my terms when I work as a physicist? Since my knowledge of physics consists entirely of concepts and observations contained in or derived from direct experience, all the terms which I use in this science must ultimately refer to the same source. If I try to define such terms, my definitions may, of course, refer to further concepts and terms. But the final steps in the process will always be: pointing towards the locus of certain experiences about which I am talking, and hints where to make certain observations. Even the most abstract concepts of physics, such as that of entropy, can have no meaning without a reference, indirect though it may be, to certain direct experiences.
>
> (Köhler, 1947, p.27)

It is worth noting that these remarks of Köhler's would have carried extra weight as it was known that he had trained originally as a physicist.

To summarize, the Gestalt theorists were opposed to sensations as data and the accompanying mosaic view of perception, to crude atomism, to introspection as a method, and to the search for a bogus objectivity in psychology. These objections will acquire more force when we outline what Gestalt psychology offered in place of the approaches and assumptions to which it was opposed.

## THE START OF THE GESTALT MOVEMENT

The start of the Gestalt movement is one of the best-known stories in the history of psychology. In fact two important Gestalt principles had been published prior to the formation of a separate Gestalt school of thought. Ehrenfels (1890) had drawn attention to the fact that many groups of stimuli acquire a pattern quality which is over and above the sum of their parts: a tune is more than the sum of its notes; a square is more than a simple assembly of lines—it has 'squareness'. Ehrenfels named this emergent property *Gestaltqualität* (form-quality), a name which was adopted by the Gestalt movement. Later, Rubin

(1915) had published his important paper on the distinction between Figure and Ground in perception, a distinction which later found an important place in Gestalt thinking.

In the summer of 1910 the person who can be said to be the true founder of Gestalt psychology, Max Wertheimer, broke a journey to buy a toy stroboscope. He then carried out some investigations of the illusory movement which such devices can create. If one exposes two stimuli alternately in rapid succession then a number of strange things can happen, depending on the exposure times, the rate of alternation and so on. At low rates of alternation two separate stimuli are seen; at higher rates one sees a displacement of a stimulus from one position to the other (this can be seen at British Rail unmanned crossings where pairs of red warning lights flash alternately): this is stroboscopic movement. But there is an optimum rate at which what is seen is not a moving stimulus, but simply movement *per se*. Obviously, this movement cannot be explained in terms of the behaviour of either of the two stimuli—each simply appears and disappears at its own location. The experience of pure movement, which Wertheimer later called Phi-Movement, arises as the result of temporal and spatial *relationships* between stimuli: something new has arisen which is more than the sum of the parts—Gestaltqualität.

Wertheimer continued to work on the phi phenomenon at Frankfurt University using as subjects two young psychologists, Wolfgang Köhler and Kurt Koffka. This trio were to create a new approach to the study of perception and a major theory—the Gestalt theory.

## AN OUTLINE OF THE GESTALT APPROACH TO PERCEPTION

### Phenomenology

There is a special way of looking at the world. To experience it follow this simple procedure: take a piece of paper and punch out a small hole in the middle about half a centimetre in diameter. Now look at any nearby surface in the normal way and note its colour. Look again, this time through the hole, with the paper held about six inches from the face. Two things may become apparent. First, the colour seen through the hole (which has the fancier name, 'reduction screen' ) no longer appears to belong to the surface, rather it seems to float just behind the hole as a film. Second, colours may appear different from those seen when looking normally: for example, someone sitting by a wall may have a portion of their face tinted in the wall's colour; grey shadows may appear coloured.

Using a pencil in front of the eyes as a referent (a trick commonly used by artists) one can quickly come to see that objects get smaller as they recede from us. And, once it is pointed out to us, we can experience this troubling fact: the nose is always visible in our field of view—whenever we choose to notice it.

The procedures above are not simply tricks. It is a fact that careful analysis of what is to be seen when we look in a special way differs from what we normally experience. Introspectionists believed that demonstrations such as the reduction screen reveal the raw material of perception, namely sensations. And it is undeniably true that retinal images of objects do in fact shrink with distance, and that we can become sensitive to these changes.

The question the Gestalt theorists raised was: Which of these two modes of perceiving should be explained in perceptual theory? Their answer was unhesitating and forceful: everyday experience. To this end Koffka asked what has become the most famous question in the history of perception:

'Why do things look as they do?'

In other words, what must be explained by perceptual theories is the stability and coherence of the world of everyday experience, the world in which surface colours are stable under different illuminants and familiar things do not change size as they recede. This is a world of objects, not sensations, and the proper approach to this world is that of the phenomenologist.

'There seems to be a single starting point for psychology, exactly as for all the other sciences: the world as we find it, naively and uncritically.'
(Köhler, 1947, opening paragraph)

This decision to try to understand the world of the unselfconscious perceiver shaped Gestalt research and led to the distinctive style of the movement. Gestalt workers concentrated mainly upon strong effects in perception, a legitimate approach, but they went further: whenever possible their readers are offered, not a table of experimental results, but a compelling illustration. The emphasis is upon experience rather than data. The reader is to be convinced, not by the results of some obscure experiment, but by what he or she actually sees whilst reading the text. The unusual power and clarity of Gestalt writings owes much to this tactic.

## Perception as a dynamic, organized process

### Figure and ground

Whenever we open our eyes we see, not sensations of light, but objects and surfaces. There is a tendency (most easily noticed in vision) to organize our percepts in a certain manner during all perceiving: we effortlessly distinguish between the *figure* in a field of view and the *ground* against which it is seen. Figures tend to be complete, coherent and in front of ground, which is seen as less distinct, is attended to less readily, and is often seen as floating behind the figure. When figure and ground share a contour (as they commonly do), then the contour is usually seen as belonging to the figure.

Figure 3.1   Ambiguous figure–ground relationships. Is the white disc superimposed on the triangle, or is it a hole through which the underlying white ground can be seen? (From a demonstration by Miller, 1964)

In Figure 3.1 the immediate organization leads us to see a black triangle (the figure) in front of a white ground. But the printed page allows us to play tricks. The white disc on the triangle, is it a figure—in which case it will be seen as over the black (which is now ground), or is it an aperture—in which case we appear to be looking through the triangle at the white ground on which the original triangle is superimposed. Notice the subtle change in the status of these figure–ground relationships when we change our attention in this way. Figure 3.2 shows how figure–ground relationships can be made entirely ambiguous: which is the figure in this case, the profiles or the vase?

Figure–ground separation occurs in all sensory modalities, for example when we abstract the voice of a speaker from the background sounds of a noisy party, or when we feel an insect crawling over our skin. And it seems that we do not have to learn how to achieve this valuable economy in perceiving. When people recover their sight after many years of blindness they commonly experience many difficulties in seeing the world as it is. But, almost without exception, the case reports say that figure–ground separation is achieved from the outset. Are we built to see in this way?

So powerful is the tendency to organize vision into figure and ground that we take it very much for granted—hence the Gestaltist's use of ambiguous material such as Figure 3.2, which is intended to shake us out of our normal habits. The magnitude of the figure–ground achievement is brought home to those attempting to make machines which can perceive. How could a computer be programmed to ignore everything but the people in a complex scene? What rules would enable it to attend only to the left-hand performance of a jazz pianist?

Figure 3.2    Figure–ground reversal: the face-vase illusion

## The laws of grouping

In one of the early discoveries in Gestalt psychology, Wertheimer (1912) demonstrated several principles by which groups of stimuli organize themselves in perception. Looking at the arrays illustrated in Figure 3.3 reveals a spontaneous tendency to organize the stimuli into wholes or *Gestalten*. For example, stimuli which are adjacent tend to be grouped together: in Figure 3.3a the stimuli could be seen as unconnected, as rows, or as columns. But the Adjacency or Proximity principle guarantees that we see them as paired columns. The figure illustrates some other laws of grouping such as Good Continuation, Similarity and Closure (the tendency to see a completed figure whenever possible). If a subset of the stimuli in Figure 3.3 were to move in the same direction then this movement would cause them to separate phenomenally and take on organized figural properties, illustrating the law of Common Fate.

These spontaneous groupings in perception are fascinating and reliable phenomena and are still being researched 80 years after Wertheimer's demonstrations (see, for example, Restle, 1979). It is difficult, having experienced these effects, to return to any view of perception which ignores its dynamic aspects. Note once again the power of demonstrating rather than describing phenomena.

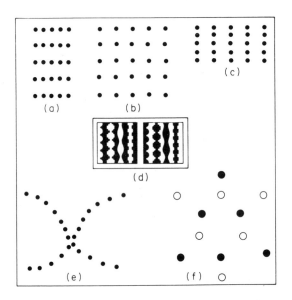

Figure 3.3  Some of Wertheimer's Laws of Grouping. (a) proximity induces grouping by rows, (b) proximity is equal and there is no dominant direction of grouping, (c) proximity induces grouping by columns. (d) Grouping by symmetry (after Bahnson, 1928). (e) Grouping by continuation. (f) Grouping by similarity

### Goodness or Prägnanz

The Gestalt theorists concluded that there must be a general underlying principle behind the numerous examples of organization which they discovered. It was as if perception was moving always towards simplicity, symmetry and wholeness, a tendency summarized by the German word, *Prägnanz*.

We now call the process of seeing novel similarities 'lateral thinking'. Remembering that Köhler had trained as a physicist helps us to understand the next stage in the development of Gestalt theory. Where else do we find processes which tend towards symmetry and simplicity? The answer is in the world of physics. Perception appears to be analogous to certain processes which we can observe in nature. For example, a raindrop is an ideal aerodynamic shape; complex wire shapes dipped into soap solutions form bubbles which are the simplest mathematical solutions to the surfaces thus formed; charges in electrical circuits and on the surfaces of condensers adjust to reduce heterogeneity of the forces involved; the field at the pole of a magnet is simple and symmetrical. It is an exciting step to wonder whether essentially similar physical forces are the cause of Pragnanz in perception. Later we shall show that this is the conclusion that Köhler eventually arrived at.

## Wholes versus parts

The claim that in perception the whole is greater than the sum of its parts is one of the most important tenets of Gestalt theory. This simple idea, elegantly illustrated in numerous demonstrations, has great significance for perceptual theory. If correct, it rules out the possibility of developing adequate theories of perception treating stimuli as single, isolatable events.

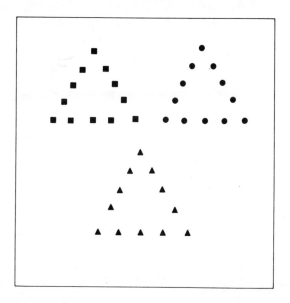

Figure 3.4   Triangularity Gestalten

As was stated earlier, Ehrenfels (1890) introduced the concept of Gestaltqualität prior to the emergence of Gestalt psychology. The importance of this concept cannot be exaggerated and it was elevated to a major principle in the Gestalt theory. When we hear a tune, the experience of the tune itself (the Gestaltqualität) is something more than the aggregate of the notes. It is not reduceable to individual notes and is not an adding together of simple sensations. For example, the last three notes of 'God Save the Queen' are the same as the first three notes of 'Three Blind Mice', but how many people who know both tunes well would ever realize this? The notes do not sound the same because they are not in the same context. And there is an interesting paradox here:

although the notes form the context, the context shapes the notes. Similarly, when a tune is transposed an octave, or played in a different key, we recognize it as the same tune, even though each individual note is different. Because the *relationship* between the notes is the same, they carry the same Gestaltqualität.

Historically, the most influential demonstration of part/whole interactions was Wertheimer's use of the phi phenomenon, which has been described earlier. Phi movement is something new, something not predictable from the behaviour of each light in isolation, but emerging as a function of the spatial and temporal *relationships* between the lights.

In Figure 3.4 the triangles have been formed from different elements, and yet 'triangularity' is evident in each display. None of the parts in isolation possesses triangularity, this emerges only in relationships. The Müller–Lyer illusion in Figure 3.5 is another example of this important point: the lines are objectively the same length, but their relationship with the arrows creates an illusion, an illusion which could not have been predicted from knowledge of the individual components.

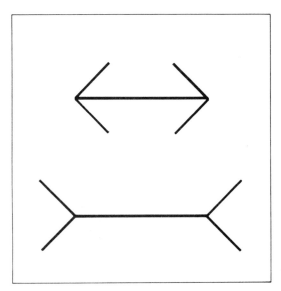

Figure 3.5   The Müller–Lyer illusion

### The constancies

The tendency for perception to be veridical, summarized by the term 'perceptual constancy', was seized upon by Gestalt theorists. When objects recede they commonly do not shrink; white paper in shadow does not look greyer; objects remain the same colour despite changes in illumination; shapes do not change when seen from new positions. All these are examples of perception going beyond the local effects of isolated stimuli. In these cases, Gestalt theorists likened the environmental context in which stimuli are lodged to a dynamic *field*, a term synonymous with that currently being developed by the physicists of the period:

> 'The constancy of brightness, for instance, depends on the the relation of the illumination and brightness of the surrounding field to the brightness of the object under observation.'
>
> (Köhler, 1947, p.121)

We shall return to the idea of a field later in this chapter.

The main perceptual phenomena which form the core of the Gestalt theory have now been outlined. During the history of the Gestalt movement the work was extended to other areas. It was found, for example, that when a chicken is trained to peck at the darker of two greys and this is now paired with an even darker grey, it is to the latter that the animal now responds—suggesting that the original learning involved a relationship rather than an absolute stimulus value. Monkeys solving problems which are more closely related to their natural lives than the laboratory mazes used by the early behaviourists do not engage in constant trial-and-error, but show periods of inactivity followed by sudden solutions of the problems. This suddenness following a latent period is characteristic of much human experience also. For example, when we suddenly see a face in a fire which we have been staring at for a long time, or when we equally suddenly solve a crossword clue. In a very different context, Gestalt theory has been applied to artistic phenomena (Arnheim, 1949, 1956, 1969). And some have tried to relate it to psychological therapies. However, it is in the field of perception that the theory has had its major impact.

It must be remembered that the ideas we have outlined above became known partly due to the flair and conviction with which they were announced. As has been said, the Gestalt phenomena were often demonstrated on the printed page. The Gestaltists were good writers and enjoyed polemics. The success of the movement is hardly surprising, and readers are urged to consult some of the texts listed at the end of this chapter to experience some of the power of this approach to perception.

## THE FORMAL GESTALT THEORY AND KÖHLER'S BRAIN MODEL

So far, we have used the term 'theory' very loosely in describing the Gestaltists' work. We have used the term to describe a movement in the history of perception, some beliefs about the nature of perceivers and the ways in which their abilities should be studied, and a set of laws describing the behaviour of stimuli during various interactions. What is missing from all this has been an account of the Gestaltists' views as to *why* perception is as they claim. This is an appropriate place to turn to the explanations which Gestalt theory advanced to explain the Gestalt laws. The explanations comprise the formal Gestalt theory.

If the word failure can be applied to any part of Gestalt psychology, this is it. Historically, the actual theoretical account of Gestalt phenomena has never achieved the status and acceptance afforded to the empirical parts of the work, and it is instructive to consider why this should be so.

Why is perception dynamic? What causes the degree of organization which we have described? How shall we predict the behaviour of stimuli in new situations—how do we know what something will look like? A set of descriptions cannot answer these questions. What are required are explanations. Not surprisingly, the Gestalt theorists, particularly Köhler, went to considerable lengths to meet this challenge.

In hindsight we can consider the problem of explaining Gestalt phenomena as a choice between three alternatives: introspection, physical Gestalten or physiological mechanisms within the central nervous system. An introspective approach to the explanation of Gestalt phenomena would have been essentially psychological or mental in flavour. But, as we have seen, the hostility of the Gestalt movement to introspection rules out any explanation of this type.

## Physical Gestalten

Köhler, a trained physicist, considered the possibility that perceptual Gestalten were manifestations of a wider set of phenomena which included physical Gestalten. If the magnetic and electrical fields studied by physicists behave in dynamic ways, exhibiting tendencies to closure, balance and Prägnanz, might not stimuli be obeying the same laws? In this way, Köhler attempted to attain 'scientific citizenship' (Petermann, 1932) for the concept of the Gestalt. Thus in his work, *Physical Gestalten*, (1920), Köhler states that when two electrolytic solutions are in osmotic contact the electrical potential which arises is a new property of the system as a whole: 'the communicating system of solutions has gestalt characteristics'. It should be obvious what Köhler was trying to do in his discussions of these physical analogies.

Unfortunately, this approach cannot be fully sustained. It is possible to collect many instances of Gestalt-like phenomena in the physical sciences, but it is only too obvious that there are many situations in which assemblies of things, including chemicals, do not show Gestalt effects. Is a pile of coal a Gestalt? What about a mixture of salt and sand—where are the Gestalt interactions here? It seems unlikely that physical Gestalten have sufficient generality or relevance to permit extrapolations to psychological phenomena; they cannot carry the theoretical weight.

Even if the idea of physical Gestalten had seemed more plausible as the basis of theory of perception, this would not have solved all the problems facing the Gestalt theorists. When we attempt to analyse a particular pattern, what can we say about its components? The Gestalt movement (at least after 1929) opposed any form of reductionism, believing that theoretical explanations in psychology should be 'from above' rather than 'from below'. More seriously, we find in Köhler (1925) the statement that in completion phenomena, which are excellent examples of the dynamic aspects of perception, 'a part will suggest a whole only if it is a genuine part'. But, as one commentator has remarked, 'it is difficult to see how [this definition] can finally avoid the tautology that 'what produces a genuine whole is a genuine part' (Staniland, 1966).

The Gestaltists found themselves forced into an even more extreme position than this. Replying to a critic, Koffka was driven to say:

'in characterising a real object as a stimulus we do not refer to an absolute property of that object, in and by itself, only to the object's relationship to a living organism.

(Koffka's Reply to Benussi, 1915, italics added)

Later, he adds:

'Hence even if there were no physical Gestalten, there might nevertheless be stimuli for Gestalt presentations.'

(Koffka, ibid.)

As Staniland (1966) comments:

' If the perceptual experience cannot be inferred from the physical data and the stimulus data are not available to introspection, the only correlation left is with the processes of the central nervous system, and it was towards this that Gestalt theory deeply committed itself.'

And in doing so the Gestalt theorists lost their chance of bringing about a permanent change in the ways in which psychologists approached the problem of explaining perceptual phenomena.


## Isomorphism

Köhler attempted to lay the theoretical foundations for an adequate account of Gestalt phenomena (see for example Köhler, 1940, 1947). His writings placed a major emphasis upon physiological/neural mechanisms as the required level of explanation. To this end he announced a 'general leading principle', that of *Psychophysical Isomorphism*, in which it was assumed that there is a correlation ('coordination') between psychological experiences and physiological events in the central nervous system.

'Experienced order in space is always structurally identical with a functional order in the distribution of underlying brain processes.'

(Köhler, 1947, p.61)

For example, if the organization of a visual display leads one to group stimuli into, say, a triangle, then the stability and Gestalt-character of the triangle is due to underlying processes in the visual cortex. These preserve the essential relationship between the components of the figure, in other words their triangularity. If the triangle is formed from three rows of dots, then the underlying processes must preserve (a) the ordering of proximities and (b) the angular relations between the sides thus formed. Similar principles relate temporal ordering of experience to temporal sequences of brain processes.

The representation, it must be stressed, is *topological* rather than *topographical*. Just as the London Underground map indicates the correct sequence of stations, but would be of little use for navigating one's way through the streets above, so we must not expect that when someone reports that an array has become organized into a triangle an actual triangle of neural responses has formed in the visual cortex. What has come into existence is a neural process underlying the spatial essence of the organized figure experienced as a triangle. It is important to recognize that Köhler did not suggest that there were pictures in the head, although many commentators have falsely accused him of this (see Henle, 1984, for a collection of the many erroneous interpretations of Köhler's position). He knew that this merely displaces the problem (what perceives the pictures?). Gestalt isomorphism was that existing between organized experience and processes in the brain.

Köhler had been struck by the tendency of some stimulus patterns to reverse after a period of prolonged inspection. It was as if perceiving involved a process in the brain which caused its own termination. What sort of process could this be?

Köhler thought about the behaviour of chemicals in solutions. Most readers will be aware that many substances decompose in solution into particles having (opposed) electrical charges. Water itself forms positively charged hydrogen ions and negatively charged hydroxyl ions: $H^+$ and $OH^-$. Common salt (NaCl) forms $Na^+$ ions, which have lost an electron, and $Cl^-$ ions which carry an extra one. Hydrochloric acid forms $H^+$ and $Cl^-$ ions. Collecting differently charged ions at two spatially separated sites forms the basis of the electrical cell, which, when short-circuited, will cause a current flow. This is the key to the Gestalt brain model. Köhler therefore speculated that the following chain of events follows visual stimulation (we shall modify one of his own examples).

Consider a stimulus array comprising a light disc on a darker background. The disc is seen as an organized figure against a ground. The neural processes associated with the perception of the disc and the background terminate in the visual cortex. The final neurons in the causal chain between the retina and the visual cortex discharge chemicals into the fluid medium surrounding them and ionic decomposition takes place. The stronger discharges associated with the disc lead to higher ion concentrations at certain sites compared with those induced by the darker ground. But both figure- and ground-induced discharges are part of the larger liquid environment surrounding the visual cortex. Thus electromotive forces will arise between the figure, the darker ground and the internal environment. These forces will maintain a current, the intensity of which will depend upon the intensity of the original visual stimulus. Further, *the currents in the visual cortex will come under the influence of physical laws*. For example, they will distribute themselves spatially according to the laws of electrostatic vectors and therefore tend towards Prägnanz (Figure 3.6 illustrates this type of analysis). Thus the dynamic tendencies which we can observe inside ourselves when perceiving reflect the influence of physical forces in our brains.

The reader should now have a good impression of the style of Köhler's thinking. It is clear that his brain model is quite a gross one, in the sense that it involves large areas of the visual cortex. (Towards the end of his career Köhler was starting to speculate that the fields which he had postulated to account for the Gestalt-nature of perception might be smaller in scale, involving activity around single synapses: see Henle, 1984.)

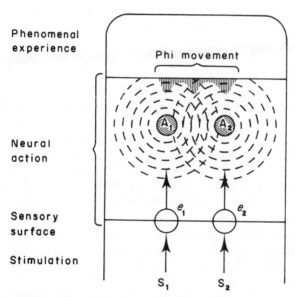

Figure 3.6   Köhler's field forces and the Phi Phenomenon. (Modified from Petermann, 1932.) $S_1$ and $S_2$ are two alternately flashing lights. $e_1$ and $e_2$ are events at the two retinae. $A_1$ and $A_2$ are points on the visual cortex from which the induced electrical fields spread. The overlap of the two fields yields a unitary percept: phi movement

The implications of Köhler's model are as follows:

(1) Context effects are explained because the very nature of the electrical processes is that they are not local and discrete but behave as *fields*. Thus the

impact of a stimulus is determined in part by the nature of the surrounding array—a fundamental Gestalt principle.

(2) The effects of stimulation can outlast a stimulus. Köhler does not claim that we can be aware of neural processes directly, but that we can adopt certain procedures which give us a clue to their nature. For example, prolonged fixation of patterns may give rise to after-effects in which it can be seen that one's perception is changed for relatively long periods. Thus when one fixates a rotating spiral for several minutes the after-effect (which is an apparent rotation of the spiral in the opposite direction) may last for hours or even days.

(3) The behaviour of the fields in the visual cortex explains the tendency of perception towards Prägnanz: it is because the underlying electrical distributions tend towards balance and symmetry that perceptual experience does the same.

(4) The dynamic processes in the visual cortex have an existence of their own— they are physical events. If electrical charges can cross gaps and distribute themselves around resistance networks in a dynamic, holistic manner, we should not be surprised to discover that perception can fill gaps or show field-like effects: the two sets of phenomena are directly related.

The temptation to look back disparagingly at Köhler's psycho-neural model should be resisted. Köhler was searching for an explanation of perceptual phenomena in terms of neural activity. There are still those, a quarter of a century after Köhler's death, who believe that the ultimate explanation of all psychological phenomena will be written in the language of physiology. His attempt was not absurd. Remember too that when Köhler first described his model knowledge of the workings of the living brain was sketchy, to say the least. It has been said that early attempts to probe the brain were like trying to understand people in the street from the top of a skyscraper, armed only with a giant needle. Köhler had to make the most of the knowledge available at that time. He wanted his model to be scientific. What could be more reasonable than to link it to some of the best science of his day, namely that associated with physics and chemistry?

To end this section on the Gestalt explanation of perceptual phenomena it must be stressed that it stands apart from the main contributions of the Gestaltists. Other Gestalt psychologists were less concerned with Köhler's psycho-neural model. Koffka, for example, was more content to describe and discuss Gestalt phemomena than to try to find a sound physiological explanation of them (see Koffka, 1924, 1935). To repeat a point made earlier, the wider meaning of Gestalt theory includes the phenomena described by Gestalt researchers and the psychological laws which they advanced. All this needs to be assessed. But for many who have supported the Gestalt approach over the years, the truth about the wider aspects of Gestalt psychology does depend upon the correctness or otherwise of Köhler's model. We must respect this distinction when examining the Gestalt contribution to perception. Incidentally, the special nature of Köhler's model, which we have called the formal Gestalt theory, explains why the theory was described at the start in terms of only two regions of our general classificatory scheme (described in Chapter 1). What we shall subsequently refer to as the Gestalt theory is broad, but Köhler's model is narrow: it links experience and the brain.

## AN ASSESSMENT OF THE GESTALT THEORY

This assessment will attempt to look at the more general Gestalt contribution to perception (which may now be referred to as the Gestalt Theory) rather than limiting itself to the brain model.

As has been shown, the Gestalt theorists held that there are certain phenomena which reveal the basic laws of perception, that perceptual processes are dynamic, rather than passive, and that the perceptual world is organized into patterns or configurations rather than a mosaic of sensations. They argued for a phenomenological rather than an introspective approach to perception, and preferred strong demonstrations to statistical descriptions. Their explanation of perceptual and related phenomena took the form of hypothetical brain processes which were part of a psycho-neural isomorphism, an explanation which is inherently nativist in its implications concerning the origins of perception in the individual perceiver.

It is now more than half a century since the first publications of the Gestalt theorists. What can be said about their contribution—how well has their work endured? We shall now review some relevant areas of research done since the development of the general Gestalt theory. We shall describe some researches which reveal flaws in the theory or in the phenomena which inspired it, and then describe some modern research which seems to support the Gestaltists' claims.

## GESTALT PHENOMENA

Most contemporary experimental psychologists would agree that the Gestalt psychologists were right about many things. Geometric illusions continue to fascinate theorists and experimenters alike; constancy in perception is undoubtedly one of its major achievements; we do seem to respond to relationships among stimuli rather than to their absolute values; context influences perception; wholes are more than the sum of their parts; stimuli become organized into patterns. The Gestaltists had undoubtedly chosen some important and reliable phenomena with which to support their claims.

## GESTALT PRINCIPLES

**Closure and balance: the tendency towards Prägnanz**

It is a prediction from Gestalt theory that, provided the influence of the actual stimulus is weakened, stimulus traces in the brain will shift towards balance and symmetry. Obviously, if one looks briefly at a crooked cross it will appear crooked: the actual stimulus is dominant. But suppose a subject were asked to remember such a cross after, say, a momentary exposure, should not subsequent reproductions of it become more symmetrical? Similarly, if someone views a circle with a gap in it under difficult conditions, shouldn't the gap tend to fill— showing the tendency towards completeness? The Gestaltists believed that both these tendencies would occur. The answer is that they do, but not always: some subjects in an experiment involving the reproduction of asymmetrical figures actually *exaggerated* asymmetries when reproducing the figures. Wulff (1922) attempted to bring both these tendencies under the heading of Gestalt principles which he called 'making precise' (the exaggeration), and 'levelling' (increased Prägnanz). But this led to the absurd position from which *any* change in a remembered figure could be explained but none could be predicted. And the detection of gaps in circles under difficult conditions is a popular way of studying visual acuity: something which would be impossible if one tended always to close the gap. These Gestalt tendencies are not wholly reliable.

There is, however, one modern piece of research which has exciting implications for Gestalt theory and the future of the idea of Prägnanz. Restle (1979) set out to quantify some effects discovered by Johansson (1950, 1977). Over a number of years Johansson has examined the ways in which subjects see simple moving dot displays. In a typical experiment three or more dots move smoothly and rhythmically back and forth across a display. The dots may move at different speeds, in various directions, and may be in or out of phase. Johansson found that the perception of these displays is dynamic in the sense that the dots are seen to be connected in some way, or to represent, say, the ends of rigid structures. In one display, for example, two outer dots move up and down in opposite directions whilst a central dot remains stationary. What one sees in this case looks likes a rigid rod swinging around a central pivot. When a row of dots move different distances, the inner ones moving furthest, one sees something like a skipping rope swinging in and out of the plane of the display. The effects are very beautiful and very compelling.

The questions Restle asked were, how can the movements of the dots be described or coded *objectively*, and how do these descriptions correlate with what viewers see? For example, one way of coding the displays would be to treat each dot as independent. Then one parameter will be required for a dot's starting position, one for its amplitude of movement, one for its phase (when it starts to move compared with other dots), one for its angle of tilt relative to the vertical, and so on. In such a manner one can produce a completely objective description of the movement of the dots, one which could be used, say, to programme a computer to drive the displays. But it is also possible to treat the dots as combinations. For example, if a number of dots move together in phase and across the same distance then a single set of parameters will code the motion of one of them and additional parameters will code the spacings and repetitions. This alternative way of coding will be equally objective, but it will of course be different.

Restle did an exhaustive coding exercise in which the various hierarchies of dot clusters used in the Johansson displays were coded, the dots treated as independent or linked in some manner. The results of this exercise are highly intriguing. Not surprisingly, the coding of dots as independent events requires the maximum number of movement parameters. When dots are treated as groups the number of parameters required to code the movement drops, and the more intimate the grouping the fewer the number of coding parameters required. The exciting finding is this: if one wishes to predict how the moving displays will be seen, then the movement configuration requiring *the fewest objective parameters* is the best bet. And the greater the discrepancy between the number of parameters needed for independent coding and for the coding of a particular grouping, the stronger is the tendency for observers to report the latter.

But the tendency to see the displays as simple, grouped and coherent is exactly what the Gestalt theorists meant by Prägnanz. The difference is that the Gestaltists proposed the principle (and gave examples) but offered no means of quantifying it. Here is an example where Prägnanz is clearly at work, and at the same time we are offered an objective measure of its effects. This is a very important development.

## Transpositional learning

The discovery that an animal trained to go to the darker of two grey stimuli will subsequently transfer this learning to an even darker grey was held to be an important extension of a Gestalt principle from human perception to animal behaviour. It was claimed that the demonstration was particularly embarrassing to stimulus-response theories of animal discrimination learning. It suffices to say that in fact stimulus-response theories can be made to account, not only for this result, but for those instances when the phenomenon does not occur (when for example the differences between the various stimuli are very large). This was demonstrated by Spence (1956).

## Stimulus ratios in perception

The Gestalt movement was correct to stress the role played by ratios between stimuli as determinants of how things will appear. Paper always looks white and coal black across a wide range of normal light intensities. What is the basis of this veridical perception? One answer adopted by the Gestaltists was that in this case the paper will always reflect *relatively* more light than coal, no matter what the level of illumination. Similar arguments were advanced to explain other forms of perceptual constancy. Stimulus ratios appear to be important in perceiving.

Let us develop this further by adding some numbers to a possible case involving brightness (or lightness) constancy. Suppose that one surface reflects 25 per cent of light falling onto it, another 50 per cent, and that light of, say, 200 units intensity illuminates both surfaces. They will reflect 50 and 100 units respectively. Now double the illumination strength to 400 units: the surfaces will now reflect 100 and 200 units to the eye—although the illumination has doubled, the *ratio* of reflected light to the eye has not changed. This is the basis of the classic explanation of constancy which the Gestalt psychologists adopted to explain the unchanging lightness or brightness of surfaces under conditions of changing illumination.

Generally, there will be few real-life situations which differ markedly from the hypothetical example above. Reflectance is a property of a surfaces: no change in illumination will alter ratios of reflection. The explanation of brightness constancy seems secure. There is, however, one situation in which ratios of reflected light can be altered, this is when additional light is added, not to the surfaces, but to stimulus energy on its way to the eye. This can happen when we look at things through a glass surface when that surface is reflecting additional light from other sources—one example is looking through the reflected glare of a shop window. To illustrate this point, consider again the second numerical illustration above: adding 100 units to the light which has already been reflected from the two surfaces will produce intensities at the eye of 200 and 300 units. The ratio has now changed from $1:2$ to $2:3$. So when we look *through* a reflection the ratio basis of brightness or lightness constancy has gone.

Gilchrist and Jacobsen (1983) noticed something which any Gestaltist could have seen: things do not seem different when we see them through reflections. They describe an elegant experiment in which scenes were viewed through a sloping glass surface onto which additional light could be projected, thus altering the ratios of lights coming from objects in the scenes. This additional light is known as a veiling luminance. The experiment showed that, provided the scene is a real one (that is, it has three-dimensional objects in it) perception is veridical through a veiling luminance. In other words, lightness constancy remains even though the ratios of reflected lights from the surfaces have changed. Thus whilst the Gestalt emphasis on ratios is probably close to the truth, this cannot be the whole story. We still do not know exacly *how* perceivers use ratios to achieve constancy in perception, nor how they cope when the ratios are corrupted, as in the above example. Similar conclusions have been arrived at by those who have examined the role of ratios of wavelengths of light in the perception of colour (see, for example, Land, 1985).

## Effects using two-dimensional displays

Because they wished to convince their readers through dramatic illustrations, and (presumably) because drawings are simpler to make than three-dimensional objects, the Gestaltists obtained many of their effects from flat patterns. Under these conditions, Wertheimer's laws of organization have not been seriously challenged: none has been shown to be actually wrong. And the general phenomenon of figure-ground organization is still recognized as very important. However, the two-dimensional drawings which have been most commonly used to investigate these phenomena are not characteristic of all our daily experience: they are not what our eyes evolved to see. It is not surprising, therefore, that when three-dimensional arrays have been studied the results have sometimes cast doubt upon the adequacy of the Gestalt laws (Kaufman, 1974, provides an excellent introduction to this more recent work). And there is at least one rival to the Gestalt view of figure ground phenomena which places much more emphasis upon learned rather than innate factors (Hochberg, 1971).

In the next chapter, and elsewhere in this book, the concept of *ecological validity* will be discussed. For now, it suffices to define the phrase as meaning the naturalness of stimuli, how representative they are of the objects and events which organisms must deal with in order to survive. It must be said that many of the displays which the Gestaltists used in their work had very low ecological validity. This does not prove that Gestalt generalizations are invalid or that Gestalt claims about the laws of perception are seriously wrong, simply that their choice of stimuli was often unfortunate and should have made them cautious about over-generalizing their findings. This criticism can be extended to the Gestalt work on illusions, which are fascinating and reliable phenomena, but how often do we experience strong illusions in everyday life?

## The Gestalt psychoneural model

Earlier in this chapter an attempt was made to give as sympathetic an account as possible of this aspect of the Gestalt theory. Even so, the reader must have felt that we were drifting into science fiction. In truth, apart from Köhler, few have taken this account of perception very seriously. It is now possible to assert that it is probably wrong. (However, see Henle, 1984, for a vigorous defence of the general principle of isomorphism.)

First, whilst it is true that the disturbance of activity in the central nervous system following sensory stimulation often outlasts that stimulation, it is not true that this involves very large fields or areas of the brain (Sperry, Miner and Meyers, 1955). Second, and more seriously, experiments have cast grave doubts on the existence in the brain of anything like the direct currents proposed by Köhler. Placing connected metal pins in the visual cortex of experimental animals should surely short-circuit such currents if they exist; the insertion of insulating mica plates into the same regions of the brain would be expected to block the spread of electricity. Both of these experiments have been performed and in neither case was the visual performance of the subjects seriously disrupted (Sperry and Miner, 1955; Sperry, Miner and Meyers, 1955). We must conclude that this important part of the Gestalt theory, in fact the basic explanation of Gestalt phenomena, is likely to be incorrect. (Once again, see Henle's, 1984, paper for a criticism of these direct attacks on Köhler's model of cortical functioning.)

## Nativism

If perceptual experience is a direct reflection of underlying (electrical) brain forces, and if these forces obey physical laws, then it follows that this experience should be as fixed and rigid as the laws of physics demand. Gestalt theorists might have been willing to concede that Köhler's field forces have not been confirmed by subsequent research, but it seems very likely that they would have clung tenaciously to some form of nativism, given the philosphical origins described at the start of this chapter. Thus the Gestalt view must be that whilst perception can be influenced by attentional processes and the effects of such variables as familiarity, practice and learning, it is basically fixed in nature. Two tests of this position are possible: first, humans and animals should not be able to reorganize their perceptions. Second, there should be perceptual competence at birth. Both these issues have been addressed in experimental investigations.

The obvious theoretical importance of these questions—whether perception is rigid or flexible, and whether it is innate or acquired—has led to much research. Animals and humans have been subjected to a number of procedures in which their sensory imputs were distorted or blocked. The severity and bizarreness of these manipulations has varied greatly.

### *The flexibility of perception*

Mild distortion has taken the form, for example, of having people wear tinted lenses for long periods. After a time (as any wearer of sunglasses knows) the tinted world reverts to normal: one has adapted to the slight change in the nature of the light entering the eye. Those who have worn prisms which tilt the world in a certain direction also report complete adaptation to this distorted input.

More severe distortion has been achieved by lens or mirror systems which completely invert the world. Here reports of adaptation must be treated with extreme caution. It is obviously difficult to know just what complete reorganization of inverted vision would look like, and many reports are extemely ambiguous. Certainly there is *adjustment* to severe distortion: in one famous experiment (I. Kohler, 1955) the subject was eventually able to ride a bicycle whilst wearing inverting lenses—but it is not clear whether this is accompanied by phenomenal reinversion of the world.

Many animals have recovered from moderate sensory distortion, but in extreme cases, such as when the eyeball of an amphibian was loosened, rotated through 90 degrees and then replaced in the socket, no adaptation took place. Flies with their heads rotated 180 degrees fail to show any adaptation to the consequent inversion of their visual inputs. (For an account of some of these dramatic experiments see Sperry, 1951.)

The experimental literature in this area is very large. At this point we will simply assert that (a) animals and humans can adapt to many forms of mild sensory distortion, (b) 'higher' animals such as monkeys and chimpanzees are better at adapting (are more flexible) than 'lower' animals such as flies, amphibians and chickens, (c) it is doubtful if any species can completely adapt to very severe distortion (although such a statement risks being tautological). Readers wishing to make their own assessments of this literature should consult some of the original publications cited above and at the end of this chapter.

Our overall assessment of the evidence is that basic perceptual organization is relatively inflexible. This accords with the nativist stance taken by Gestalt theorists, although it must be added that some contemporary workers might disagree with this conclusion; many would argue for the old Scottish verdict, Not Proven.

## The innate versus the acquired in perception

The relevant literature here is enormous. Fortunately, it is well reviewed in most basic texts on perception to which the reader should turn for detailed reviews. Basically, the types of evidence which have been examined with this question in mind are human and animal deprivation experiments and studies of the competence of young infants.

*Animal deprivation experiments* no longer seem to hold the promise they once did. Rearing an animal without, say, vision, and then testing its visual perception is probably not the way to discover whether visual capacities are innate: the animal is an abnormal animal; suddenly acquiring vision may be frightening; the animal may not be motivated to do well with its new sense. These problems may be insuperable.

*Human deprivation* studies examine the visual performance of those who have recovered from blindness and compare it with that of the normally sighted. Here too problems of adjustment and motivation are to be expected, and this is borne out in many reports. Here is a tentative summary of the literature.

The newly sighted are not simply people who have lacked vision, but people who have learned to live with their other senses. In this they are atypical perceivers when their vision is restored. What does seem to be generally true is that such people have great difficulties in organizing and making sense of their new visual world. A nativist would not be dismayed by this discovery, for reasons such as those outlined earlier. However, where the nativist position gains some limited support from these studies is in the general finding that most subjects who have been studied appear to perceive lines, edges, brightnesses and colours without difficulty (see, for example von Senden, 1960; Gregory and Wallace, 1963; Valvo, 1971). Equally striking is the fact that in most reports it appears as though the organization of the world into figure and ground takes place quickly and spontaneously, as the Gestaltists would have predicted. This evidence suggests that at least some of our visual capacities are innately organized and require little or no learning.

*Infant vision studies* are probably the best way of examining the relative importance of innate versus acquired factors in the development of perception. To the student of the history of perception this is a most fascinating area. If one looks at the literature of the 1940s and compares it with contemporary work one becomes aware of a steady swing from the empiricist emphasis of the early workers such as Hebb (1949) to a growing belief that the newborn is amazingly competent. It is not the infants who have changed in this 40-year period, it is the skill of experimenters. The great difficulty has always been how to communicate with the newborn. As the techniques for doing this have improved—using conditioning methods, measuring eye-movements, habituating the infant to one stimulus before presenting a different one, recording changes in heart rate—so the age at which infants can be shown to have certain perceptual abilities has moved inexorably downwards. Newborn infants show shape constancy (Slater and Morison, 1985); they prefer their mothers' voices (De Casper and Fifer, 1980); they will follow with their eyes a head shape bearing normal features more intently than one with the features scrambled—this within five minutes of birth (Goren, Sarty and Wu, 1975; Dziurawiec and Ellis, 1986); their colour vision resembles that of adults (Bornstein, Kessen and Weiskopf, 1976).

None of these studies proves that the world of the newborn is the same as ours. It must certainly lack associations, meaning and familiarity. Perhaps their experience is like ours during those first few moments when we awaken in a strange room: we see everything, but nothing makes sense. And it is likely, particularly from animal studies and from studies of children born with perceptual defects (for example, Blakemore and Cooper, 1970), that there are *critical periods* following birth during which experience of the world moulds the developing senses. For example, if an infant is born with a squint and this is corrected immediately, normal stereoscopic vision will develop. But if there is a delay in treating the squint, then when the deviant eye is brought into line surgically the child's visual performance may be permanently impaired: it looks as though those cells in the visual cortex which are binocularly driven must receive appropriate input in the first eighteen months of life if they are to develop correctly.

But even if the existence of critical periods is recognized, there remains a mass of evidence to show the existence of perceptual abilities shortly after birth. This throws doubt on the claim that we must learn to perceive and is strong evidence in support of the nativist position adopted by the Gestalt theorists.

Clearly, the above reviews have been biased to studies of humans and the 'higher' primates, for obvious reasons. It is important to say at this point that a very strong version of nativism can be defended if discussion is restricted to the perceptual abilities of simpler organisms. Many creatures show complex behaviour the moment they emerge into the world, and as this may involve things as complicated as flying through the environment, it is clear that their visual powers must be intact from the start: insects mostly do not bump into things. There is no doubt that perception can be innately organized, but the interesting question is whether this is the case in us and species similar to us.

## Cross-cultural similarities in perception

If perception is shaped by innate brain processes, and if all human brains are essentially alike, originating as they have from some common stock, then perceptual processes should be similar in all peoples, irrespective of the particular environments in which they live. It is true that some differences have emerged when people from so-called primitive cultures are compared with Western subjects. Generally these differences have been demonstrated when the stimuli used are quite artificial, for example drawings, photographs and even illusory figures. There is little evidence that there are any major differences between cultures when it comes to fundamental forms of perceiving such as depth perception, colour vision, pitch perception, sound localization and so on.

More importantly, there are some striking agreements between cultures in matters where it was possible that major differences might have emerged. For example, children in cultures which range from the highly sophisticated to the non-literate tend to draw people in the same way: the familiar matchstick figures of our own childhood drawings are to be found all over the world: this looks like an untaught, universal convention (see Arnheim, 1956). Children in very different cultures form similar impressions of schematic faces (Gordon, Zukas and Chan, 1982). In a series of highly ingenious researches, Ekman and his colleagues (Ekman, 1971; Ekman and Friesen, 1967, 1971) have shown that there are strong cross-cultural similarities in human facial expressions and, significantly, in the perception of these patterns. (There are of course cultural differences in facial expression: during the Second World War a Japanese woman was expected to smile politely on learning of the death of her soldier husband.)

The evident cross-cultural agreement in this area is impressive and provides additional evidence for innate components in perception.

Finally, we must point out that Arnheim (1949) and others have claimed that much of our perception of expressiveness—in objects, works of art and music—is due to underlying field effects in the brain. It must be said, however, that the evidence for and against this position is rather inconclusive.

In view of the evidence listed above, we can assert that there are good reasons for believing that a major part of our ability to perceive is innately determined. Whilst this evidence could be marshalled to support *any* nativist theory, it remains true that it is the Gestalt theorists who put foward the most explicit and influential version of nativism and provoked much of the stimulating research which we have attempted to outline.

## FINAL REMARKS ON THE GESTALT THEORY

Subsequent research in perception owes a great debt to the movement started by Wertheimer, Koffka and Köhler. Each of these men had a good eye for important phenomena. Little of what they researched seems trivial in retrospect. Indeed, many of the phenomena which they uncovered are now seen to present some of the major challenges to perceptual theory. The Gestalt theorists had breadth. They wrote well and with conviction. Their phenomenological programme—to explain everyday perceiving—was a valid one. Their belief in the innate basis of much of perception may well turn out to be true. The recognition of similarities between perceptual processes and aspects of problem solving was a valuable gain.

What then of the flaws in the Gestalt approach to perception? In the first place the central explanatory device, the brain model, is almost certainly incorrect. Had the contemporary knowledge of neurophysiology been more advanced Köhler would probably have avoided this trap. But the remainder of the Gestalt theory (in contrast to Gestalt research) is faulty by modern standards, and it is worth trying to explain why this should be so.

At the start of this chapter it was stated that the Gestalt psychologists were motivated by a philosophical conviction that perception must be a centrally organized dynamic process. The rate at which supporting evidence for this position was accumulated is a very impressive achievement. Most of the key Gestalt phenomena had been described and explored within twenty years of the first statements of the theory: figure ground, relational effects, whole-part interactions, the constancies, laws of grouping, the effects of Prägnanz—all these had been presented to a wide readership in lucid books and papers.

But too much of a scientist's time can be spent demonstrating the correctness of a theory. We have already listed some of the inadequacies of the Gestalt theory, experimental results which should have provoked, not argument, but further research: the investigation of Prägnanz is a good example of this. The

Gestalt psychologists were fine polemicists, but debating skilfully is not the same as being right.

Too much of Gestalt theory is circular. For example, having demonstrated the powerful tendency to organize perceptual inputs into simple, coherent experiences, the Gestaltists allowed descriptions of this phenomenon to serve as explanations. Prägnanz is a good example: perception tends to be as good as conditions allow and this is Prägnanz. Why? Because of Prägnanz (a tautology) or field forces in the brain (speculative and untestable at the time).

Gestalt psychology contains few references to Darwin. As a result there is little concern in Gestalt theory for what we would now term the ecology from which stimuli arise. The dangers of this have been outlined earlier. In terms of the general model offered in Chapter 1, it can be said that the Gestalt psychologists should have included more regions in their theory: then they might have been forced to think more about the real-life stimuli which shaped the evolution of perception.

Finally, as has been said earlier, the Gestaltists tended to concentrate upon strong effects which can be reliably demonstrated. But much of perception may not be like this. In the real world, the world of unreliable, uncertain stimuli, perceiving may involve processes of a statistical nature (this will be the theme of the next chapter). This is an unfortunate complication for the researcher, but if it is the truth it must be handled by an adequate theory. Gestalt theory did not find a place for such ideas.

These then are some of the criticisms which occur to one who looks back over the Gestalt movement. But the importance of this body of work cannot be doubted. Gestalt psychologists exerted a permanent influence on the psychology of perception. All who follow are indebted to the theory in some manner. And, despite what now look like strategic errors in their approach, the Gestalt movement still stands as a model of the literate, enthusiastic and creative approach to the problems of perception.

## NOTES ON CHAPTER 3

Gestalt writings on perception are clear, accessible and extremely interesting. Readers wishing to learn more about this approach should start by reading original Gestalt documents, particularly the Köhler and Koffka references given in the text. (It may seem strange that a number of the references given below appeared so long after the start of the Gestalt theory. Many of these are English translations which appeared after the Gestalt theory became more widely known and the Gestalt psychologists had moved to the United States.)

Köhler's Field Theory of neural action is described in his book, *Dynamics in Psychology (1940)*

The source book by Ellis (1938) is invaluable and contains some of the best-known replies of Gestalt theorists to their critics. See particularly Koffka's

*Reply to Benussi* and Köhler's *Reply* to Müller.

Petermann (1932) provides a useful description of Gestalt work on dynamic aspects of perception. Part 1 of this book contains a description of Köhler's views on physical Gestalten and his brain model.

Haber and Hershenson (1980) provide a valuable introduction to studies of the development of perceptual mechanisms. See their Chapter 13 for a discussion of infant studies.

One Gestalt psychologist who has not been referred to in the main text, but whose work deserves mention is David Katz. See, for example his book *Gestalt Psychology* (1951).

Readers who enjoy the style of the best Gestalt writings will also enjoy reading Michotte's work on the perception of causality (Michotte, 1946). This shares some of the characteristics of Gestalt research and the demonstrations, which are easy to set up, are extremely compelling. The Johansson (1964) reference describes experiments which would have been of great interest to Gestalt theorists.

The distinguished contemporary psychologist Julian Hochberg has attempted to extend and improve some Gestalt ideas on visual perception. See Hochberg (1968, 1973) for an account of some highly interesting perceptual researches.

Interesting applications of Gestalt theory to the arts are described by Arnheim (1949, 1956, 1969)

Figure 3.7

For a recent defence of Gestalt views on brain processes see the article by Henle (1984).

We have run the risk of over-emphasizing the Gestaltists' nativism. In fairness it should be pointed out that, for example, Koffka (1924) was willing to consider the possibility that experience and language could influence the development of colour vision in children. In the same book, Koffka takes a very moderate position when discussing human development from empiricist and nativist viewpoints.

The enduring validity of Gestalt laws is demonstrated by a display to be seen with increasing frequency in public buildings in Britain. The reader may care to say which laws of organization underly the way we perceive Figure 3.7.

# Chapter 4

# Brunswik's probabilistic functionalism

The second theory to be described is probabilistic functionalism, which was essentially the work of one man, Egon Brunswik (1903–1955). Brunswik left no school of followers, his work is rarely cited in modern writings, and no subsequent group of workers has ever assumed the label, 'Probabilistic Functionalist'. There are, however, three reasons for including this short chapter on Brunswik's work.

First, Brunswik was one of the first experimental psychologists to believe that perceptual research should reflect the complexity of the phenomena it was trying to explain. The maxim for most earlier researchers (with the exception of some Gestalt psychologists) seems to have been, 'simplify and control'. The desire to copy other sciences caused researchers to adopt classically simple designs in which all variables save that under investigation were carefully controlled. This led inevitably to a concentration upon laboratory research, the use of trained subjects and the need to use highly artificial stimuli. Brunswik was convinced that imposing such simplicity upon perception blinded researchers to its true complexity and power.

Second, Brunswik was a functionalist, mindful always of the fact of evolution. To achieve a full understanding of any living perceptual system we must remember that behind the system lie millions of years of evolutionary development. The investigation of a perceptual system should be guided by the fact that the system must have survival value. The system cannot be understood except in relation to the perceiver's environment or ecology. It was not until the work of J. J. Gibson and, later, the work on the computational theory of vision (both of which will be described later in this book) that this important point was fully accepted.

The third reason for writing about Brunswik's theory is the stress he placed upon the uncertain nature of the perceiver's world. Helmholtz and later empiricists claimed that evidence arriving at receptor surfaces is often imperfect; visual images, for example, are not perfect copies of objects, they may be blurred and incomplete. The accounts of perception which arose from this discovery invoked higher, reasoning-like processes which constructed percepts from sensory evidence. Brunswik's position is even more extreme than this: he held that

76

cues arising from the world are essentially statistical or probabilistic in nature. Perceptual evidence is more than incomplete, it is uncertain. Perceiving is a series of gambles. Brunswik's emphasis upon the world from which stimuli arise, together with his suggestions for new quantitative methods for studying perception, will form the basis of this chapter.

## EGON BRUNSWIK

Brunswik's career began in Vienna and ended in California where he died in 1955 at the age of 52. His work in perception is described in a number of papers in English and German. Detailed statements of his theoretical position are to be found in 'The conceptual framework of psychology' (1952) and *Perception and the Representative Design of Psychological Experiments* (1956), which was published posthumously.

Brunswik's views on perception evolved during his lifetime and would certainly have been modified further had he lived. In what follows the aim is to convey the essence of Brunswik's ideas, at the risk of some over-simplification. The reader who then wishes to work at a more detailed level through Brunswik's difficult writings should consult the references cited at the end of this chapter.

## PROBABILISTIC FUNCTIONALISM

In Brunswik's writings a perceiver resembles a boxer who is fighting to survive. On no account must he take a hard punch to a critical area, but he must always be ready to seize his own opportunities to attack. It is vital to anticipate the opponent's moves: which is the real threat, which the feint. The boxer needs clues, ways of predicting what will happen in the next fraction of a second. The opponent will inevitably give some hints—movements of the arms and legs, changes of expression, shifts of gaze—but none of these is entirely to be trusted. The fight is in part a gamble: the first fighter to predict accurately will survive; errors will be punished. And there is no set of rules, no textbook of boxing, which can guarantee success. It all depends on getting things right at the time, with speed rather than precision.

Brunswik's theory of perception may be outlined using the concepts and terminology which he used in his writings.

### Distal and proximal cues and the achievement of stability

As we study a perceiving organism it becomes increasingly obvious that its behaviour is directed not to the pattern of stimulation on the sense receptor, but to the world beyond. Although it is possible to list *proximal* variables or *cues*, such as the sizes and shapes of retinal images, behaviour is directed not to these but to the actual properties of things and events out in the world, to *distal* variables. The researcher's main task is to discover the basis of this achievement. Further, all that we know about our own perceiving (and what we can infer about perceiving in other species) tells us that the central achievement of perception is *stability*. Although our retinal images are constantly shifting because of the ways we move our heads and eyes, the world we experience is a stationary one.

### The probabilistic nature of cues

The environment, to use Brunswik's term, 'scatters its effects'. The cues which arise in the external world are only *probabilistic* and not fully dependable. An example (not Brunswik's) will reinforce this important point. Suppose we are searching for edible fruit. Let us assume that edible fruit is in fact generally (a) darker, (b) redder, (c) softer and (d) sweeter. Obviously, darker and redder are visual cues, softer is tactile, sweeter is gustatory: the environment is scattering its effects. And these cues, the only ones available, are all imperfect: all carry some risk. Not all ripe fruit is red, nor is all red fruit edible. Sweetness often indicates edibility, but some poisonous fruits are sweet. Some fruit is less edible when soft, some soft fruit will be rotten.

### Vicarious functioning and the perceiver as an intuitive statistician

What can the perceiver do, faced with such uncertainty? We must remember that for millions of years such problems were, literally, a matter of life or death. Brunswik's answer was that in order to survive, the perceiver must be able to act as an *intuitive statistician*. The perceiver must weigh and combine cues and shift from ones which are not available to others which are. As cues are varied and commonly have reliabilities of less than 1.0, the environment is described as being *vicariously mediated*. The response to vicarious mediation is *vicarious functioning* in the perceiver.

Flexibility in perception must be accompanied by flexibility of response: organisms are clearly goal-directed. An experimental animal, prevented from gaining access to reward in a usual manner, will find another solution to the problem: a rat which has learned to run through a maze will swim if it is flooded.

Perception then is *uncertainty-geared*. It aims for 'smallness of error at the expense of the highest frequency of precision'. And as perception involves the evaluation of evidence from different sources, the estimation of relative probabilities and decisions about the attainment of goals, it clearly shares many of the properties of thinking. There are differences though. Thinking aims for definite answers, it is 'certainty-geared'. Thinking is deterministic and discontinuous; it is characterized by 'sudden attainment', often following lengthy pauses. These qualities are sufficiently different from those of perceiving for the latter to require a special term: *ratiomorphic*. Thus a clever person will not necessarily be a better perceiver. And illusions commonly persist even when they have been 'explained' to us (Brunswik once referred to this as 'the stupidity of the senses').

## The validity of cues

Validity is an important concept in Brunswik's theory. The nature of the physical world, and the structure of the various sense organs, creates relationships between distal and proximal variables. For example, one impressive aspect of vision is its stability. Researchers can measure the size, distance and position of any object in a field of view. From this list of distal variables we can calculate the sizes and positions of retinal images (or, more conveniently, we can take photographs from the observer's position and use these as substitutes for the retina). These new values tell us about proximal variables. In Brunswik's opinion, the task remaining for the researcher is to discover the relationship between the distal and proximal variables, for here must lie the key to the achievement of perceptual stability. The relationship will seldom be perfect and simple, of course: distant objects usually form smaller images than near objects, but very small objects form small images even when they are near.

But how can the relationship between distal and proximal variables be quantified? Brunswik suggests that the *correlation coefficient* is the most appropriate measure. The magnitude of the coefficient offers a useful index of the *ecological validity* of a particular cue—retinal image size in the example above. Ecological validity will seldom be perfect, as we have shown, but obviously some cues will be better than others and this will be reflected in higher correlations.

The ecological validity of a cue indicates its potential usefulness for an organism, but does not reveal whether or not the cue is actually used. The researcher must now ascertain whether or not a potential cue has *functional validity*. For example, consider the role of the two eyes in stereoscopic vision. It is known that this form of depth perception is based upon the small differences between left- and right-eye views which exist because of the lateral separation between the eyes. The resulting *retinal disparity* is a powerful source of information concerning an object's position in the third dimension: it has high ecological validity. But it is of no help to a small minority of people who lack the ability to fuse information from the two eyes. For these 'stereo-blind' individuals the ecologically valid cue has no functional validity. In contrast, many people have been shown to base their judgements of the intelligence of others on aspects of their appearance. For example, wearers of spectacles tend to be judged as cleverer. But as this is not in fact true, we can say that spectacle wearing may have high functional validity (it is used as a cue), but low ecological validity (don't trust guesses about intelligence based on appearance).

### The lens model of perception

Brunswik considered this to be an important part of his theory. The model was meant to illustrate how perception involves a kind of focusing: the scattered and mutually substitutable cues arising from the environment must somehow be gathered together for possible use. Perception invoves a focusing of cues, it 'achieves' distal objects and it is towards these that responses are directed.

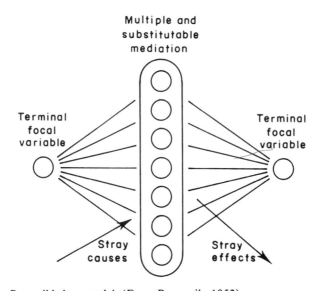

Figure 4.1   Brunwik's lens model. (From Brunswik, 1952)

In its original form the lens model treated perception as analogous to a single bi-concave lens (Figure 4.1). Later versions reflect Brunswik's increasing recognition of the importance of central, ratiomorphic processes: habits, evaluations and predispositons can all influence behaviour. And it is (trivially) true that central factors must underlie mutually substitutable responses: we can respond to a stimulus by speaking or pushing a button if asked to do so. For these reasons a pair of bi-convex lenses may be more appropriate as a model of perceptual processes (Figure 4.2).

Brunswik believed that his lens model could guide the quantitative assessment of particular perceptual achievements and thus assist researchers. In an illustrative exercise (Brunswik, 1956, Figure 10) data from a study of size constancy were placed within a lens model. Photographs of a real scene were taken and the actual and retinal (photographic) sizes of objects were compared. Other cues to distance were recorded. Subjects then judged the sizes of objects from the photographs. Correlations between object and image sizes yielded values for ecological validities, and correlations between cues and judgements yielded functional validities. The various cues available in the photographs (for example, size and vertical position) could then be ranked in terms of their relative importance. Although Brunswik did not do this (though he did elsewhere), it was now possible to use the correlation coefficients to trace 'principal rays' through the lens, revealing the basis of the form of perceptual stability represented by size constancy. In other words, people can judge sizes from photographs—the overall reduction in the sizes of depicted objects does not trouble them—and the lens model can reveal the basis of this attainment.

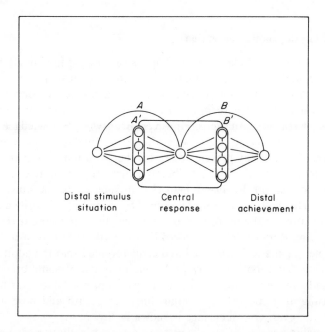

Figure 4.2   A double-lens version of Brunswik's model. *A* and *B* are functional areas. *A'* and *B'* are central processes which mediate between substitutable stimuli. High correlations between responses (verbal report, pointing, button-pressing etc.) suggest that they too are substitutable and arise from central goal-directed processes, represented by a circle in the figure. (From Leeper, 1966)

The lens model will not be discussed further. As a way of conceptualizing various aspects of perception it can be useful; it shaped the opening parts of this book. As a means of gaining deep insights into perception the lens model appears to have little to offer; a conclusion which is reinforced by experience with students who appear to gain little understanding even of Brunswik's own work by concentrating on this single part. It should be said of the lens model, however, that it is one of the earliest examples of this type of thinking in the history of perceptual research. And Brunswik himself thought it important.

## BRUNSWIK'S RESEARCHES

A good way to understand Brunswik's style of thinking is to study some of his own empirical investigations. Some of these are valuable less for what they achieved than for what they attempted. This review will omit Brunswik's earlier, more orthodox researches and concentrates on three of his most original publications.

### A study of physiognomic perception

Brunswik was critical of classical psychophysical designs in which all variables save the one under investigation are kept constant. Just as no psychologist investigating personality should generalize from a restricted sample of people, so generalizations about perception are invalid if the stimuli are not in some way typical of real-life situations. However, Brunswik acknowledged that pure *representative design*—the ideal—was often unattainable. Real faces, or even photographs of faces, may present the researcher with too many variables; such complex stimuli also make it impossible to achieve representative samples from such a vast population. Brunswik held that in such cases one must look for a compromise. He chose the factorial design. The study to be described represents Brunswik's claim for the usefulness of such designs in perceptual research.

Brunswik and Reiter (1937; reworked in Brunswik, 1956) constructed a number of simple schematic faces. Trial and error revealed that the addition of hair made all such faces look similar, whilst the omission of some other features, such as pupils, made the faces look unreal. A compromise face was finally constructed using an oval outline, straight lines for mouth and nose and simple ellipses for the eyes. One such face is shown in Figure 4.3.

The following aspects of the faces were systematically varied: nose length, forehead height (horizontal position of the eyes), mouth height and eye separation. When the full ensemble was examined certain combinations of features appeared unacceptably unreal or grotesque and these were rejected. The final ensemble comprised 189 schematic faces, some of which are shown in Figure 4.4.

Subjects' descriptions of the faces were recorded and used as the basis for the final descriptive scales: gay-sad, young-old, good-bad, likeable-unlikeable, beautiful-ugly, intelligent-unintelligent, energetic-unenergetic. Next, subsets of the faces were ranked on each of the seven scales. Finally, the rank scores were converted to indices ranging from 0 (least favourable) to 100 (most favourable).

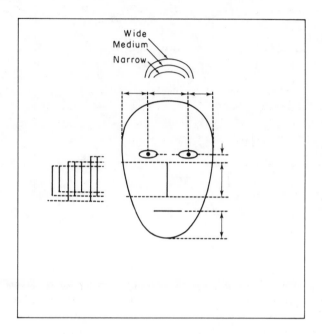

Figure 4.3   The Brunswik–Reiter schematic face. (Redrawn from Brunswik and Reiter, 1937)

The results of this experiment revealed co-variation or grouping between (a) apparent mood and age, (b) character, likeability and beauty, (c) intelligence and energy. Variations in mouth height elicited the most extreme response: the higher the mouth the gayer and younger the face (and vice versa) but the lower the apparent intelligence. Widely spaced eyes and short noses had a similar effect to high mouths. The longest noses had unfavourable effects throughout. Higher foreheads generally received favourable judgements. A subsequent analysis of variance showed that all main effects were significant, the order of importance of the physiognomic cues being (1) forehead height, (2) mouth height, (3) eye spacing.

These are very interesting results. Brunswik and Reiter had discovered that strong impressions, of the type we form everyday when looking at other people, can be induced by very simple patterns. And small changes in these patterns induce marked changes in the impressions they induce. It is now natural to ask about the interactions between the various parts of the faces. For example, are there interesting Gestalt interactions in which, for example, nose length enhances or diminishes the effect of close-set eyes?

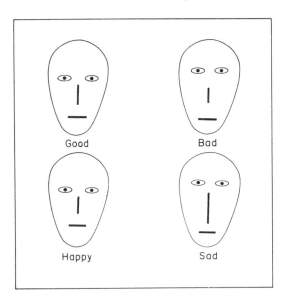

Figure 4.4   Four faces from Brunswik's experiment which were associated with judgements of Good, Bad, Happy (Gay) and Sad. (Redrawn from Brunswik and Reiter, 1937)

Strangely, Brunswik veers away from such an analysis (other than reporting the significance levels of certain interactions), his excuse being the incomplete nature of his factorial design due to the exclusion of certain faces at the start. This is regrettable, particularly as a study of the ensemble of faces used by Brunswik would convince the reader that although the number of features used is minimal, the resulting configurations are indeed face-like, showing how little information we need in order to achieve an impression of facialness. (Many years after Brunswik's study, the present author and colleagues (Gordon, Zukas and Chan, 1982) found that children in British, African and Chinese cultures produced strikingly similar responses to the Brunswik–Reiter faces, suggesting that the stereotyped responses which they induce may be in large part unlearned and universal.)

It is also of interest to observe the nature of the effects produced by small manipulations of certain features: some of the faces do indeed look sadder, more threatening and so on. The Brunswik–Reiter faces appear to offer powerful opportunities for understanding what it is in a face which can induce impressions of emotion and mood, and yet this work was not extended and developed. Brunswik had struck gold but left the mother lode unworked.

### Size constancy under real-life conditions

The traditional psychophysical method of measuring size constancy requires the observer to adjust a near stimulus until it matches the apparent size of a distant one. Typically, the measurement takes place in a large room or a long corridor. The variables manipulated include the attitude of the subject, the distance of the far stimulus, the use of one or two eyes, and so on. This of course is the type of design to which Brunswik objected because of its artificiality, its failure to sample the real environment.

In an experiment published in 1944 and reworked in his 1956 book, Brunswik describes a very different approach to the phenomenon. A student was followed outdoors for a period by a psychologist who asked her to estimate the size of that object which was currently dominant in her field of view. From the resulting sample of 174 estimates a number were selected for further analysis, which involved measuring the actual sizes and distances of the judged objects.

The size range of the objects was very large, 105:1, much greater than any that had ever been used in a laboratory study. (Brunswik was clearly correct about the unrepresentative nature of much of the research in this area.) Brunswik's reporting of his main results leaves much to be desired. The main finding, however, is of some interest: the correlation between object size and image size (the angle subtended at the eye by an object) was only 0.7 over all objects, dropping to 0.1 when small objects were excluded from the analysis. Thus the ecological validity of image size is low. But the overall correlation between object size and judged size was extraordinarily high: 0.99. Clearly the subject had achieved true and valid distal focusing despite the relatively poor utility of one well-known cue to size constancy.

At this point we await a lengthy discussion by Brunswik on how the sizes of objects in the real world are 'attained': his work has uncovered an important paradox and we await his speculations on this with interest. Disappointingly, we are offered only a brief description of distance cues in general and reference to a proposed experiment using photographs.

This is not the place for a lengthy discussion of the perception of size: interested readers should consult the admirable review in Kaufman (1974, Chapter 9). But there is a problem here which Brunswik does not face up to. A common technique used in the study of size constancy is to provide the subject with a variable stimulus within arm's reach. The subject looks at a distant target and adjusts the variable so that it matches it. Various instructions are used: the subject may be instructed to try to achieve a 'retinal match', that is, to make the two stimuli subtend the same visual angle, or he or she may be asked to match the actual size of the distant object. Interestingly, it is hard to achieve true retinal matches because of the tendency to respond in terms of true object size: in other words, because of size constancy. And we all notice in daily life that people do not shrink when they walk away from us; that is, there is phenomenological evidence to support the claim that size constancy is a basic tendency in visual perception.

But Brunswik's outdoor subject could not be given a variable with which to match real distant objects: this would have to be extendable to 20 metres or more. So she gave a verbal estimate of perceived size. But is this what we mean by size constancy? To the author, a high-flying 747 looks very small indeed: his size constancy is clearly breaking down when looking upward through empty space. But asked to judge the size of the aircraft (rather than set a retinal match on a variable display) he would reply that it was about 50 metres long. This could be taken as evidence of size constancy, but it is not. It does not agree with phenomenal experience. It seems a pity that someone with Brunswik's research aims did not think this particular problem through more thoroughly. In fact, a convincing account of the basis of size constancy, this very important aspect of vision, did not emerge until twenty years after Brunswik's death.

### Grouping and spatial proximity

This study is a rarity in psychological research in that it did not employ an experimental subject.

An important principle in Gestalt psychology is that of Nearness or Proximity. Wertheimer's (1923) classic demonstration revealed that stimuli arranged like those in Figure 3.3 in the previous chapter become organized patterns. For example, it is conceivable that Figure 3.3a might be seen as a widely spaced inner pair of lines flanked by additional lines, or as four independent vertical lines. But neither of these organizations occurs: the figure is seen as two adjacent pairs of lines.

The Gestalt theorists explained this powerful tendency to group elements according to their proximity by postulating underlying fields in the brain which followed principles of attraction and repulsion. Thus grouping is seen as a basic property of experience caused by lawful brain processes.

Brunswik's novel question arising from his functionalist approach was: Might grouping by proximity occur because it has survival value? Is it the case that in the real world adjacent parallel lines tend to be associated by forming the boundaries of objects? The question can be answered by a simple analysis of parallel lines in a sample of the environment.

As an approximation to a representative sample of the 'existing ecology', Brunswik and Kamiya (1953) obtained several stills from a popular motion picture. The number of adjacent straight (or nearly straight), parallel (up to a deviation of 5 degrees) pairs of lines was counted and their separations in the photograph measured. The pairs of lines were then classified by what they represented in the photographed scenes.

The results of this study are quite revealing. The (geometric) mean distance in the photographs between pairs of lines common to actual objects was 1.2 mm;

that between lines representing 'ornamental divisions'—that is regular markings on surfaces—was 1.3 mm; lines delineating holes, gaps or spaces between objects had a mean separation of 2.8 mm. A correlational analysis restricted to separations of lines representing objects and those representing spaces between them yielded a coefficient of +0.34. This significant result confirms Brunswik's guess: *proximity has ecological validity*.

Wertheimer's discovery can now be seen in a new light: it has functional value. Grouping is useful because it will commonly lead to the delineation of objects. It works because of the way the world is. A valuable insight has been gained by examining the relationship between perception and the environment in which it takes place. This is one of Brunswik's most original and successful contributions.

## AN EVALUATION OF PROBABILISTIC FUNCTIONALISM

Brunswik's approach to perception has been presented as simply and convincingly as possible. If this attempt has been successful the reader may agree that Brunswik had some stimulating and novel ideas, ideas which are the more impressive when one considers how long ago they were formulated. Why then has he had so little subsequent influence on theory and research? Those who knew Brunswik testify to his originality and cleverness, and yet his influence has been slight. A number of factors seem to have led to this state of affairs, the main ones are listed below.

### Style

Brunswik's first languages were Hungarian and German. His English, whilst always correct, is often difficult and even turgid. Compare the opening of Köhler's highly influential *Gestalt Psychology*, which was written by one whose first language was German, with the ending of Brunswik's best-known work, *Perception and the Representative Design of Experiments*.

> 'There seems to be a single starting point for psychology, exactly as for all the other sciences: the world as we find it, naively and uncritically'.
>
> (Köhler, 1947)

> 'Perception, then, emerges as that relatively primitive partly autonomous, institutionalized, ratiomorphic subsystem of cognition which achieves prompt and richly detailed orientation habitually concerning the vitally relevant, most distal aspects of the environment on the basis of mutually vicarious, relatively restricted and stereotyped, insufficient evidence in uncertainty-geared interaction and compromise, seemingly following the highest probability and smallness of error at the expense of the highest frequency of precision.
>
> (Brunswik, 1956)

The Brunswik paragraph is in fact a remarkable summary of an original theory, achieved in 68 words. And it is hoped that anyone who has worked through the present chapter will find it entirely comprehensible. It is, however, a hellish sentence.

The style of Brunswik's English would matter less had he been more considerate in his reporting of experiments. Several diagrams in his publications are all but incomprehensible. It is commonly very hard to know what exactly happened in one of his experiments. The choice of symbols is often unfortunate and sometimes quite surreal. In one case, U-variables are so named because u is a vowel in the middle of the word 'population'; S represents the environment in the lens model, U now standing for individual differences. For every reader who learned to cope with this sort of thing there must have been dozens who decided that Brunswik was not for them.

## Brunswik's views on experimental design

Brunswik was opposed to 'classical psychophysics' in which all variables save one are controlled. The history of perception suggests, however, that such designs can be very fruitful ways of discovering the laws of perception. For example, much of what we know about colour vision has come from experiments using carefully controlled beams of monochromatic light; major researches into hearing have used only pure tones. As we have seen, Brunswik was interested in faces. Years later Hess (1965, 1975) showed that simply enlarging the pupil in a photograph of a face makes that face seem more attractive, even when the alteration remains unnoticed. This very simple (classical) experiment yielded a result as intriguing as any of Brunswik's.

## Brunswik's experiments

Brunswik often strayed from the ideal course he advocated for perceptual research. Consider his experiment on physiognomic perception. We may ask, what is representative about an ensemble of schematic faces? Brunswik's study of the phenomenon of grouping by proximity was a good idea and provided a critical test of the Gestalt explanation of the phenomenon, and hence of a whole aspect of Gestalt theory. The aim was clear: look at the disposition of adjacent lines in the world and see whether there is a functional basis for the grouping tendency in perception. But how representative were the photographs? They were not from the real world but from a film studio. They were pictures of constructed film sets. It is not necessary to labour the point, but anyone who reads Brunswik's experimental work after learning his views on the importance of ecological sampling will be surprised by the frequently contrived and artificial nature of his visual displays.

### Some general criticisms

We shall not offer an exhaustive examination of all aspects of Brunswik's work. Interested readers may consult the Hammond (1966) reference cited at the end of this chapter. But it is proper to ask whether Brunswik's programme for perceptual reseach is at all feasible. If one was sufficiently impressed by the arguments for probabilistic functionalism what research would one do?

Brunswik emphasized the need to sample the environment or the ecology of the organism. But here we meet a major difficulty: what is 'the' ecology? Are outdoors and indoors part of the same niche? We evolved in one and came to inhabit the other, so should we perceive them in a common way? Brunswik is silent on this point and it is clear that he greatly underestimated the problems associated with Representativeness.

The idea of the perceiver as intuitive statistician is one of Brunswik's main ideas. Perception involves making the best bet from imperfect information. Cues are weighted according to previous success or failure, a claim which emphasizes learning. Of course, certain cues such as pain-inducing stimuli might be responded to reflexively, but generally the weighting of cues must depend upon experience. Brunswik wrote at a time when much of American academic psychology was engaged by the problems of animal learning and the 1940s produced several major theories in this area. At the same time workers such as Hebb (1949) were stressing the role of learning in perception. Not surprisingly, Brunswik's theorizing reveals the influence of this zeitgeist. However, subsequent research has shown that organisms, including humans, are surprisingly capable perceivers very soon after birth (evidence for this was reviewed in Chapter 3). If this shift of emphasis towards the innate aspects of perception continues, approaches such as Brunswik's will require important modifications.

## FINAL REMARKS ON PROBABILISTIC FUNCTIONALISM

The desire to communicate complex ideas clearly and convincingly should be strong in any theorist who wishes to influence others. The neglect into which Brunswik's writings has fallen is partly his own fault. We wish to assert once again that Brunswik's view of perception is stimulating and original and that any reader who is now prepared to work through his writings will find that the ideas therein amply repay the effort.

Throughout this chapter we have maintained a fairly critical attitude towards Brunswik's work, particularly his empirical researches. Why, if there is so much to criticize in probabilistic functionalism, have we included Brunswik's difficult theory in the present selection? What is the point of describing Brunswik's best known factorial experiment when it is clear that he made a botch of it?

The answer to these questions is that Brunswik should be valued, less for what he achieved than for what he attempted. We believe that this was the first researcher to face up to the true complexity of perceptual processes, to recognize what a great achievement is represented by perceptual stability in an inherently uncertain world. The workings of our senses have been shaped by a successful evolutionary past just as their structures have. And this shaping has been done by the complicated rich environment in which evolution took place: we must take this into account when thinking about perception.

Brunswik's assertion that to simplify stimulus situations in the classical psychophysical manner was to ignore the properties of real-life stimulation, is convincing and well-argued. The alternatives he offered—ecological sampling of stimuli, factorial designs, correlational assessment of performance—led to problems which he could not solve. But that does not detract from the originality of his ideas and the wisdom of his advice. And the complexity of his writing reflects not the confusion of a fool, but the vigorous efforts of someone who is trying to capture the complex truth as he sees it. Anyone who takes the trouble to read *Perception and the Representative Design of Psychological Experiments* will finish the book puzzled but with a new and valuable perspective. And in the years which have elapsed since the book's publication powerful statistical techniques have been developed which offer the chance to design and analyse experiments as rich and complex as Brunswik hoped for.

The emphasis which Brunswik placed on the study of the ecology is re-emerging in contemporary work in perception. Workers who have adopted the direct perception paradigm have, as we shall show later, followed J. J. Gibson's lead in claiming that light and sound reaching the perceiver are rich in information. The task for the psychologist is to find within this richness invariant patterns which are capable of specifying a stable external world. Attention must be directed to the environment and its relationship to the perceiver. Indeed, Gibson's last book was entitled *The Ecological Approach to Visual Perception*. And when we describe the computational approach to vision we shall show that it is by carefully studying the environment that theorists can arrive at plausible constraints on their models of perceptual processes, a discipline which has been particularly fruitful. All this might have happened earlier had Brunswik attracted the amount of attention which we believe his theory deserved.

## NOTES ON CHAPTER 4

Brunswik's *Perception and the Representative Design of Psychological Experiments (1956)* is a difficult book, but contains the core of his ideas and is thus essential reading.

Hammond (1966) is a useful source book, containing essays by a number of psychologists who were contemporaries of Brunswik. Some evaluate parts of Brunswik's theory and others attempt to relate his ideas to their own researches. The modification to the lens model shown in this chapter is explained more fully in Hammond's collection (see Chapters 2 and 3). Part 3 of the book is a reprint of some of Brunswik's papers. All Brunswik's publications are listed in an appendix.

The following references are not cited directly in the text but may be useful in understanding Brunswik's approach: Brunswik, E. (1938, 1939, 1948, 1955).

Petrinovich (1979) offers a modern comment on some of Brunswik's ideas.

# Chapter 5

# The neurophysiological approach to visual perception

This chapter will describe some areas of perception research in which it has been suggested that psychological hypotheses can be replaced by models based on known neural mechanisms. There are good reasons why a significant number of perceptionists have always been in favour of this shift. In the first place it is manifestly true that neural mechanisms underlie all behaviour: in an important sense *they* wrote these words and are now reading them. And there are those who believe that psychological knowledge is more secure when it can be linked to known physical structures. For example, the acuity of the eye falls off dramatically as one moves away from the central (foveal) region. The function linking lowered acuity with degree of eccentricity is known sufficiently precisely to allow the prediction of visual performance in the periphery. But the reason *why* this falling-off takes place is now known: it is because of the increased ratio of rod to cone cells in the peripheral retina. The high degree of connectedness of the rod system results in high sensitivity through summation of outputs, but the price for this is the lowered resolution of the system. For many this is satisfying knowledge.

Another reason for preferring neurophysiological explanations is simply that some researchers find it easier and more satisfying to think in terms of neural mechanisms rather than in more abstract psychological terms.

The fact that perception, memory and thought are all mediated by the central nervous system does not, however, force us to accept reductionism. The neural structures underlying mental events may be interacting in ways of which we cannot conceive and which could never be described using only the language of neurophysiology. This is said simply to warn the reader against too ready an acceptance of some of the claims to be outlined later in this chapter.

The approaches to be described have one thing in common: they attempt to use neural mechanisms to explain perceptual phenomena. We have of course met such an approach in the earlier chapter on the Gestalt theory. But this modern work differs from the Gestalt approach in two important ways. First, Köhler's physiology was highly speculative and, as it happens, largely incorrect; modern theories are much more securely based. Second, the Gestaltists, as phenomenologists, wanted to explain the richness of everyday perception; modern neurophysiological theories of perception are usually more modest in their aims. Typically, what they try to explain are basic sensory discriminations: how perceivers process some of the basic information contained in, say, the visual image, how this is coded and in what form it is sent onwards into the higher regions of the visual pathways. Such questions are very different from asking, for example, how familiarity affects our perception of objects or why blue is almost certainly the world's favourite colour. Thus in terms of our basic model the areas of interest are joined by a very short arc—that connecting what arrives at the receptor surface with peripheral and (sometimes) central processes of the nervous system.

None of the theoretical work to be described would have been possible without the remarkable gains in the understanding of the nervous system which have been achieved during the past 150 years. This is clearly not the place to undertake a history of neuroanatomy and neurophysiology, although this is a fascinating story and well worth reading. But we shall attempt to provide those readers who are unfamiliar with neural structure and physiology with sufficient knowledge to be able to appreciate the material of this chapter. Other readers will skip the next section; those wishing to learn even more about the workings of the nervous system should consult the basic references given at the end of the chapter.

## THE NERVOUS SYSTEM

The term 'nerve' is used somewhat loosely. Major nerves are in fact bundles of nerve fibres: the human optic nerve, for instance, actually comprises approximately one million separate fibres. But 'nerve' is sometimes used to describe the basic unit of the nervous system, the *neuron*.

Neurons are specialized cells having a variety of shapes and sizes. Basically, each neuron comprises a cell body with a nucleus, a complex arrangement of branching structures or *dendrites*, and one or more long processes or *axons* which run either to other neurons or to muscles or glands. The neuron receives stimulation via its dendrites and passes on stimulation via the axon. A typical neuron is shown in diagrammatic form in Figure 5.1.

The connection between two neurons in a sequence is not direct. Activity in the first leads to temporary changes in a minute gap or *synapse* between neurons. Whether or not the stimulation from the first neuron is passed on depends upon the strength and timing of the changes at the synapse. Many neuronal endings may terminate on the dendrites or cell body of a single neuron.

When a dendrite receives sufficient stimulation the characteristics of its membrane at a local site suddenly change. As a result of rapid chemical processes, the permeability of the membrane alters in such a way that ions pass into and out of the cell. This results in a wave of electrical disturbance, or *depolarization*, which spreads away from the site of stimulation. This wave of electrical disturbance is *decremental*, tending to die away over distance. But if several stimulating events occur within a short time or within a small area the electrical wave may be strong enough to reach the site where axonal conduction begins.

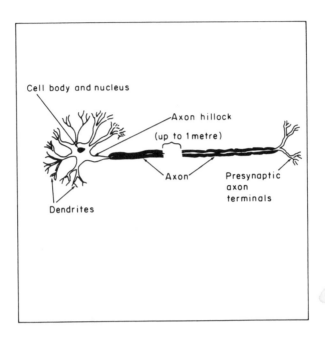

Figure 5.1    Diagram of a typical bi-polar neuron

Once a disturbance reaches the axon it is propagated according to a different principle: now the wave of electrical conduction is no longer decremental but *all-or-none*. That is to say, if an impulse begins to run along an axon it will continue to the end. And the size of the impulse is independent of the strength of the original disturbance, just as the speed of a bullet is independent of the strength of the trigger pull, provided this exceeds the threshold of firing. Neurons tend to code strength of stimulation as frequency, the stronger the stimulus the more impulses per second. From the end of the neuron activity spreads into the next synapse and, of course, this can lead to graded stimulation of the next neuron. Thus the rapid all-or-none conduction down an axon fibre can be seen as a means of conveying graded information, translated into a frequency code, to another site in the body.

The preceding account of the causal sequence between adjacent neurons has omitted an important phenomenon. We have described the pattern by which one neuron excites another, increasing the chance of the latter's firing. But neurons can also interact in an *inhibitory* manner. Thus one neuron's activity, far from inducing a wave of depolarization in another neuron, may actually cause a *hyperpolarization* of the next membrane, thus lowering the chance that the second neuron will fire.

When we put these basic facts together, we can see that the activity between successive neurons permits (i) threshold effects resulting from summation over space and time, (ii) positive (excitatory) and negative (inhibitory) interactions between these basic units of the nervous system. These facts are very significant for it means that groups of neurons can behave in ways directly analogous to *logical gates* (see Figure 5.2).

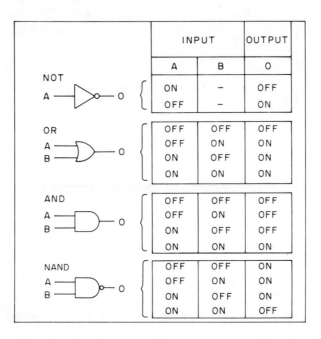

Figure 5.2   Four common logical gates. The function of the OR gate, for example, is to give an output if either or both its inputs are active; the AND gate gives an output only if both its inputs are active. Combinations of various gates can be used to build computing devices

In engineering terminology, an AND gate, for example, is a switch-like device which produces an output only when all its inputs are positive; an AND-NOT gate will not give an output if all inputs are simultaneously positive; an EXCLUSIVE-OR gate will give an output if either of two inputs occurs, but not if both occur. With such simple switching devices it is possible to build elaborate logical networks. It is now possible to link these facts and draw an exciting conclusion:

(1) Neurons interact in various ways. One neuron can excite or inhibit another, increasing or decreasing the chance that the latter will fire.
(2) Logical gates are switches and can be used to build computing devices.
(3) Because of the ways in which they interact, neurons can simulate logical gates.
(4) Therefore neurons can do something akin to computing.

This is a very important development in the history of neurophysiology. Some of the implications of this idea will be described later in this chapter.

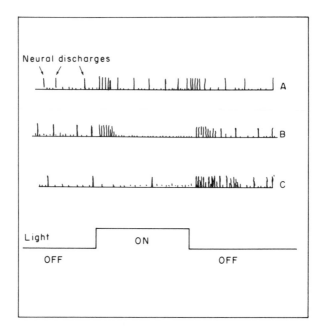

Figure 5.3   Three types of response from neurons in the optic nerve of the frog. Each spike represents a single neural discharge. Fibre A responds to light onset and maintains a steady discharge rate. Fibre B responds maximally to light onset and offset. Fibre C responds maximally to light offset. The combined effect of these responses is that the visual system responds most strongly to *changing* illumination. (Diagrammatic, after various authors)

It should be remembered that neural processes take time. The discovery by Helmholtz in 1850 that the speed of conduction down a sensory nerve was in the order of 100 metres per second was vitally important. Neurons do not conduct with the speed of light (as some had believed), they are relatively slow. 'The speed of thought' is not instantaneous, but is commonly slow enough to be measured, as is the speed of perceptual processes. Were this not so, psychologists would not have been able to discover nearly as much as they have about perceptual processes, and neurophysiologists would have had a much harder time trying to understand the ways in which neurons respond and interact.

This necessarily brief review of neural action may be completed by stating a final major principle which researchers have discovered: sensory neurons seem to have evolved to deal with *change* (see Figure 5.3). In numerous regions of the afferent nervous system it has been found that the onset or offset of stimulation produces a rapid and marked increase in neural firing. But should the stimulation continue then, typically, the neural response returns to a value close to the resting base-line. We know that change is important in psychological terms: if one looks into a completely homogenous volume, for example if the head is inside an illuminated white sphere (known as a Ganzfeld), then vision fades within seconds—the surface of the sphere softens to a fog, eventually there is no sensation of seeing at all (interested readers may experience the Ganzfeld effect by placing half a table tennis ball over each eye and looking towards a source of illumination). A similar fading occurs when the eye is effectively prevented from moving: this is known as the Stabilized Image phenomenon. Analogous effects occur in touch: an object placed on the skin is felt very clearly at first, but within a few seconds the tactile impression fades. These effects seem to reflect an underlying basic principle of economy of response. Change is always potentially important and there is an obvious evolutionary advantage in concentrating neural resources so as to maximize responses to it.

## NEUROPHYSIOLOGICAL EXPLANATIONS

The question asked in this chapter is, How far can the knowledge outlined above be employed in the solution of perceptual problems? Can one by-pass psychological theory and go straight to a causal, physiological account of sensory and perceptual phenomena? There are those who believe that this may be possible and it is to their work that we now turn.

To date, neurophysiological explanations in visual perception have been of various kinds. We shall draw examples from three areas of research: (i) the direct substitution of known neural/physiological mechanisms for hypothetical constructs, (ii) the discovery of neural feature detectors, and (iii) work which reinforces the growing belief that structures in the visual system can perform elaborate syntheses as well as analyses of incoming sensory data. This three-fold classification is somewhat arbitrary, but it does provide a structure within which to describe a selection of modern researches.

Although elegant neurophysiological work has been done in other sense modalities, all the following examples are drawn from visual studies. The neural region of the vertebrate eye, the retina, is actually an outgrowth of the brain and is thus a region of formidable neural complexity. We should not be surprised by some of the extraordinary processes which neurophysiologists have discovered there in the past few decades.

### Neurophysiology and colour vision

The following examples of this substitution of known mechanisms for psychological hypotheses are both drawn from the area of colour vision. They are good illustrations of the successful application of neurophysiological knowledge to classical psychological problems.

The two most important facts about colour vision in humans (and some other vertebrates) are, first that our colour vision is trichromatic, second that we experience highly predictable contrast and fatigue effects.

The *trichromacy* of colour vision means simply this: any hue which a person is capable of perceiving can be matched by suitable mixtures of three wavelengths of light. These *primary wavelengths* need not be precisely specified, provided that (a) they span the visible spectrum—there is a wide range of choices amongst the blues, greens and reds, and (b) no two primaries should be exactly complementary: the test of this is that when they are added the resulting mixture must not be achromatic.

Most people are greatly surprised when their trichromacy is first demonstrated to them. It is a memorable experience, particularly when it is seen that equal amounts of the three primaries mix to produce white: as the intensity of the third light is increased all colour simply fades away. Moreover, the matches made are highly stable. For example, if one produces yellow by mixing red and green light, the yellow can be made indistinguishable from that seen in the 'yellow' portion of the spectrum (a wavelength of approximately 560–580 nanometres). If one then biases colour perception by fatiguing the eye with, say, orange light, *both yellows change in exactly the same way*. The stability of the match is also maintained when an additional coloured light is added to both yellows.

*Colour contrast and fatigue* effects are equally remarkable phenomena. If a red square is placed on a grey ground and fixated for a few moments, one comes to see a greenish tinge surrounding the red. An intense green light induces a reddish after-image; blue light induces yellow, and vice versa. Note that red and green and blue and yellow are complementary hues in that they mix to form neutral greys. Anyone can experience these effects by simply staring at a coloured light (*not the sun*) for a few moments and then looking at a white surface. A related phenomenon may be observed on brightly lit snowscapes where it can be seen that shadows are blue (a phenomenon first brought to general attention by the Impressionists).

In the nineteenth century these very reliable and interesting phenomena gave rise to a number of theories of colour vision. The first, known now as the Young–Helmholtz Three-Factor Theory (Helmholtz, 1909–1911, translated

1924–1925) attempted to explain trichromacy as follows. Suppose that the eye contains three types of receptor each maximally sensitive to a portion of the spectrum (Young originally proposed three pigments, Helmholtz three types of retinal cones. Historically, the difference is trivial). Then if the eye is illuminated by a particular hue the type of cell whose sensitivity is closest to the wavelength of the hue will fire strongly whilst other types of receptor will respond less vigorously. Yellow light will stimulate the cells sensitive to the red and green parts of the spectrum about equally. White light will stimulate all three types of receptor, evoking the achromatic response (see Figure 5.4).

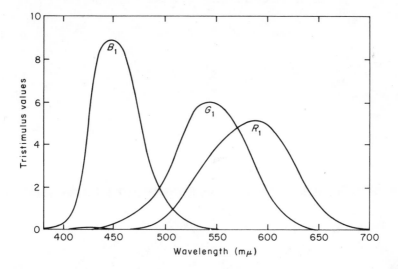

Figure 5.4   A diagrammatic illustration of a typical three-component theory of colour vision. $B_1$, $G_1$, $R_1$, describe the hypothetical short- medium- and long-wavelength receptors postulated by the Young–Helmholtz theory. The vertical axis can be interpreted as the relative absorption efficiency of each pigment as a function of wavelength. (From Judd, 1951. © 1951 John Wiley & Sons Inc. Reproduced by permission.)

The Young–Helmholtz theory of colour vision does have weaknesses. It does not readily explain the stability of yellow, a hue which is still seen in intensely strong light when all other hues apart from blue vanish: how can the yellow remain when the contributing receptors (in the red and green regions) do not appear to be functioning? And the theory has some difficulty over certain forms of colour vision deficiency. Nevertheless, the Young–Helmholtz three-factor theory has proved to be very useful and durable. It is the most widely cited theory in the history of colour vision research.

Historically, the major rival to the Young–Helmholtz theory was Hering's Opponent Process Theory (Hering, 1890). This theory postulated the existence in the optic nerve of three processes capable of functioning in, as it were, opposite directions. In the 'anabolic' direction the processes give rise to the sensations of red, yellow and white; in the 'catabolic' direction these same processes give rise, respectively, to green, blue and black. Thus the phenomenon by which complementary hues mix to grey is accounted for in terms of a balanced neutral point in the relevant opponent process. Fatigue and contrast effects are handled just as easily, as is the fact that one cannot see, for example, blue and yellow at the same time in the same place. And whilst there are bluish greens, there is no blue-yellow sensation; nor are there are any reddish greens or blackish whites.

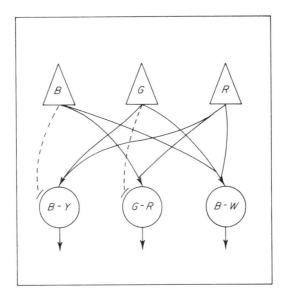

Figure 5.5   A modern opponent-process model. Three types of receptor (*B*, *G*, *R*) responding to short-, medium- and long-wavelength light send outputs to opponent cells (*B–Y*, *G–R*, *B–W*). These outputs may be excitatory (→) or inhibitory (– – –<). For example, the *B–Y* cell receives an inhibitory signal from the short-wavelength detector and this results in a 'Blue' output from the cell. Yellow light will stimulate the *G* and *R* receptors equally: they excite the *B–Y* cell which produces a 'Yellow' output. (After various authors)

Hering's opponent process theory also has its weaknesses. For example, it predicts a form of yellow-blue colour blindness which has never been found, and the theory does not yield a satisfactory account of the brightness of colours. Nevertheless, it provides an explanation of some very important phenomena.

The debate between these two very different theories (or their more recent counterparts) has been lengthy. And one can see why: each explains some of the data of colour vision but not others. But the theories are very different: how could they both be right?

We now know that *both* the Young–Helmholtz and the Hering theories are essentially correct. Our confidence that this is the case is one of the triumphs of visual research. An account of the work which confirmed both three-factor and opponent-process theories will demonstrate the way in which actual neural mechanisms can replace hypothetical constructs.

## The search for the visual pigments

Human (and animal) data from colour vision experiments have led to the construction of quantitative models of colour vision in which various triads of hypothetical pigments are evaluated. By constructing absorption curves for these hypothetical pigments one can test whether it is possible to account for various aspects of colour performance—particularly matching tasks, the colour confusions made by colour-deficient judges, and the relationships between hue and other aspects of colour, such as lightness, brightness and saturation. As a result of many years of careful measurement there are now good data which can be used to predict various colour phenomena. However, the hypothetical pigments in this research are selected to give the best fit to the performance data: there is no direct evidence that pigments in the eye exactly match them. How satisfying it would be to locate the real pigments and to know once and for all what underlies human trichromacy. This is a goal which eluded visual researchers for many years.

No one researcher can be given sole credit for solving this classic problem. However, many would agree that an important breakthrough came when Rushton (1964) perfected a technique which made it possible to search for pigments in the living eye.

In essence, *microspectrodensitometry* entails shining a narrow beam of pure, monochromatic, light onto the cells of the retina, trapping the returning beam and measuring the difference between the two. In this way it is possible to assess the absorption properties of retinal cells. Described so baldly the work sounds relatively simple; in fact perfecting the technique took many years of intensive research.

Rushton's work was extended by MacNichol (1964) and Dartnall, Bowmaker and Mollon (1983) working on isolated cone cells. When these various researches were combined it became certain that the cone cells of the retina do in fact contain three different pigments. Each has a wavelength to which it is maximally absorbent and the three peak sensitivities are at 420, 530, and 560 nanometres (see Figure 5.6 and compare it with Figure 5.4). This is a most satisfying result. It enables us to call cells containing the pigments the short-, medium- and long-wavelength colour receptors of the eye. This is exactly what is required by trichromatic theories, such as the Young–Helmholtz theory outlined earlier. Helmholtz was essentially correct (that he chose cone types, rather than pigments, doesn't matter). The basis of visual trichromacy has been discovered.

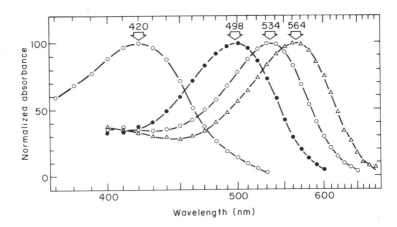

Figure 5.6 Actual absorption data obtained from isolated cells from a human retina. Microspectrophotometry has revealed the presence of three distinct cone pigments with absorption maxima at 420, 534 and 564 nm (the filled points are absorption data from the rod pigment, rhodopsin). The basis of human trichromacy has been discovered. (From Bowmaker and Dartnall, 1980. Reproduced by permission of the Physiological Society.)

The story just told represents a remarkable gain in our knowledge of colour vision. It is not, however, an adequate explanation of all the basic sensory colour vision phenomema. The existence of a cone type containing a long-wave (red absorbing) pigment does not by itself explain how we distinguish between different reds, how our colour discrimination is so good, nor does it readily explain those phenomena which prompted the opponent-process theory outlined earlier. Two further discoveries filled this gap.

*The search for the opponent processes*

Success here came when Svaetichin (1956) discovered an electrical potential in cells of the fish retina which responds differentially to coloured light in the following manner: at short wavelengths the potential responds positively, at long wavelengths negatively (see Figure 5.7). Other cells in the retina produce a similarly selective response to blue and yellow light. Then DeValois (1960) found cells in the lateral geniculate nucleus (a relay station between the retina and the visual cortex) of the monkey which also respond in an opponent manner to wavelength. These cells respond by increasing their firing when the eye receives light from one end of the spectrum and decreasing their firing when the light is from the other end of the spectrum. Refinements in this research have now uncovered +Blue −Yellow, −Blue +Yellow, +Red −Green, and +Green −Red lateral geniculate cells, *all behaving in a manner suggested by opponent-process theory*. Once again, neurophysiological work has demonstrated the essential correctness of an abstract theory of colour vision, and has yielded a satisfying explanation as to why the theory works and also complements very different three-factor theories. That is to say, retinal cone cells in the eye do absorb light by the action of three pigments and these three pigments underly trichromacy. At the same time, cells in the visual pathways located inwards of the cone cells use the outputs of these cells and respond differentially to them, producing the sharpening postulated by opponent-process theory (see Figure 5.5).

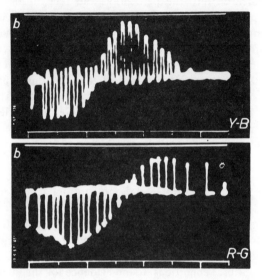

Figure 5.7   Svaetichin and MacNichol's discovery of opponent-process responses in the cells of the fish retina. The slow electrical potential (the S-response) changes its polarity according to wavelength. In this figure the vertical axis shows the direction of the S-response, the horizontal axis represents the wavelength of the stimulus. Note the differential effects of Red versus Green and Yellow versus Blue light. (From Svaetichin and MacNichol, 1958. Reproduced by permission of the Annals of the New York Academy of Sciences.)

Taken together, these two sets of researches justify the claim that theoretical constructs at this level of colour vision research can be replaced by known neurophysiological mechanisms. This in turn allows research to be directed to new problems: how the various pigments and opponent-process cells are arranged in other species. What is lacking in those people who have impaired colour vision? And so on. Of course, the discoveries do not signal the end of colour vision research and theory. Many questions remain, in particular how we perceive coloured surfaces where texture and hue interact; how the 'true' colours of things can be perceived when illumination is changing; why some animals, such as the cat, have cone cells and visual pigments in the retina but find it difficult to learn colour discriminations. But at the basic sensory level of explaining trichromacy and contrast and fatigue effects, neurophysiology has given us definite answers. Small wonder that some believe this to be the eventual fate of many other perceptual phenomena.

## Feature detectors in the visual system

As an example of another type of neurophysiological theorizing in perception some modern research into the perception and recognition of shape will be described, with particular emphasis on the search for feature detectors. Recognition of the importance of shape perception and discrimination came early in the history of psychology. Mach (1836–1916), aware that contours play an important role in delineating shapes, solved some of the psychophysical problems of contour extraction. He established that contours appear whenever a gradient of lightness or brightness changes suddenly (technically this is the second differential of the intensity gradient). The Gestaltists demonstrated how figures emerge from ground, they stressed the importance of shape constancy in perceptual stability, and they showed how priority appears to be given in perception to balanced, simple, symmetrical shapes according to the law of Prägnanz.

By the early 1950s there were enough facts to fuel a theoretical controversy. Some workers, for example Hebb (1949) claimed that there was evidence to support a learning interpretation of shape perception. Hebb's theory assigned an important role to eye movements in the creation of 'cell assemblies' mediating subsequent shape recognition. But at the same time ethologists, studying animal behaviour under natural conditions, found evidence for the innate recognition of certain shapes. For example, compound shapes comprising only large and small discs induce unlearned gaping responses in nestling thrushes which are the same as those induced by parent birds. The ethological literature contains many other examples of this kind of innate responsiveness to shapes (see Tinbergen, 1951).

Another development in the 1950s was the advent of digital computers capable of restricted pattern recognition. This encouraged the development of psychological models of shape perception and recognition (generally subsumed under the heading, 'pattern perception'). What eventually emerged were two main types of model: template matching and feature detection.

*Template matching models*, for example those of Selfridge and Neisser (1960) and Uhr (1963) recognize patterns or shapes by noting their similarity to canonical forms. This is not unlike those educational toys in which solid shapes can be posted only through the correct apertures in a box. However, such template matching models have some major flaws: how is it, for example, that we can recognize a certain letter even when it is presented in an unusual typeface, or in a different size, or at a different retinal location? Our ability to do all these things presents serious problems for this type of model.

*Feature detection models* were designed to avoid these difficulties. They work by analysing shapes into component parts or features. For example, Selfridge's well-known Pandemonium model (Selfridge, 1959) postulates peripheral, low-level feature detectors, many of which are triggered by shapes falling onto a receptor surface. The outputs of these detectors are weighed at higher levels of the system, with the detector (actually called a demon) which 'shouts' loudest having the best chance that its output will be accepted for further processing. The shape finally arrived at is based on combinations of features detected by the demons.

Sutherland (1957) claimed that those shape discriminations of which the octopus is capable can be explained by assuming that visual stimuli are analysed in terms of horizontal and vertical features, but not by oblique ones. In yet another context, human perception and thinking, Bruner (1957) suggested that patterns are examined for key attributes which are then related to categories created by the perceiver beforehand. Hence some cognitive activity is believed to precede actual shape recognition.

A valuable discussion of much of the work described above will be found in Neisser (1967). For now it suffices to say first, that the importance of shape perception and recognition has long been recognized by psychologists; second, that this is still a live issue. For example Marr (1982) whose important work will be the subject of Chapter 8, stated quite explicitly that he was attempting to formulate a theory 'in which the main job of vision was to derive a representation of shape' (Marr, 1982, p.36).

These then are some of the theories which have arisen in response to the challenge of shape perception. We shall now attempt to show how such thinking is being influenced by discoveries in neurophysiology.

## The receptive field

In a pioneering study of the responses of the nervous system, Adrian (1928) found that tactile sensory fibres in the limb of a monkey respond whenever a region of skin is stimulated. Adrian coined the phrase *receptive field* to describe the relationship between a region of a sensory surface, such as the skin, and neural cells inwards of the surface which receive messages from it. The concept of the receptive field is now centrally important in neurophysiology.

Adrian's work on the tactile receptive fields was quickly extended to other areas. From the work of such distinguished researchers as Hartline (1938, 1940), Barlow (1953), Kuffler (1953), Lettvin, Maturana, McCulloch, and Pitts (1959) and Maturana, Lettvin, McCulloch and Pitts (1960), knowledge of receptive fields grew rapidly. It was found, for example, that receptive field organization exists in the frog retina and in the optic pathways of the cat (whose visual system shares many important characteristics with our own). Many visual receptive fields have a circular organization. In some of these fields central excitatory areas are surrounded by concentric inhibitory regions. The result is that stimulation in the centre of a visual area results in increased neural activity, but this can be inhibited by stimulation of the surrounding area—the on-centre/off-surround fields (see Figure 5.8). The opposite organization is found in what are described as off-centre/on-surround fields. The quality of these researches was recognized in the award to Hartline and his colleagues of the 1967 Nobel Prize.

The possible relevance of this research for the psychology of perception was further demonstrated by the work of Lettvin *et al.* and Maturana *et al.* on the frog's visual system. Recordings from fibres in the optic nerve produced a very exciting discovery: the frog's visual system appears to respond in a very limited but selective manner to stimulation at the retina. Some cells produce a prolonged response to edges. Others respond when small dark objects are moved across the visual field (hence their name, 'bug detectors'). There are cells which respond maximally to changes in contrast in the visual field. Others respond when their visual fields are darkened. Finally, there are cells which respond inversely to light intensity and thus appear to be dark detectors.

These remarkable findings are doubly significant. First they show that the *visual world of the frog may be very different from our own.* It appears to be a simple world, restricted to those stimulus attributes which are vital to the frog's survival: the presence of small prey, the shadows of possible predators, the safety of darkness. Second, these aspects of the world which the frog must perceive in order to survive are extracted automatically. The frog does not have to search for areas of darkness, or for small moving objects, these important stimulus patterns are extracted directly by the cells of the peripheral visual system.

Neural mechanisms in the frog retina extract features from the visual image. That this processing is thus peripheral rather than central may be explained in part by the fact that the frog does not have a very complex brain—for example, it lacks a cortex. But warm-blooded vertebrates do have complex central nervous systems. When some of the researchers listed above turned their attention to the visual system of the cat (which, like many other warm-blooded vertebrates, has a well-developed visual cortex) they found that receptive fields can also be found in more central regions of the nervous system. We shall now describe what has become a classic set of experiments. The work by Hubel and Wiesel (1962, 1977) to which we now turn has been described by some psychologists as the most important set of discoveries in the history of physiological psychology. The quality of this research was recognized in the award to the authors of the 1981 Nobel Prize.

Hubel and Wiesel (1962, 1977) succeeded in recording the electrical responses of living cells in the visual cortex of the cat and the monkey to various patterns of stimulation. To appreciate the magnitude of this achievement one must realize that cortical cells are microscopically small, so that to record from them without destroying the cells requires the use of exceedingly fine microelectrodes. (These are so fine that the tip is invisible, even under a microscope.) Then the electrode must be positioned very carefully in the cortex using precision stereotactic instruments. The aim is to make contact with the outer wall of the cell without puncturing and destroying it. The researchers must be certain that they are actually recording from a living cell—which of course they cannot see. Finally, the experimental animal must be kept alive and well under anaesthetic whilst the retina is stimulated in a controlled manner. It took researchers many years to overcome these formidable technical problems.

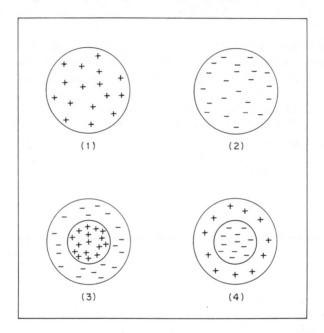

Figure 5.8  Examples of types of receptive field organization in the visual system. Each diagram represents an area of the retina monitored by a retinal ganglion cell. The signs represent the responses of the ganglion cell (+ = excited, − = inhibited) when light falls onto the receptive field. (1) and (2) represent the simplest forms of receptive field; (3) is an on-centre off-surround field; (4) is an off-centre on-surround field. Receptive fields are also found in more central regions of the visual system. Not all fields have such clearly circular arrangements. (After various authors)

Hubel and Wiesel have described how one day, whilst trying vainly to induce a response in a cortical cell, they accidentally moved the slide in their projector so that the edge moved across the experimental animal's visual field. The cortical cell immediately responded to this moving edge. Subsequent experiments showed that what had been discovered was a receptive field organization in the cat's visual cortex. However, unlike the simple, circularly organized receptive fields found previously in the retina and lateral geniculate body, these cortical fields are thinner and more elongated in shape. They respond to the presence in the visual field of moving edges or contours *having a particular orientation*. Some cortical cells respond to vertical lines and their response falls off as the lines are changed away from the vertical. Other cells respond to horizontal or oblique lines and edges.

Not all the cells explored in the cortex by Hubel, Weisel and others have receptive fields, but subsequent studies of those that do uncovered some remarkable facts about the visual cortex of the cat and, later, the monkey.

(1) Some cells in the visual cortex exhibit a vertical, columnar organization. As one penetrates deeper into the cortex below a particular site the column of cells produces similarly specific responses to, say, a particular orientation of the stimulus.

(2) Cortical cells show different types of responsiveness. In some the receptive field is an elongated area with excitatory and inhibitory regions. Others respond positively to appropriate stimulation anywhere in the relevant portion of the retina and have no inhibitory regions. Still other cells are indifferent to the orientation of the stimulus but respond selectively to patterns of a particular height and width.

(3) Many cortical cells are binocularly driven and can be induced to fire by stimulation of either eye.

(4) The responsiveness of some cells is bizarrely specific: for example, Gross, Rocha-Miranda and Bender (1972) found cells in the macaque monkey's inferotemporal cortex (a region of the brain at a distance from the visual cortex which is implicated in certain forms of visual recognition) which respond selectively *to the image of a hand*.

(5) Receptive fields are present at birth, a finding which gives some support to the nativist view of perception advanced by Gestalt psychologists. However, early experience can modify the nature of the fields. For example, Blakemore (1974) reared kittens in artificial environments comprising either vertical or horizontal striped surfaces. After varying periods of time in such environments the kittens were examined in two ways. First their ability to discriminate contours was tested. It was found that kittens reared in a vertical striped environment showed impaired acuity to horizontal stripes, and vice versa. The animals were not blind to the unfamiliar stripes, but their performance made it obvious that the stripes were not perceived as clearly as those in the familiar orientation. Second, when receptive fields were examined in the visual cortex of these animals cells were found which responded normally to stripes in the familiar orientation, but the cortical responses to stripes in the other orientation were severely reduced. It was not that the cortex had actually lost a number of

functional units, but rather that an abnormal number had developed to match the orientation of the striped rearing environment.

Thus overt behaviour and the cellular responsiveness of the visual system both indicate that some early experience is needed for normal development of receptive fields, and that abnormal experiences can bias them. There is, moreover, a critical period during which experience is particularly important and this exists between approximately three weeks and three months after birth. Similar conclusions emerge from variants on this work in which, for example, animals are reared with one eye permanently closed for a period to see the effects this has on binocularly driven cortical cells. Thus this neurophysiological research seems to support a modified nativism, in which the elements of perceiving are present at birth, but not in a rigid or unmodifiable form. To date, it is not yet safe to extrapolate this important conclusion to human perception (although the evidence is very suggestive): the obvious experiments are rendered impossible by ethical and technical considerations.

Readers wishing to learn more about this important research will find excellent accounts in the source books listed at the end of this chapter. Next, and later in Section iii, we shall show how the discovery of receptive fields has influenced psychological theory.

One obvious interpretation of the discoveries by Hubel and Weisel and subsequent researchers is that *the feature detectors suggested by theories of shape perception have been found*. Just as some had supposed, it seems that neurons in the brain (at least in cats and monkeys) are capable of responding selectively to certain aspects of stimuli. These can be simple features, such as lines in particular orientations; more complex relationships, such as particular lengths *and* widths; and very complex combinations of features such as a hand shape. Small wonder that this research quickly attracted the attention of a great many psychologists.

One of the best known psychological and theoretical researches to follow Hubel and Weisel's discovery is that by Julesz (1981). Julesz has investigated the properties of visual textures to see which can and cannot be effortlessly discriminated. Following a long series of investigations, Julesz claims that the basic building blocks of visual texture are dots, elongated blobs and terminations of lines. And in describing the role that these *textons* play in perception he makes specific reference to the work of Hubel and Weisel—not surprisingly, for these are exactly the aspects of stimulation which their feature detectors can extract from images. Here then is clear evidence of what is known to occur in the visual system having a major influence in an important area of perceptual theory.

The emphasis so far in the two strands of research described above has been on neural *analysis* of sensory data—how information about colour and shape might be extracted from the visual image by simple neural mechanisms. We shall postpone further comment on these researches until we have given one more example of the impact of neurophysiology on perceptual theory. In this we shall attempt to explain how neural mechanisms might be capable of synthesis as well as analysis. The work to be described followed quite naturally from that above, and some of the researchers have worked in both areas.

**The visual system's response to spatial frequency**

Spatial frequencies are associated with lines and edges, features which are of vital importance in visual perception. The concept of spatial frequency may be explained in terms of one of the widely used research tools in this area, *the visual grating*.

*Gratings*

A grating is a display comprising alternate light and dark stripes. In visual research these stripes commonly do not have sharp edges but vary smoothly from light to dark and vice versa (Figure 5.9). Such *sinusoidal gratings* have the advantage that they are not affected by imperfections in the refractive surfaces of the eye and thus arrive at the retina in an uncorrupted form.

Any grating can be described in terms of four independent properties.

(1) The *contrast* of a grating is simply the difference in brightness (or luminance or reflectance) between the light and dark areas; low contrast gratings are harder to see, other things being equal.

(2) The *spatial frequency* of a grating is a function of the width of the stripes, which in turn defines the number of alternations of light and dark across unit distance. Convenient measures of spatial frequency are the number of changes per degree of visual angle or the number of stripes falling across one millimetre of the retina.

(3) The *orientation* of a grating simply describes whether it is horizontal, vertical or oblique.

(4) The *phase* of a grating is taken from any arbitrary starting point: is the stripe in that position light or dark?

*Simple gratings* are those formed from a single spatial frequency. *Complex gratings* (Figure 5.9) are formed by adding simple gratings. Conversely, complex sinusoidal gratings can be analysed into their simple components. The procedure for doing this is known as *Fourier analysis*.

It is obvious that one can have gratings with stripes that cannot be seen, *either* because the stripes are too fine to resolve, *or* because the contrast between the light and dark areas is too low. It follows that there are two distinct thresholds associated with the detection of a grating.

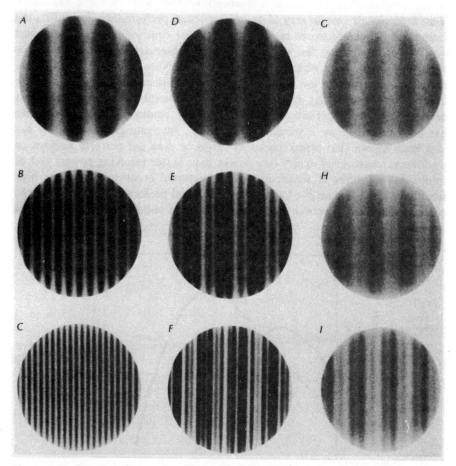

Figure 5.9 Simple and complex sinusoidal gratings. The top row of simple gratings differ only in contrast, the left column differ only in spatial frequency. The remaining complex gratings are formed by adding the simple row and column gratings. (Reproduced by permission of Alfred A. Knopf, Inc., from Sekuler and Blake, 1985)

In what has become a classic study on spatial frequency detection, Campbell and Robson (1968) measured these two thresholds in human observers. Using electronically generated sinusoidal gratings, Campbell and Robson selected a particular spatial frequency and set the contrast so low that the grating lines could not be seen. The contrast was then raised until the stripes were just visible. Then the spatial frequency was changed and the process repeated.

Campbell and Robson presented their threshold data in a new form of graph, the *Contrast Sensitivity Function*, which has provided valuable insights into the process of seeing. As Figure 5.10 shows, the interrelation between threshold contrast and resolution of spatial frequency takes the form of a curve. This curve is an exceptionally useful way of describing visual performance. It predicts the fineness of detail which can be seen at particular contrast levels, it is the best way yet of comparing the vision of different observers, and it allows us to compare human vision with that in other species. Note in Figure 5.10 that the cat is very sensitive to low spatial frequencies. This means that cats are able to see faint shadows that we cannot, which might explain the long association between cats and supernatural phenomena. The contrast sensitivity function has been described as 'a window of visibility'. Interestingly, although it has long been known that other species can rival or even out-perform humans on traditional measures of acuity (the hawks have better resolving power) and on traditional measures of sensitivity (some nocturnal creatures have very high sensitivity ), the human eye has the best all-round performance in terms of the contrast sensitivity function: it has the largest area under the curve, the largest window.

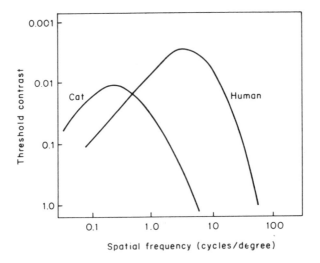

Figure 5.10   Contrast sensitivity functions. The contrast of a grating is defined as a ratio: $(I_{max} - I_{min})/(I_{max} + I_{min})$ where $I_{max}$ and $I_{min}$ are the intensities of the lightest and darkest regions of a grating. The contrast sensitivity functions are obtained by selecting a particular spatial frequency grating and raising the intensity of the lighter regions until the grating is just detectable. This is continued over a range of spatial frequencies. Note that although the human function is better overall than the cat's, the latter is more sensitive to low spatial frequencies

The use of gratings heralded a new approach to the measurement of visual performance, an approach which was to yield important new theoretical insights into the process of seeing, and which quickly led to the discovery of new and important phenomena. Three examples will illustrate the intriguing nature of these discoveries.

First, Campbell and Robson (1968) investigated the perception of complex gratings in a series of threshold determinations. Remember that a complex grating can be formed by adding a series of simple sinusoidal gratings (Figure 5.9). However, when one looks at such a grating the components are not obvious—they do not appear in consciousness—and in a sense they cannot be perceived. But when Campbell and Robson examined the contrast sensitivity functions for complex gratings they made an interesting discovery. As the contrast of a grating is raised the subject becomes able to detect the lowest spatial frequency. Further increases in contrast reveal the influence, one by one, of the other spatial frequencies contained in the complex grating. And each threshold is the same as it would be if that particular spatial frequency had been presented in isolation. This is a most intriguing finding, particularly when one looks again at Figure 5.9 to remind oneself that the component frequencies are not perceptually distinguishable.

Second, Blakemore and Campbell (1969) then discovered an interesting adaptation phenomenon. When a subject fixates a particular grating for a period of time and then has his or her contrast sensitivity function assessed, a drop in sensitivity is observed. Such fatigue effects are common in vision and this one was not surprising. However, the strange thing is that the effect is not general but is limited to those spatial frequencies close to that of the adapting grating. Similarly, fixating a horizontal grating reduces sensitivity to nearby frequencies, but only when these are horizontally arranged; there is no loss of sensitivity to vertical gratings. In both cases fixating has presumably fatigued some process, but the process is not general: it is orientation- and frequency-specific.

Third, it has been found that fatigue/bias effects are not limited to threshold stimuli. Fixate the left half of Figure 5.11 and then look between the two right-hand gratings. It will be found that the apparent spacings of these two (identical) gratings will have changed, a supra-threshold effect first reported by Blakemore and Sutton (1969).

These discoveries provoked an exciting idea: *the visual system conveys information about spatial frequencies in tuned channels.* This was an insight which was to have a considerable impact upon subsequent theorizing about the visual system, as will be shown in Chapter 8.

The model of perception to emerge from the work described in this section is that vision proceeds in two distinct stages. Demonstrations such as that in Figure 5.12 prove that a scene can be physically analysed or decomposed into a set of component spatial frequencies. But it is obvious from Figure 5.12 that this process can be reversed: addition of spatial frequencies yields complete pictures. And if complete pictures can be formed in this manner might not the same be true of complete *percepts*? As yet, there is no strong evidence as to where the necessary syntheses take place in perception, nor do we have certain knowledge as to how this process is achieved, although we shall describe some hypotheses concerning this in a later chapter on the computational approach to visual perception. We can say, however, that the researches described above have been a rich source of ideas about vision and that the earlier work on visual analysis is beginning to be complemented by ideas as to how such analyses are later combined to form percepts.

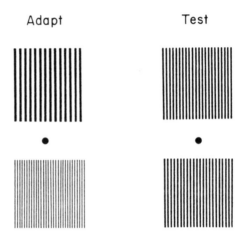

Figure 5.11   The Blakemore Sutton after-effect. Fixate the left dot for about one minute, then look at the right dot. The upper right grating will then seem more narrowly spaced than the identical lower right grating. (This illusion was first described by Blakemore and Sutton, 1969.)

Figure 5.12 (*opposite*)   Computer-processed images. (a) The original photograph (of a famous Psychology department). (b) The area of the original selected for processing, after conversion to pixels. (c) The results of processing the sample through a low-pass filter: the picture now contains only low spatial frequences. (d) The result of processing (b) with a Laplacian filter. This has revealed those regions in the picture where zero-crossings occur. In this case the 'receptive field' comprised a central excitatory region of one pixel surrounded by eight inhibitory pixels arranged in a square with weightings of $+8$ for the excitatory centre and $-1$ for each of the 8 surrounding pixels. (e) is similar to (d) except that the receptive field or mask applied to (b) comprised a central excitatory square of $3 \times 3$ pixels surrounded by a further 72 pixels weighted so that the excitatory centre was again balanced by its inhibitory surround. Thanks are due to Professor M. J. Morgan of London University College for producing the filtered versions in this illustration.

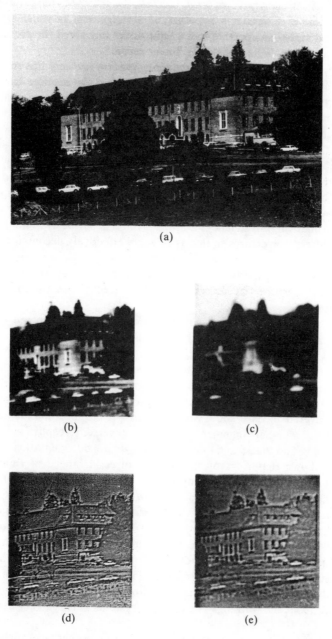

Figure 5.12 (*caption opposite*)

*Neural mechanisms and spatial frequencies*

What sort of neural structures could mediate the responses to spatial frequency described above? Consider a hypothetical arrangement in which two gratings were moved across an aperture and a light meter measured the energy reflected from the aperture. What would the meter reveal?

Clearly, the stripes of the high-frequency grating are very fine relative to the aperture. Therefore the meter would simply record the average luminance (or reflectance) from the light and dark stripes. Moving the grating would have no effect upon this average output.

But were the low-frequency grating to be moved across the aperture it is clear that the larger stripes would exert changes which would be detected. Dark stripes would fill a large portion of the aperture to give a low signal on the meter; light stripes, when they appeared, would produce a sudden change in output. Thus the aperture is acting as a *filter* biased to low-frequency gratings. It is easy to see how a smaller aperture would allow the light meter to respond actively to finer (high-frequency) gratings. And it is obviously a simple matter to combine different apertures so that they could effectively decompose a complex grating, responding selectively to particular bands of spatial frequencies. Thus we can consider the aperture as a component in a spatial frequency detection model, with aperture size determining which frequencies the system is most sensitive to.

The question now is whether there is a known neural mechanism which could act in a manner analogous to an aperture. The reader has probably anticipated the answer to this question: *receptive fields could perform this function.*

It was for this reason that so much space was devoted earlier to the discovery of receptive fields. They are known to possess many of the properties required for spatial frequency analysis. Remember that those receptive fields discovered to date show various forms of organization: some have on-centre/off-surround arrangements, others the reverse. Receptive fields have different shapes and sizes, and many are known to be orientation specific. As it can be shown that pairs of slit-like apertures, arranged at right-angles to each other, can detect *any* grating (within their frequency range), it follows that we can now begin to understand how the visual system's responsiveness to spatial frequency may be mediated. During scanning movements of the eyes lines and edges will move across the retina; thus large numbers of overlapping receptive fields will be stimulated by features within the visual image. There is therefore a very plausible set of mechanisms which could do the required job of spatial frequency analysis, and spatial frequency information can be recombined to form percepts. Perhaps we are starting to learn something very important about the workings of the visual system. This is a very exciting state of affairs.

Of course, no one has claimed that this is a comprehensive theory, even of low-level visual perception. Nothing has been said regarding, for example, the relation between spatial frequency and colour or texture; nor have we referred to depth or motion perception. But there is now a convincing account of how one important aspect of seeing might be mediated, and a major portion of this account uses the language and concepts of neurophysiology.

## An assessment of the neurophysiological approach to perceptual theorizing

The gains in knowledge used to illustrate the theme of this chapter have followed a rough progression. Ingenious new techniques of measurement led to the discovery of the visual pigments suggested by psychophysical studies of colour vision. Then another major problem, the 'opponent' aspect of colour vision, was solved by the use of microelectrode probes which enabled researchers to study living neurons in the visual system. Knowledge of nerve excitation and inhibition, combined with the results of microelectrode studies, provided hard data on the characteristics of receptive fields. Finally, it was discovered that further psychophysical data on the perception of spatial frequencies could be explained by extending the concept of the receptive field.

Evaluation of this style of theorizing involves a degree of personal choice. There have always been those who prefer to think in terms of concrete entities rather than hypothetical constructs, and this preference is not restricted to perceptionists.

One may also feel sympathy for the understandable desire to continue what is best about all this work, namely the fruitful interaction between psychology, where many of the problems of perception first become apparent, and physiology and neuroanatomy, where there are workers who are in a unique position to perform direct tests on sensory mechanisms. What have been described in this chapter are examples of the best sort of cross-fertilization between disciplines. But can the language of neurons and their physiology provide a full and final answer to problems in perception? Some think not.

First, to repeat a phenomenological argument made elsewhere in this book, colour is, amongst other things, an experience; a pain is not only activity in certain sorts of neuron, it hurts. But 'redness' and 'hurting' are part of our conscious lives. How much we hurt depends, in part, on our upbringing and upon the mores and attitudes of those around us; that is to say, upon other events and experiences which have taken place in the external world and which must be described in a language appropriate to that world. A full description of colour and pain must surely take this into account.

Then it must be recognized that to try to account for perception using the neuron as the basic explanatory device pushes one inevitably towards a reductionist point of view. It is an obvious possibility that sensory aspects of seeing—what happens in the retina, the optic nerve and the primary visual cortex—may indeed be explicable in terms of relatively simple mechanisms and systems. But the ways in which large groups of neurons interact are simply not known. Vision probably utilizes a significant proportion of the total ensemble of cortical cells, in which case the numbers involved are very large indeed: billions rather than millions. There could be interactions in such groupings too complex for the language of neurology, now or in the foreseeable future. Might it not be better to keep an open mind about the neural aspects of vision and to feel free to invoke hypothetical constructs when and where they seem appropriate? To do this would be to respect a long tradition in which supporters of Holism have long claimed that, as the brain is one vast interacting system, it is pointless to look for places where specific functions are performed or to simplify hypotheses to the level of components.

These remarks are very general in nature and the thoughtful reader will already have opinions about the issues raised. At this point we will turn to a much more specific evaluation of the neurophysiological approach to psychological problems. An example may be drawn from Marr (1982). Marr's work will be considered in more detail in Chapter 8; at this point we repeat something which Marr says in his important book *Vision*: namely that the great excitement felt when some of the neurophysiological discoveries were published has died down; some of the promise has not been borne out in subsequent work. Why should this be?

Consider again the work by Hubel and Weisel alluded to earlier. It must be re-emphasized that the papers in which they announced their discovery of orientation-specific receptive fields in the visual cortex of the cat have become probably the best known neurophysiological papers in the history of perceptual research, certainly among psychologists. Hubel and Weisel appeared to have solved an important problem in pattern perception, namely the basis of the detection of features. But finding a mechanism is not always the solution to a problem. Frisby states this well:

> 'it is dangerous to assume that a property of a neuron can be directly equated with its functions; "line detectors" have the property of responding optimally to a line of a given type but this does not mean that they are "line detectors" in the full and proper sense of this term, that is that their function is to detect lines.'
>
> (Frisby, 1979)

This criticism may be developed further. To repeat: the language of neurophysiology must remain 'inside' the organism. But the raw material of perception comprises things and events in the external world. Specifically then, Hubel and Weisel's detectors are neural mechanisms which detect lines or discontinuities *in the visual image*. But this does not mean that their job is to detect edges in the world; it might be, but nothing we know of them renders this certain. The same remarks apply to the theoretical elaboration of receptive fields into spatial frequency channels.

But there is one case in which a solution has been found to the problem of how the visual system can go beyond the retinal image to provide reliable information about the environment. This solution, which will form a fitting end to this chapter, has important implications for explanation in perception generally. For this reason we shall anticipate a later chapter and mention here one aspect of Marr's theory of vision.

The problem is to be sure that some property of the visual image represents something in the world, that a contour on the retina is associated with a real edge. Marr and Hildreth (1980) suggest the following solution. One aspect of any two-dimensional image is the distribution of intensities across the surface. Sometimes the intensity value between two adjacent regions changes abruptly. The abruptness of this change can be measured in terms of what are known as first- and second-order differentials of intensity, and from these it is possible to extract a measure of change in intensity known as the 'Zero-Crossing'. (All this may seem rather obscure: it will be explained more fully in Chapter 8.)

There is then a property of an image, known as the zero-crossing, which is associated with regions of rapid change in intensity. As such, it is rich in information. In a lengthy analysis, Marr and Hildreth show how spatial frequency filters can extract zero-crossings, and how combinations of neurons can act as the filters. They then adopt the reasonable assumption (in view of the spatial frequency research reviewed earlier) that a zero-crossing might be extracted simultaneously from different spatial frequency channels. Now, if a range of contiguous sizes of channel all detect a zero-crossing in the same location then *it can be proved that there is an intensity change in the image arising from a single external cause*.

This is a marvellous result. It shows one way in which vision could go beyond the visual image to permit valid inferences about the external physical world. But it also tells us something about the nature of explanation: the necessity of coincidence between contiguous spatial frequency channels in order that the Marr–Hildreth model can operate is a *rule*; it could not have arisen purely from within the language of neurophysiology. It is a rule stated at a level of explanation which is of necessity more general than that of neurophysiology and could not have come from neurophysiological knowledge alone. Might not this be a warning about the inevitable limits on neurophysiological explanations of perceptual phenomena?

Some readers may have found this chapter a rather difficult one. It has been necessary to describe some very technical researches briefly and in simple terms, and this is not easy to do. And we have had to refer on occasion to later chapters, for it is here that certain links with neurophysiological research and perceptual theory will re-emerge. After this explanation to the reader it is time to ask what the work described in this chapter amounts to. What can be said finally about the neurophysiological approach to perceptual theory?

For a start, it is clear that this is not a general theory of perception. Most of the solutions to problems described in the preceding sections have been very local ones. Many of these are satisfying in that they confirm the essential truth of some early perceptual theories. This is most clearly demonstrated in the research into mechanisms of colour vision, but an equally good case could have been made by describing comparable work in other modalities, particularly hearing. These solutions or explanations involve very few regions of the general model described in Chapter 1. For example, they may relate retinal outputs to the wavelength distributions of incoming light, or to brightness gradients across the retinal image. But the arc connecting the proximal stimulus and the receptor surface or structures adjacent to it is a very short one.

Nowhere in such accounts of vision can there be any place for phenomenal experience. The contrast between, for example, the type of thinking outlined in this chapter and that which characterizes Gestalt theory could hardly be greater. Nor is it possible to see how some of the important Gestalt phenomena could be subjected to neurophysiological investigation: how to explain size constancy, figure-ground effects or Prägnanz? And it is clear that most of the work described assumes a direct causal link between events in the retinal layers and perceptual responses. But if Brunswik was correct in his insistence upon the probabilistic nature of perception then such causal links cannot be the whole story.

What has emerged from modern neurophysiological research is something of a consensus among leading workers about the basic nature of vision. This is that it begins with a series of analyses in which aspects of the visual image are converted to neural codes. These analyses must be relatively independent: the mechanisms for coding colour must be different from those coding spatial frequency, for example. But knowing *that* such coding takes place is not the same as knowing *how* the nervous system does it: this will be the theme of Chapter 8. But it is also agreed that neural analysis must be followed by some sort of neural synthesis, and here there is much more uncertainty concerning possible mechanisms. This is hardly surprising, not least because such mechanisms, because of their later position in the chain of visual processing, must lie deeper within the central nervous system. They are going to be harder to find. But the process of synthesis may prove to be even more interesting as a research topic than anything described in this chapter. It is a striking fact that in all our experience of seeing, we never notice colour and shape drifting apart. A red object never splits into its shape plus a misaligned colour, the registration is always perfect. How remarkable that these aspects of the stimulus object remain so tightly locked. How can the vital timing of colour and shape processing be synchronized to this impressive degree? It will be fascinating to try to solve problems of this calibre.

We end this chapter by asserting, once more, that reading of the discoveries which form the material of the present chapter is an exciting experience. These major researches will have a permanent place in the history of perception. And even if it becomes accepted that the true explanation of perceptual phenomena cannot be arrived at using only the language of neurophysiology, then this too may be an important step in our understanding.

## NOTES ON CHAPTER 5

Those readers to whom the work described in this chapter is quite new should consult these excellent texts: Thompson (1967) for a lucid introduction to the early work on receptive fields, Ludel (1978) for a very clear account of neural structure and function.

The debate over three-factor versus opponent-process explanations of colour vision is described in most general perception textbooks, including Sekuler and Blake (1985).

Sekuler and Blake (1985) should also be consulted for their excellent descriptions of receptive field and spatial frequency research. Kaufman (1974) contains a very clear and interesting exposition of the relationship between spatial frequencies and the filtering characteristics of various sized apertures.

Frisby (1979) can be recommended as a demonstration of how knowledge of neural action can form the basis of a theory of shape perception.

A warning: some readers who consult the papers on single-cell recording referred to in this chapter may find details of the experimental procedures distasteful.

# Chapter 6

# Empiricism: Perception as a constructive process

'whilst part of what we perceive comes through our senses from the object before us, another part (and it may be the larger part) always comes out of our head'.

(William James 1890)

In 1959 a Canadian psychologist, Robert Sommer, described an incident leading to a trial at which he was a juror. Here is Sommer's account of the incident.

'A hunting party went out one afternoon looking for deer. While driving through a field, their car became stuck in the snow and eventually the transmission broke. Of the five men in the party, two volunteered to go to a nearby farmhouse for help. Of the remaining three, one remained in the rear seat while the other two stood at the front of the car. Meanwhile, one of the two men on the way to the farmhouse decided that there was no reason for both of them to go, and he thought he might be able to scare up a deer. Unknown to the men in the car, he circled around down a hill in front of them. At that point, one of the men standing outside the car said to the other, "That's a deer, isn't it?" to which the other replied in the affirmative. The first then took a shot at the deer. The deer pitched forward and uttered a cry which both men heard as the cry of a wounded deer. When the deer started running again, the second man implored, "Don't let him get away, please get him for me". The first man fired again and the deer went down but continued its forward movement. A third shot brought the deer to the ground and both men started running towards it. By this time the third man in the car, who had been trying to find and focus his field glasses, suddenly called out, "It's a man".'

(Sommer, 1959)

The ideas in this chapter attempt to explain what happened on that tragic afternoon.

After that real-life story, consider two simple demonstrations. Look first at Figure 6.1. What do you see? Most readers will interpret the figure as a row of numbers crossed by a column of letters. Now notice that the numeral '13' and the letter 'B' are identical. Interpretation of the patterns is affected by their context.

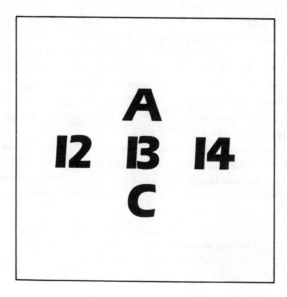

Figure 6.1

Turn now to Figure 6.2. For many readers this will appear as a random jumble of black shapes on a white ground. If this is what you see your perception of the figure will now change.

Figure 6.2   The hidden face. See the text for instructions on how to find the face. (From Porter, 1954)

The first hint is that the figure contains a face: can you see it? If not, then note that it is a Christ-like or Cavalier face occupying the top third of the rectangle and looking out of the page. Now can you see it? If not, note that the figure is strongly lit from one side, has two penetrating eyes, long hair and a beard. If you still cannot see the figure look at Figure 6.3 which contains a more explicit plan of the face. If you happened to see the figure immediately, show it to a friend and then help the friend to see it by a series of hints. Seeing the face can occur quite dramatically and is a fascinating experience. Once seen the face will always emerge from Figure 6.2.

It is clear that in both these demonstrations one's perceptions are not predictable simply from the parts which form the 'B', the '13' or the face. Something—the context, the hints—seems to have come between the registration of the stimuli and our final response to them. Is this an essential part of perceiving?

Many who have worked in the field of perception, possibly the majority, have not been committed solely to the testing of one particular theory. Researchers have had their imaginations triggered in a variety of ways. They may have read about some new phenomenon and decided to set up equipment to enable them to see it for themselves. It is then a small step to make small changes and explore the effects of these on the phenomenon. Soon, a research programme for the next few years has crystallized. Similarly, people can simply notice something odd about their own perceiving under unusual or unfamiliar conditions and decide to investigate what nature has tossed into their laps. And much research is still of the 'What will happen if ...?' variety. What will happen if chimpanzees learn sign language? What will happen to perception under conditions of weightlessness? What will happen if an animal is prevented from using its eyes for the first three weeks of life? And so on.

In this sense it is almost possible to be a-theoretical in perceptual research. Almost, but not quite. The *framework* within which one thinks, the attitudes one brings to experimental designs, and even the ways in which one expects subjects to respond, are all subtly influenced by the current zeitgeist. All who study perceptual phenomena carry around with them a set of beliefs concerning the fundamental nature of perceiving. To this extent, nobody is really a-theoretical. And when such a set of beliefs and assumptions becomes widespread and strongly influential it qualifies for the label, 'paradigm'. (See Kuhn, 1970, for a discussion of paradigms in scientific research.)

We now assert that the dominant paradigm in perceptual research this century has been *empiricism*, which is the subject of this chapter. The thoughts which may have been suggested by the opening demonstrations at the start of this chapter are the same as those which led to the spread of empiricism in psychology: the idea that perception is something more than the direct registration of sensations; that somehow other events intervene between stimulation and experience. We shall attempt to show just how fruitful this idea has been.

In terms of the simple classificatory scheme outlined at the start of this book, psychological empiricism is concerned with (i) the relationship between the external world and events at sensory surfaces and (ii) how events at these surfaces interact with more central processes to produce meaningful perceptions.

At this point it would be as well to warn philosophically informed readers that empiricism in psychology is not identical with the tradition which developed in the writings of Locke, Berkeley, Hume and Mill—the British empiricists. Locke, for example, was concerned with the origins of *ideas*. His writings stress that ideas can come into the mind only as the result of experience. Locke did not argue, as is sometimes claimed by psychologists, that we have to learn to see. But, as we shall show, some psychologists have in fact claimed that this is indeed the case. Empiricism in psychology is therefore somewhat coarser and more extreme than the philosophical version. An excellent discussion of this topic will be found in Morgan (1977).

## HISTORICAL BACKGROUND

Helmholtz (1821–1894), one of the founders of perceptual research, was probably the most gifted, original and successful perceptionist to date. The list of his discoveries and inventions is staggering: the first scientific account of hearing; the first scientific explanation of musical effects; probably the best book yet on seeing, *The Physiological Optics*; a major theory of the workings of the inner ear; a major theory of colour vision; the invention of the opthalmoscope— Helmholtz was the first person to look into a living eye.

In mid career, Helmholtz discovered an interesting problem. He had noticed that if a small piece of grey paper is laid over a red surface it becomes tinged with green. Where does this green come from? Subsequent discoveries permit an explanation of the induced green in terms of known physiological mechanisms. But Helmholtz knew only that green is the *complement* of red. (In colour vision research, two hues are said to be complementary if they yield an achromatic grey when mixed.) Helmholtz therefore offered an explanation of the induced green in terms of the viewer's *knowledge* of the fact that the grey paper, when adjacent to the contrasting red, should yield its complement.

With this explanation of a perceptual effect Helmholtz brought empiricism into experimental psychology. He argued that between sensations (when our senses first register the effects of stimulation) and our conscious perception of the real world there must be intermediate processes of a constructive nature. These processes resemble thinking, in particular inferential thinking, and because of them perception can go beyond the evidence of the senses—evidence which is often inadequate or distorted. But when we introspect we are not normally aware that we are making inferences, nor can we change our perceptions at will: the inferences must be *unconscious*. Armed with this simple idea one

Figure 6.3   A key to the hidden face

can begin to explain a variety of important phenomena. For example, if the brain can calculate object distance, possibly by a process resembling triangulation, then this might be a way of compensating for the reduction of image size with distance. This would provide a basis for size constancy. In a similar manner, it is possible to understand why rectangular objects maintain their apparent shape when viewed obliquely. And so on.

Helmholtz did not fully explore the implications of unconscious inference. He offered some rules about the inferences—that they were the result of associations and experience, that they were inferential, that they were the result of association and experience—but the central idea is not fully developed in his subsequent writings. However, the idea of unconscious inference did enable Helmholtz to avoid nativist solutions to the problems of perception (we see things at their proper size because we are built to see in this way, which is hardly an explanation), and this may have been his main aim.

## EMPIRICISM AFTER HELMHOLTZ

Helmholtz's prestige, added to the basic appeal of empiricism, made this way of looking at perception almost irresistible. It is true that another great physiologist, Hering (Helmholtz's contemporary and rival), adopted a nativism which was totally opposed to empiricism. And, as we have seen, the Gestalt movement had little sympathy for the idea that perception was based upon associations. But despite these important exceptions, a major paradigm had emerged: perception was to be thought of as an indirect, constructive, inferential process.

We will now describe a selection of discoveries made during the years between Helmholtz and the present which have reinforced the empiricist view of perception.

### Attention and set

In a classic study of human attention, Külpe (1904) used a tachistoscope to deliver brief exposures of displays of variously coloured letters. The subjects in the experiment were directed to attend to some aspect of the display, say the position of certain letters. When asked subsequently to describe some other aspect of the display, for example the colours of the letters, they were unable to do so. The significance of this famous demonstration is that although all the information from the brief display must have reached the eye, at some point between the formation of the retinal image and the production of the final report, selection had taken place: what is taken in from a display depends not only upon the properties of that display but on the 'set' which the viewer has adopted. Perceptions are not simply inputs.

### Drives and perception

Sanford (1936) showed ambiguous pictures to groups of schoolchildren and asked them to write down what they had seen. The experiment was run at different times of day. It was found that twice as many food-related responses were made before compared with after meal times. Hunger can influence what is seen.

### The influence of stereotypes

Early in his famous book *Remembering* (1932) F.C. Bartlett describes a demonstration which he ran during the first open day at the new psychology laboratory in Cambridge. Visitors were asked to look into a tachistoscope and report what they could see. The picture in the tachistoscope was that of a man wearing a naval officer's cap. Many viewers reported, wrongly, that the man had a beard:

the current stereotype of a British naval officer. Prior expectations had influenced what they had seen. (In the subsequent researches for which he became famous, Bartlett was able to show that stereotypes and expectations exert an equally striking influence on long-term remembering.)

## The New Look experiments

In the years after the Second World War a group of American psychologists, many of whom had an interest in Freudian or other psychodynamic theories but had also received training as experimentalists, reported a series of researches which became known, collectively, as the New Look Psychology (after a popular contemporary fashion in clothes). Here are three of the most famous of their findings.

First, Bruner and Goodman (1947) carried out an investigation into children's ability to judge the size of objects. Now size estimation of familiar objects is something which humans are quite good at. However, the objects to be judged by Bruner and Goodman's young subjects were American coins—that is things which the children knew to have *value*. It was found that size estimation was imperfect. The children tended to overestimate the sizes of valuable coins, and poor children overestimated them to a greater extent than richer children. This finding may be analogous to an experience which many readers may have had: on the rare occasions when one sees a very famous person in the flesh (a well-known film star, for example) they look surprisingly small.

Second, McGinnies (1949) performed a word-recognition experiment using tachistoscopically presented materials. Among the items presented were a number of 'taboo' words. Thresholds for these taboo words were higher, that is, it took longer to recognize them. But how did the subjects know the words were taboo if they had not yet recognized them?

Third, Lazarus and McCleary (1951) paired certain words with electric shock. These and other words were then presented tachistoscopically. Throughout the experiment the subject's Galvanic Skin Response was recorded. (The GSR is an autonomic reaction of the body during emotional changes and is not under voluntary control: it is recorded as a sweat reaction from the palms or the fingers.) Recognition thresholds were higher for the shocked words and these words (not surprisingly) induced the strongest GSR responses. Interestingly, the subjects started to show GSR responses to the shocked words *before they could say what the words were*.

Each of these typical New Look studies has been criticized (as has the entire movement). For example, as the value of American coins increases with their size, the behaviour of Bruner and Goodman's young subjects wasn't *that* irrational. Taboo words are rarer in printed English and recognition thresholds are known to be higher for infrequent words. The idea (Lazarus and McCleary, 1951) that some sort of censor is coming between perceptual inputs and consciousness is not a very satisfactory one as we are told so little about the characteristics of the censor: how does one recognize words in order to censor them? However, the popularity of this sort of research in the years between 1947 and 1960 shows that the idea of perceptions as essentially indirect in nature, and not tied directly to sensory inputs, had become a very powerful influence on psychological thinking.

## The Ames demonstrations

During the 1940s Adelbert Ames of the Dartmouth Eye Clinic, Connecticut, developed some of the most compelling illusions ever seen. The most famous of these are the Ames room and the Ames window (see Ames, 1949).

The Ames room is shown in plan view in Figure 6.4. It is an irregular shape with a receding rear wall. But the room is decorated in a special manner: the decoration of the rear wall is such that it projects an image to a viewing point in the front wall which is identical to that which would be produced by a wall at right-angles to the two side walls; in other words by a normal wall.

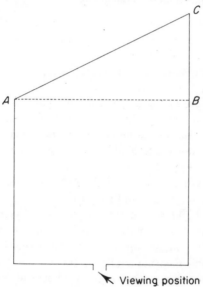

Figure 6.4    The Ames room seen from above. The wall *AC* is shaped and decorated so as to appear to be in position *AB*. Viewed monoculary from the front, the room appears to be rectangular. However, an object moving from *A* to *C* will appear to shrink

When one looks into the Ames room, one sees it as normally proportioned. But if a person walks from one of the two farther corners of the room to the other, the room remains apparently rectangular, *but the person appears to change size.* This wonderful illusion does not disappear when one learns the true shape of the room.

The Ames window is simply a trapezoidal shape with a window design added to it in such a way that when the window is viewed obliquely from 45 degrees the outline and the details appear rectangular. When such a window is rotated one sees, not rotations, but *oscillations*, the window appearing to change its direction of rotation half way through each cycle.

The original explanation of these two Ames illusions was in terms of our familiarity with rectangular rooms and windows. It must be said that this explanation has been challenged (see for example, Day and Power, 1965). But note how powerful a demonstration of the vulnerability of perception is contained in these ingenious inventions. How could one deny that perceptions are modifiable constructions, rather than direct responses to patterns of stimulation, when one has been made to doubt the evidence of one's senses in such a captivating and compelling manner?

### The work of J. S. Bruner and his colleagues

In the 1940s and 1950s the distinguished American psychologist J. S. Bruner and various colleagues undertook a programme of research into human thinking. Bruner was particularly interested in the ways in which problem-solvers utilize information. For example, in several studies, a large number of patterns were displayed to subjects. The experimenter had chosen a category of which only some of the patterns were exemplars. The question of interest was: when subjects form hypotheses about the category, do they test these by choosing positive or negative instances from available evidence? In Bruner's experiment testing against a negative instance could often yield information which would lead to rapid solution of the problem. However, subjects showed a distinct bias in favour of positive instances, even though such tests were not always helpful. Bruner was interested in the use and weighting of cues in problem-solving, the role of categories in thinking, and the formation of hypotheses by subjects in problem-solving tasks. It was a natural but ingenious step to extrapolate from such questions about thinking to questions about perceiving.

Bruner, Postman and Rodrigues (1951) carried out a tachistoscopic recognition experiment. Two things were unusual about this experiment. First, the materials presented were playing cards. Second, and even more unusually, some of the cards were wrong: some had black hearts, others red clubs, and so on. The question asked was, how would subjects perceive the unnatural cards? The outcome was that (a) some subjects made correct reports of these cards, but (b) others reported strange compromise perceptions: for example, the incorrectly coloured hearts were sometimes described as purple. It was as if a compromise had been reached between the actual properties of a stimulus and the perceivers' knowledge of its normal appearance.

Using these and other results, Bruner arrived at the following theory of perception (Bruner,1957). A perceiver meets the world (or processes sensory inputs) via a set of hypotheses. Sensory input is used as evidence against which a hypothesis is tested. A strong hypothesis requires less evidence to confirm it and more evidence to infirm it; the reverse is true of a weak hypothesis. In everyday terms, one would require a lot of sensory evidence (it would take longer) before deciding that the floor one was standing on had become rubbery—a much more likely conclusion would be that something was amiss with one's legs. On the other hand, if a telephone operator were to answer 'rumba please', it is very likely that one would hear this as normal. We have then a theoretical statement linking perception and thinking via the specific proposal that the basis of perceiving is the formation of hypotheses. The theory is clearly testable, although it is not necessarily the case that hypotheses will always be explicit or reportable.

## Attention and perception

Some very famous studies of human attention were published during the 1950s and 1960s. We shall not attempt to review this large literature. It must be stated, however, that influential books by Broadbent (1958) and Neisser (1967) made a powerful case for the selective nature of much human perceiving. A subject asked to monitor one of two aural messages delivered simultaneously will subsequently be unable to say very much about the other. The subject will, however, hear his or her own name in the non-attended ear. In another widely used experimental situation, a subject who has just scanned rapidly through a visual array for a target will be able to say very little about the non-target items scanned through.

These and many other reliable effects illustrate the selective nature of perceiving and seem to show that perception is open to control by central factors and is not determined solely by local conditions of stimulation. This is very suggestive evidence from the point of view of those who support an empiricist view of perception. This then was the state of thinking concerning the indirect, constructive nature of perception 100 years after Helmholtz had formulated the doctrine of unconscious inference.

To summarize: empiricism in psychology conceives of the perceiver as being not unlike the captain of a submarine. He has knowledge of the medium in which he is submerged but cannot experience it directly. So he must plan according to the knowledge which experience and training have given him. From time to time indirect samples of the environment are taken: instruments show the distance from the ocean floor, the vessel's heading, the presence in the area of other submerged objects. The better (the more alert and experienced) the captain, the more skilfully will he evaluate the evidence from his imperfect sensors. He must guide the ship through water he can never touch.

The sections above outline the history of empiricism in psychology and show some of the varied evidence adduced in favour of this paradigm. But the alternative theories within this tradition have been sketched only in bare outline (except of course Brunswik's which, although written by someone calling himself a functionalist, clearly makes assumptions of a constructivist nature). We turn now to a detailed account of a modern version of empiricism, a contemporary theory of perception which can be traced back to the work of earlier psychologists such as Bruner. The theory of perception developed by the British psychologist R. L. Gregory will show the state that empiricism has reached in the 100 years since Helmholtz's introduction of the idea into the psychology of perception.

## R. L. GREGORY

Richard Gregory (b. 1923) is an experimenter of unusual originality. He has also invented a microscope, a telescope, a new type of hearing-aid and several other ingenious devices. In Gregory's experiments, subjects have been hurtled down tunnels, swung on giant swings and baffled by illusions. His lectures are distinguished by the use of novel demonstrations which are so compelling that one comes away convinced that what he says about perception must be right. He has inspired the building of a 'hands on' science fair, and is a frequent broadcaster. The quality of his writing and his demonstrations matches the standards set by the Gestalt psychologists and Ames and his co-workers—which is to say, they are as good as any in the history of perception. Gregory has enabled countless individuals to experience some of the delights which the study of perceptual phenomena affords. It is hardly surprising that his views on perception should be so well known.

## PERCEPTIONS AS HYPOTHESIS: GREGORY'S VERSION

In addition to being well known as a highly original experimenter, Gregory is interested in the classical philosophical problems associated with perceiving. In an article published as part of a debate between psychologists and philosophers (Gregory, 1974), he describes some of the properties of perceiving which, he claims, force the conclusion that this is an activity resembling hypothesis formation and testing.

The essence of Gregory's hypothesis theory is this. Signals received by the sensory receptors trigger neural events. Appropriate knowledge interacts with these inputs to create psychological data. On the basis of such data, hypotheses are advanced to predict and make sense of events in the world. This chain of events is the process we call perceiving.

One of the merits of what Gregory calls *the hypothesis theory* is the clarity of its presentation. Another is the care with which Gregory presents the evidence in support of his views. Gregory's main arguments for this most recent version of empiricism will now be summarized.

(1) *Perception allows behaviour to be generally appropriate to non-sensed object characteristics.* We respond to certain objects as though they were tables, having, that is, four legs and rectangular tops, even though all we can 'see' are three legs and the trapezoidal projection of the top. Mustn't we be using more than just sensory inputs to achieve these percepts?

(2) *Perception can, in familiar situations, mediate skills with zero time delay.* In a typical tracking experiment the subject is asked to keep a pointer aligned with a moving target. This would seem to be an essentially visual task, and visual processes are known to require a finite time. However, if the target position in a tracking task is made regular and predictable, then the subject will be able to track the target with zero time delay. How is this possible without a degree of anticipation entering into the perception of the target?

(3) *Perceptions can be ambiguous.* Look for a moment at Figure 6.5, the Necker cube. As one stares at this familiar figure its orientation may suddenly change: it is unstable. If a single physical pattern can induce two different percepts, perception cannot be tied to the stimulation in a one-to-one manner.

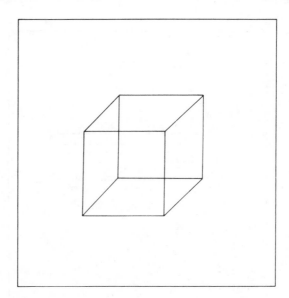

Figure 6.5 A reversible figure: the Necker cube. If fixated in the centre the orientation of the cube will change quite suddenly

(4) *Perception can extract familiar objects from background clutter.* Gregory uses as an example our ability to extract one person's voice from others in a crowded room. This is something which no machine has ever been able to do, although we find it relatively easy. Is this because there is a limited repertoire of acceptable speech sounds which we and the speaker share? If so, our knowledge of the language is reducing the informational demands of the task. The achievement which this form of perceiving represents is more obvious when we consider experiences in a foreign country: after a few repetitions it slowly dawns on one that the sound, 'atoo talur', is the phrase, 'A tout l'heure'. Perceiving appears to be aided by knowledge.

(5) *Highly unlikely objects tend to be mistaken for likely objects.* One of Gregory's best-known demonstrations involves a hollow mask of a face. When suitably illuminated, such a mask is generally seen as normal. Interestingly, even when one knows the true orientation of the mask (and even when one has constructed it) the illusion remains, recalling Helmholtz's description of unconscious inferences as 'irresistible' and Brunswik's phrase, 'the stupidity of the senses'.

(6) *Perception can be paradoxical.* Figure 6.6 is the famous Penrose design. In this case, the 'impossibility' of the figure seems to depend upon false assumptions about triangles which we have brought to the perception of the diagram.

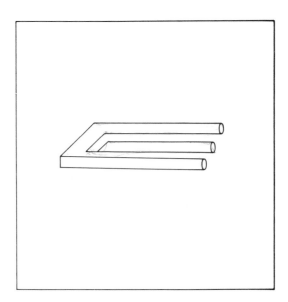

Figure 6.6   An impossible figure. (After Penrose and Penrose, 1958)

(7) *Perception can be of one thing representing another.* The perception of any picture is in a sense ambiguous: we see the lines and the surface and also the object depicted, even though the latter may in reality be many times larger than its depiction. Therefore there must be a large cognitive component in the perception of pictures.

(8) *Perception is not essentially based on what is experienced.* In many experimental situations subjects may be influenced by stimulus characteristics of which they are unaware. If one shows two photographs of a person, in one of which the pupils have been enlarged, this will tend to be seen as the more attractive version. Interestingly, subjects are often unable to notice any physical difference between the two pictures.

(9) *People experience hallucinations.* Quite simply, we can have vivid experiences of a perceptual nature in the absence of external stimulation.

These then are some of the key reasons which Gregory advances in support of the idea that perception is an indirect, constructive, hypothesis-like process. His case is clearly a formidable one. Notice also how well supporting instances are presented: the statements above concerning empiricism and perception are some of the most explicit ever.

### An application of hypothesis theory

Gregory has used his theory that perceptions are hypotheses to develop an explanation of certain well-known illusions. The Muller–Lyer illusion, which appeared in our account of the Gestalt theory (see Figure 3.5), is one of the most famous of all the geometric illusions. For many years psychologists have attempted to explain the shortening and lengthening of the main parts of this figure, without, it must be said, much success. Gregory's suggestion is an interesting application of hypothesis theory to an old and hitherto intractable problem.

Suppose that the feather ends of the Muller–Lyer lines are acting as cues to depth and that they provoke the hypothesis that one line, that with the out-turned feathers, is the inside corner of a junction of two surfaces. Look now at the ceiling of the room in which you are reading this and note how the corner formed by the two walls and the ceiling resembles the out-turned feathers. Now inspect an object which has a corner or edge pointing towards you (say a book standing vertically on a horizontal surface), the outside corners of the book can be seen to resemble the in-turned arrows of the Muller–Lyer figure. In the real three-dimensional world such inward and outward facing corners reveal whether an edge juts towards or away from us, that is to say they are cues to *distance*.

In real scenes, the shrinking of the retinal image of a receding object is opposed by the mechanism of *size constancy*, which, by enabling us to see things as the same size despite changes in distance, helps us to perceive a stable world. But if the Muller–Lyer arrows trigger this constancy mechanism, they are doing so in an inappropriate situation: the lines are actually equidistant from us on the page. So, instead of the equality of the lines being preserved over different distances, the constancy scaling mechanism induces a perception of unequal size at a fixed distance, and this is the Muller–Lyer illusion: an adjustment of perceived size triggered when it is inappropriate. This original and ingenious explanation follows quite naturally from the assumption that perceptions are hypotheses, and is a good example of Gregory's ingenious use of his theory.


## AN EVALUATION OF THIS VERSION OF EMPIRICISM

Gregory's theory that perceptions are hypotheses is the most explicit and fullest treatment of the central idea of empiricism. We shall now offer some criticisms of the theory.


## GENERAL CRITICISMS

### The nature of perceptual hypotheses

If perceptions are hypotheses, what sort of hypotheses are they? In one formal approach to the philosophy of science it is held necessary to abandon a hypothesis when a single contradictory fact appears (see, for example, Popper, 1960). However, it is commonly accepted that this is not how scientists actually behave. Nor do perceivers: we do not mistrust our senses following exposure to a single illusion. Scientists modify and elaborate hypotheses according to their success, or lack of it. But how do perceivers modify *their* hypotheses? Is this done according to the frequency of positive and negative tests, or is the modification based upon the strikingness of confirmatory and invalidating experiences? For example, learning that a photographed face is that of a mass-murderer certainly seems to effect a permanent change in one's perception of the face. And the reader has had experience of very rapid perceptual learning when discovering the face in Figure 6.2. On the other hand, learning to adjust to the effects of lenses which distort the world may take hours or even weeks of exposure. What is the difference between these forms of learning? We are not told. And, as we have seen, illusions persist even when we have full knowledge of the inducing conditions. Why doesn't this knowledge enable us to modify our hypotheses in an adaptive manner? Generally then, there is a serious problem concerning the relationship between knowledge and hypotheses, and it is difficult to see how this can be resolved in the current version of hypothesis theory.

That it is in fact possible to offer detailed guesses concerning the role of central constructive processes in perception will be proved in Chapter 8. In the artificial intelligence approach to vision it is common to refer to 'top-down' processes which control and structure information delivered by input processes. As will be shown in this later chapter, work in this area has made it possible to be quite explicit about the characteristics of hypothetical top-down processes and it will be asserted that this is a real gain in understanding and rigour compared with earlier theories of visual perception. Hypothesis theory cannot yet match this degree of explicitness concerning central processes.

## Hypotheses and language

How do hypotheses relate to language? Hypotheses, in the normal use of the term, must be statable if they are to be tested against evidence. But we often have perceptual experiences that are hard to describe. It can be the case that only after considerable thought by the observer can he or she describe what was seen. But the seeing came first. It would appear that perceptual hypotheses may be closer to intuitions than to formal statements. We can say that we dislike someone without being able to say why. We can walk down a flight of stairs without looking at our feet and without even noticing what the stairs look like. The hypothesis that the stairs are regular does not appear in consciousness. If hypotheses are not necessarily verbal or even conscious, then finding out about them is going to be difficult.

## Hypotheses and evidence

If we accept for the moment the idea that perceptions are hypotheses, a little thought reveals another serious problem: what is the *evidence* against which they are tested? Gregory is not clear on this point, and it is a difficult one. One of his own examples can be used to show the problem. He says, rightly, that we frequently 'see' a table when its retinal image must be distorted and incomplete. We go beyond the partial evidence of our senses via the (reasonable) hypothesis that there is a rectangular table in view.

Such a table is in view as this is being written. The top is built from parallel rough planks (university salaries being what they are), and three legs of a different wood are visible. It would be a shock to discover that this familiar, shaky object was not a table: the hypothesis seems to be a strong one. But what is the nature of the supporting *evidence*? Presumably it lies in the perception of the planks and the legs. But what guarantee is there that actual legs and planks are there? Is it not necessary first to have hypotheses to 'acquire' these components; and doesn't this lead to a regress of hypotheses concerning finer and finer details of the world? But if the Gestalt psychologists were right, the perception of the parts of a table does not simply add up to give the whole: they are seen in a manner partially determined by this whole. This and related criticisms of Gregory's theory are discussed more fully by the philosopher G. E. M. Anscombe (in Brown, 1974). Anscombe reminds us that a hypothesis is typically something which is answerable to data. What are the data to which Gregory's hypotheses are answerable?

### Starting to perceive

This is a problem which seems at first to be rather trivial, but on reflection can cause complete bafflement. If perception is essentially constructive, how does it ever get started? How does the naive, newborn perceiver ever establish a grasp on reality? One wonders if perception can be such an individual and chancy process. One's real-life experience suggests a great communality among the perceptions of different people. Where did this come from if all have had to construct their own idiosyncratic worlds? As demonstrated in Chapter 4, Brunswik would have an answer to this question: the selection of appropriate cues is vital to survival and organisms which get things wrong are unlikely to survive. That is to say, the world is common to all perceivers, and it may be this single fact that regularizes the perceptions of all creatures sharing a particular ecological niche. But hypothesis theory does not engage in such functionalist explanations.

The next general criticism of hypothesis theory may be somewhat unfair in that a theorist is not obliged to consider all possible ramifications of a theory; what follows should be read as a statement of opinion rather than a formal criticism.

### Human and non-human perceivers

There is a trap awaiting all whose work in perception concentrates upon the human subject: this is to suppose that all perceivers are like us. But all species are the product of a long evolutionary history which shaped the structures *and* the functions of the senses. It is as well to remember that, on several criteria, humans are not the most successful creatures to date. They are certainly not the most numerous, nor does their history match the duration of other groups such as dinosaurs and arthropods. All animals perceive, and must do this well enough to survive.

When we learn of the perceptual abilities of other creatures we find much that is strange:

> 'The mayfly lives but a day as an adult. It may, for all I know, experience that day as we live a lifetime.'
>
> (Gould 1980)

Our natural self-centredness should not blind us to the remarkably different lives of such creatures. Has the mayfly time to form and test hypotheses? Has it the neural equipment to do the necessary statistical assessments? Probably not. But mayflies can see their world, and have been doing so well enough for millions of years.

There are certainly major qualitative differences between our perceptual systems and those of many other animals. The long period of post-natal helplessness in humans may be the price paid for perceptual flexibility, and in this they differ from many other species who can function well at birth but who are relatively inflexible in their subsequent behaviour. But at what point does perception cease to be reflexive and become constructive? In how many species can we apply the theory that perceptions are hypotheses? Might it be that our long evolutionary history enables us too to perceive the world more directly and automatically than hypothesis theory suggests? This is certainly the view of some theorists whose work we shall review later in Chapter 7.

## Empiricism versus nativism

Any theory which stresses the role of knowledge in perceiving must clash with a nativist account of the origins of perception in the individual. Such an account has already been described in the Gestalt chapter (Chapter 3), when some of the evidence suggesting innate components in perceiving was reviewed. Should more evidence accrue in favour of nativism, then this can only be at the expense of approaches such as Gregory's.

## Appropriate stimuli for perceptual research

Nineteenth-century physiologists pioneered scientific work on the senses. In much of this early work the stimuli used were extremely simple and precisely controlled. This was a proper scientific tactic. If one wishes to understand the skin's responsiveness to, say, changes in temperature, then it is obviously useful to apply warm and cold stimuli to small regions without simultaneously touching the skin or triggering a pain response. In this way important facts, such as the punctate nature of skin sensitivity, were quickly established. This tradition is still to be found in contemporary sensory physiology.

But are simple stimuli appropriate in the study of perception? To repeat a point made earlier: perception evolved in an environment. It was, presumably, the ability to deal with the real external world which gave the evolving perceptual systems their selective advantages. And in this world warm stimulation often comes from objects which we are actively touching. So in real life contact and temperature may be closely linked. When perceptual abilities (as opposed to sensory thresholds) in the tactile sense are being explored, would it not be wiser to use more complex representative stimuli? We shall return to this point at the end of this chapter.

*The computer as a model of the mind*

This comment on hypothesis theory is a very general one and applies to many constructivist/empiricist approaches to perception. If one believes that sensory evidence is inadequate as a basis for valid perception of the world and needs augmenting, then it is natural to see perception as a number of functional stages. An image on the retina cannot specify the absolute size of an object. Therefore elaboration of this sensory evidence is required and this must take place somewhere and will require a finite amount of time. It is a small step to assume that we are dealing with *stages* between which *information* flows. This in turn leads quite naturally to the adoption of a new metaphor for the brain (or mind): the digital computer.

The digital computer is a relatively new model in psychology, but it has been enthusiastically adopted by many psychologists. This is not the point to develop a major criticism of the computer analogy. However, it must be stressed that there are those who think that the classical computer is not a suitable model for perception (or other psychological processes). These objectors argue strongly that this way of thinking about human performance represents a new and harmful form of mentalism. Should such objections prevail it seems certain that this will tend to discredit the empiricist paradigm within which the computer model has been applied. This important point will be dealt with at greater length in Chapters 7 and 8.

*The inadequacy of sensory evidence*

As has been stressed several times in this chapter, many theorists since Helmholtz have accepted his claim that sensory inputs alone are insufficient to specify the world. In support of this claim it has been pointed out that, for example, because the retinal image of an object shrinks as the object recedes, the correct perception of the unchanging size of the object implies that the sensory evidence has been supplemented from other sources. This constancy example has been used several times in this book—quite deliberately as it is a classic illustration of the empiricist argument.

But are retinal images really so impoverished? In the world (in contrast to the laboratory) retinal images will only rarely contain projections of single isolated objects. They will be much richer than this, typically including projections of other objects, the background to the objects, even the distant horizon. They will be rich in detail.

Some modern research has shown that complex images of real scenes commonly contain information which can be used to tell whether or not a receding object has or has not changed its size. Basically, what seems to be important is that some part of an otherwise changing image remains *invariant*. Similarly, although the shape of an object may not be uniquely specified by any single view of it, multiple views may deliver an unambiguous and correct solution to the true shape. And movement is a vital part of perceiving, a truth which has often been overlooked in laboratory research. The search for invariants, the importance of multiple views, and the difference which movement makes to seeing will be discussed at some length in Chapter 7. For now it suffices to say that empiricists may have underestimated the richness of sensory evidence when perceivers operate in the real world.

## OTHER VERSIONS OF EMPIRICISM

This chapter has concentrated upon the version of empiricism developed by R. L. Gregory. This has enabled us to mention current work within the constructivist paradigm. It is also true to say that Gregory's is probably the best-known and most thoroughly developed version of empiricism to date. The reader should be aware, however, that the broad appeal of empiricism and constructionism is such that several different general theories have emerged within this paradigm. Here is a list of some of the authors whose work should be consulted by anyone who wishes to know the various ways in which the central idea of this chapter—that perceptions are constructions—has been developed and refined.

(1) It is clear that Brunswik's theory, in which the perceiver acts as an intuitive statistician, uses some constructivist ideas. The theory outlined in Chapter 4 should be re-examined from the more general position described in the present chapter.

(2) Bruner's work on the role of categories has already been mentioned (see for example Bruner, Goodnow and Austin, 1956), as has his work on needs and values in perceiving (Bruner and Goodman, 1947). Here is a very good example of a theory which claims that perception is active rather than passive and that the perceiver copes with the complexities of the world by meeting sensory inputs with ready formed classificatory systems.

(3) As a result of his experimental studies of visual perception carried out at the Dartmouth Eye Institute, USA, Adelbert Ames developed Transactional Functionalism. His experimental findings suggested to Ames that we carry around with us knowledge of the 'typical' size and shape of familiar objects, which we usually see over a very restricted set of distances. If unusually large or small versions of familiar objects are illuminated in the dark, their apparent distance is determined partly by their actual distance, partly by the visual angle they subtend under natural conditions. Similar explanations can be advanced to explain illusions such as the Ames room and the Ames window. Thus perception is a dynamic interplay between current stimulation and expectations based upon our previous dealings with the world.

(4) In our opinion, some of the most interesting perceptual experiments of the

past 20 years are those described by Hochberg (see for example Hochberg, 1968). Hochberg is clearly impressed by the various Gestalt demonstrations of coherence and stability in perception, although he disagrees with Gestalt interpretations of perceptual phenomena. In some of his own researches Hochberg has studied the perception of objects when these are viewed through moving apertures. Interestingly, provided the size and speed of the moving apertures are adequate, complex percepts can be achieved even though visual information is spread over time. For example, it is quite easy to see a Necker cube when it is shown behind a moving slit: it even reverses on occasion.

From such studies Hochberg concludes that perception involves the creation and use of *schemata*. That is, in daily life we build up plans or cognitive structures which later serve to guide and control the ways in which we sample the world. This means that the partial samples of objects taken during sequences of eye movements and fixations can make sense only when they are referred to existing schemata. The fact that the perception of large complex things must inevitably be sequential (given the small angular size of clear central vision) means that successive inputs must be stored before being synthesized to whole percepts. It is during this storage that central organizing effects come into play, and this is the constructive aspect of seeing.

(5) In his earlier writings Neisser (for example Neisser, 1967) also made use of the concept of the schema in his account of the constructive nature of perception. Neisser is concerned with the general nature of cognition and this leads him to an analysis of the role of attention in perception and eventually to many stimulating ideas concerning the processes of synthesis which, he claims, underlie pattern perception. Later (Neisser, 1976) he develops a model in which schemata guide the perceiver's exploratory activities whilst the information sampled during these explorations is used to modify schemata. It is of interest that in this later account Neisser attempts a rapprochement between the constructivist/empiricist account of perception and some of the markedly different ideas developed by J. J. Gibson which are the subject of the next chapter.

(6) There is a theorist whose work is seldom referred to by perceptionists: this is George Kelley, whose theory arose out of his work as a clinical psychologist. Kelley's Personal Construct Theory is strikingly similar to some of the ideas which have been outlined in this chapter. He held, for example, that we perceive other people through, as it were, a series of filters which he called Constructs. Much of Kelley's work (see, for example, Kelley, 1955) was an attempt to discover the ways in which these constructs shape perception, how they differ between individuals, how they affect behaviour and how they relate to the emotions. Kelley's Repertory Grid technique for the exploration of construct systems is in use

to this day. It is very odd that Gregory, for example, makes no mention of Kelley's work, for this would undoubtedly have enabled him to extend the range of application of his own theory.

(7) In Chapter 8 an account will be given of Marr's computational theory of vision. Much of this modern research, as we shall see, concentrated upon the ways in which information is extracted from the visual image on the retina. But Marr was mindful of the fact that analysis must be followed by synthesis, and he acknowledged the role which knowledge can play in contributing to such a synthesis. It is clear that empiricism is alive and well.

## FINAL REMARKS ON EMPIRICISM

The theoretical writings which have emerged within the empiricist paradigm have tended to use psychological rather than physiological concepts. Gregory's theory, for example, is closer to Brunswik's than to the Gestalt theory. We have argued earlier that this is a good thing: problems in the psychology of perception demand explanation at the appropriate level. Pain is something we feel. Although it is undoubtedly caused by neural impulses, these are not part of our awareness. Pains may be sharp or dull, neural impulses are neither.

The tradition (or paradigm) which has been outlined in this chapter has been a vigorous one. A mass of results has been obtained from highly ingenious experiments. Very little of the literature in the area can be dismissed as trivial or dull—quite the reverse, as anyone may confirm by reading, for example, Gregory's own publications. That words may affect us below the threshold of awareness is a strange fact. The effects of set and attention are fascinating, as is the fact that we can be so completely fooled by an oddly shaped room or a hollow face. It is a rewarding experience to introduce people to such phenomena, as any teacher of perception will confirm. And, as has just been stated, the empiricist or constructivist approach is still to be seen in perceptual theorizing.

Early in this chapter an account was given of some of the discoveries which inspired empiricism. Later, some criticisms were put foward concerning Gregory's hypothesis theory. At this point it seems reasonable to offer a general opinion about empiricism as a paradigm for perception.

First, it must be said that nobody is yet in a position to make a final judgement between contructivist and rival approaches to perception. The deep mysteries of perception remain and it requires an act of faith to believe that they will ever be solved. What follows is a speculation of the kind which must have occurred to many who have tried to evaluate empiricism.

The evidence adduced in favour of constructivist accounts of perception, such as hypothesis theory, comes in the main from one of two types of experimental situation: the stimuli employed are either meaningful, in an abstract sense, or they are products of the built or cultural environment. Consider: the perception of patterns under conditions of brief exposure, drawings which could represent the corners of buildings, oddly shaped rooms, hollow masks, twin-track tape recordings, glowing objects in darkened corridors. These are the sorts of situation faced by subjects in many of the classic experiments which have sustained empiricism. But none of these existed in the African grasslands where human perceptual systems reached their present state of evolutionary development. The point has been made earlier, but it is worth repeating: the evolution of the modern human being antedated human civilization. Has this research been appropriate?

This general point may be reinforced by another example. Consider the problem of flying. Most people could be taught within minutes to keep a light aircraft straight and level under conditions of good visibility. In fact, people have stolen aircraft and taken off successfully without ever having handled the controls before (most of them died when attempting to land, however). But nobody can fly for long in cloud without special instrument training—a claim which is borne out by a long list of fatalities. Why is this? The reason is that when an aircraft starts to deviate from its heading, for whatever reason, detectors in the inner ear correctly signal the initiation of the turn. But as the turn continues the lack of change in radial acceleration causes these same detectors to signal that the body is now travelling straight ahead. At this point any attempt to straighten the aircraft will be perceived *as a turn in the opposite direction*. The situation is now out of control and can only worsen. The pilot, who cannot get back into step with the manoeuvres of the aircraft, is about to become an accident statistic.

For a trained pilot the situation is completely different, and quite safe. He or she has practised ignoring sensations from the inner ear in order to concentrate upon the readings from the flight instruments. In time, these seem to become the 'natural' source of information about the behaviour of the aircraft. But this takes much learning. And it is of course highly artificial and almost completely cognitive, at least in the initial stages of training.

It is hard to resist the conclusion that perception under blind flying conditions is learned, interpretative and constructive. And this may be true of perception *whenever the situation is in any way artificial or unnatural*. This must happen whenever meaning must be extracted from a symbolic display. Meaning clearly implies knowledge, but a word does not signal directly what it stands for: 'fin' is part of a fish in English but means 'end' in French. One could not possibly perceive the meaning of a word without learning.

Hence it is possible that we perceive constructively only at certain times and in certain situations. Whenever we move under our own power on the surface of the natural world, and in good light, the necessary perceptions of size, texture, distance, continuity, motion and so on, may all occur directly and reflexively.

The claim that this is in fact the case is a tenet of the theory to be discussed in the next chapter.

The relative brevity of this chapter should not be taken as an indirect evaluation of the importance of empiricist explanations of visual perception. On the contrary, it would be quite possible to write an entire volume on this topic alone. This account has been kept as short as possible for two reasons. First, the empiricist approach dominates modern thinking. The reader has only to consult any standard general perception text to find all the main empiricist demonstrations and interpretations stated with clarity and conviction. It can be claimed that this paradigm has been so dominant during the past 40 years that, until recently, it *was* the general theory of perception. Second, when describing a radically different approach to perception in the next chapter it will be necessary to describe again many of the claims made by modern empiricists. So we have not yet finished with the general topic of empiricism or the specific version of it represented by Gregory's hypothesis theory.

## NOTES ON CHAPTER 6

The following additional references may be useful.

Boring, E. (1950) for an account of empiricism in psychology and a good description of Helmholtz's speculations about the inferential nature of visual perception.

Many of Gregory's publications are collected in Gregory (1974).

Gregory's position regarding the brain/computer analogy is described in Thorpe and Zangwill (1961). See his paper entitled *The brain as an engineering device*.

For a philosopher's reaction to the claim that perceptions are hypotheses, see the comment by G. E. Anscombe published in Brown (1974).

Chapter 7

# Direct perception and ecological optics: the work of J. J. Gibson

'... perceiving is an act, not a response, an act of attention, not a triggered impression, an achievement not a reflex.'

(Gibson, 1979)

The theoretical position to be described in this chapter owes a great deal to the work of one man, the distinguished American psychologist J. J. Gibson. His claim that perception is in an important sense direct, and his development of what has been called Ecological Optics, are among the most interesting theoretical developments in modern perceptual research. Since his death, Gibson's ideas have been refined and developed and he himself changed his views during the course of his career. In what follows we shall give a general account of what seem to be the most important aspects of this approach to perception; for the sake of clarity and economy we shall not always indicate whether a particular idea or argument belongs to Gibson or to a follower of his, although major theoretical differences will be pointed out. The general term, Direct Perception, will be adopted. This has been given to the body of theory developed by Gibson and his followers which, it has been claimed, represents a new paradigm. The reader will note that, once again, visual examples dominate the account of a theory. However, extensions of the theory to other modalities will be mentioned.

## J. J. GIBSON

Gibson was born in 1904 and died in 1979. His education in psychology gave him, initially, a behaviourist approach to his subject, although by the 1960s Gibson had come to disagree fundamentally with the assumptions of behaviourism. In fact, as his friend and colleague, R. B. MacLeod, has pointed out, in one sense Gibson was a functionalist of the old pre-behaviourist school.

The term functionalist has already been used in the description of Brunswik's theory in Chapter 4 and the reader will have acquired a working knowledge of the term. At this point it may be said that the more general use of the term in psychology embraces a number of different attitudes or assumptions.

(i) Many functionalists allow their thinking to be guided by the fact of evolution. That is, when studying any part of an organism's structure or behaviour, the fact that this has a long evolutionary history should be borne in mind; the structure should be seen in the context of the environment that shaped its evolution.

(ii) Functionalism is also a doctrine which holds that functions can be studied independently of structure: this is very true of extreme behaviourism where, for example, psychologists may be interested only in the relationship between patterns of reward and punishment and measurable responses; no attempt is made to understand what is going on 'inside' the experimental subject.

(iii) A modern version of functionalism is seen in artificial intelligence research (see Chapter 9). Theorists in this discipline are often interested in processes that can be embodied in any number of structures and cannot be defined in terms of any one of them. To use a familiar example, the process of time measurement can be embodied in a sundial, a water clock, an egg timer, an electronic watch. These have nothing in common except the fact that they all mediate the measurement of time.

We shall see later how the description of Gibson as a functionalist in some of the above senses is quite apt. It is also worth noting that Gibson came into contact with the distinguished Gestalt psychologist, Kurt Koffka, towards the end of the latter's career, and came to hold his work in high esteem.

As a young experimental psychologist Gibson worked on a variety of problems. He was interested in the effects of mental set on performance, he studied human conditioning, and he did orthodox psychophysics. He was then an empiricist, a theoretical position which he gradually abandoned after studying adaptation effects in perception.

It was known that if an observer wears lenses which distort the world, prolonged exposure to the distortion leads to a degree of recovery. For example, if the spectacles cause vertical lines to appear curved, the lines become straight again after a period of practice. Removal of the spectacles then causes the world to bend in the opposite direction for a time. The usual explanation of this adaptation to distortion was that the brain gradually comes to reduce the discrepancy between the distorted visual input and normal tactile inputs: in Berkeley's original sense, touch teaches vision.

However, Gibson found (to his surprise) that adaptation occurs even if the observer simply sits and stares at vertical lines. Further, simply staring at curved lines without using lenses causes their curvature gradually to lessen. Such effects convinced Gibson that the empiricist interpretation must be flawed. Much of the remainder of Gibson's career was devoted to attacking what he considered to be the misleading and harmful assumptions of empiricism, in particular the role assigned to sensations in that theory.

During the Second World War Gibson worked on problems of pilot selection and testing. Flying clearly demanded accurate perception of space. But:

'as I came to realise, nothing of any practical value was known by psychologists about the perception of motion, or of locomotion in space, or of space itself. The classical cues for depth referred to paintings or parlour stereoscopes, whereas the practical problems of military aviation had to do with takeoff and landing.'

(Gibson, 1967b)

Gibson became convinced that perception from aircraft made important use of information from the ground and the sky (particularly when there was a covering of cloud), and that this information lay in patterns of movement, the flowing textures which arise as a result of motion relative to the ground. An analysis of this situation is shown in Figure 7.1.

Figure 7.1   Optic flow during an approach to a landing. This is the sort of visual phenomenon which was brought to Gibson's attention during his involvement with flying training. (From Gibson, 1950)

In 1950 Gibson expressed these views in detail in his book, *The Perception of the Visual World*. This has become a classic and its main findings are now included as standard in most textbooks on the perception of space. The importance of movement in perception and the usefulness of considering perception under real-life conditions, as opposed to simple laboratory experiments, were beliefs which remained with Gibson for the rest of his professional career. Gibson's theoretical position evolved over the years and the following account will tend to emphasize his later ideas. However, all his writings are original and interesting, and well worth reading.

## AN OUTLINE OF THE THEORY OF DIRECT PERCEPTION

A good way to appreciate the arguments for direct perception is to understand what it is that Gibson and his followers have objected to in the most popular contemporary approach to perception, namely a form of empiricism. We have given an example of this approach in the previous chapter on Perceptions as Hypotheses. Here, as a reminder, is a summary (some would say a parody) of this position.

(1) We cannot be directly aware of the real physical world. Colour, for example, resides not in objects but in our heads. The sensation of tickle does not resemble the objects which induce it.
(2) Illusions force us to accept that perception may be non-veridical.
(3) Sensory inputs are usually too impoverished or too degraded to specify external scenes or objects.
(4) Human visual perception takes the form of sequential samples or fixations. Therefore, if we are to achieve unified perceptions there must be integration of visual input over time.
(5) Because sensory inputs (or sensations) are not rich enough to mediate perception, the perceiver must add to them. The elaboration of sensations involves inferential processes utilizing memory, habit, set, and so on. Survival pressures require that inferential processes deliver 'correct' solutions most of the time—we successfully go beyond the sensory evidence—but sometimes inferences fail and we experience illusions or other 'errors' of perception. Illusions also confirm the constructional nature of perceiving.

The essence of this approach is that awareness of the world is *indirect*: something must be added to the incoming stimulus information before the final perceptual response is attained; sensory inputs must be elaborated into images, schemata, models. Gibson's followers have argued that this assumption leads inevitably to a particular research strategy: if the visual image is the starting point for elaboration, study visual images; if successive samples of the world are important, present such samples under controlled conditions using brief exposures; in order to present brief exposures in a controlled manner, keep the viewer's head still; the use of brief exposures will eliminate errors due to eye movements. And so on.

Data from such studies must then be fitted into some sort of model. As events take place 'in' time (the time of Newtonian physics—even, unbroken, unidirectional) the perception of these events includes the perception of their sequence and of time itself. Thus the model chosen for perception will inevitably involve *stages*: successive samples must be stored before being elaborated. This in turn requires the involvement of different types of memory: iconic, short-term, long-term, and so on. And as the model now includes stages it is natural to think in terms of *information* flowing between them. Almost inevitably there will be the conceptual leap into believing that perceptual processes resemble the workings of the *digital computer*.

It was acknowledged in the last chapter that this has been a fruitful way of thinking about perception. The indirect perception approach has led to many ingenious experiments yielding important data. But the question remains: is awareness only indirect? Is our perceiving really mediated by internal representations? Do we see only images of the world and not the world itself? Direct perception theorists think not.

Gibson and his followers (see, for example, Costall, 1981, and Reed, 1987, for valuable discussions of what follows) argue that the constructivist, indirect paradigm can be traced back through a long history, which explains in part why it is so pervasive. The Galilean doctrine that nature is composed of matter residing in physical space and time led to the Cartesian doctrine of the essential separation between the mental and the physical. This raised, inevitably, the major philosophical and psychological question of how the realms of the physical and the mental meet: if our minds are essentially different from the world, then we cannot know it directly; all we can know are images of the world—sensations arising from it which are used to represent it.

Reed (1987) points out that psychologists still tend to view space and time as the 'receptacles' of objects. There is thus an automatic tendency to separate psychological activity from the biological and physical aspects of the perceiver. Seen from this perspective, the physical world is meaningless and neutral. Gibson's aim was to find out how organisms become aware of this world, how they come to behave as though the world is sensible and meaningful. Hence, although he was against Cognitivism (the postulation of mental representations formed from sensations etc.), what Gibson attempted was a cognitive theory: he wanted to explain how organisms come to know the world. But in seeking this explanation Gibson was determined to avoid the dualism inherent in the traditional view of the perceiver, which separates perceptual experience from the objective world. His work thus represents a radical challenge to the existing philosophical framework within which most theories of perception have arisen.

To achieve his aim Gibson had to reconsider the nature of stimuli and their ecologies, and their relationships with perceiving organisms. We shall see that by the end of his career Gibson had arrived at a new way of describing stimulation, he had rejected sensations as useful explanatory concepts, he had abandoned the distinction between sensory and motor aspects of behaviour, and he had given a new impetus to the study of the environment and its inhabitants. More fundamentally, Gibson was able to claim that because appropriate ways of describing perception had been found, many of the problems which had engaged earlier theorists had evaporated.

In terms of our original classification, the regions emphasized in Gibson's approach are (a) the world, which he describes with a clarity and thoroughness unusual in perceptionists, (b) incoming stimulation and (c) the brain. Gibson was not interested in events at receptor surfaces or in the peripheral transmission of sensations.

As a starting point for an attack on the idea of indirect perception, Gibson and his followers would begin with a discussion of the nature of light.

## LIGHT AND THE ENVIRONMENT

In the usual textbook discussion of, say, the problem of size constancy (to use our familiar example yet again), the starting point is usually a simple optical diagram. Single lines, representing rays of light, are drawn from an object to the eye (see Figure 7.2). When the object is drawn as further from the eye, the ray diagram shows how the visual angle at the eye is diminished, as is the (inverted) visual image on the retina. Why then doesn't the object appear smaller to the viewer?

The problem changes, however, when we consider a real scene. The viewer is in, say, the centre of a room, with a light source overhead. The light source (a window, a lamp) emits light in many different directions. This emission may comprise several million rays, in contrast with the one or two shown in a classical

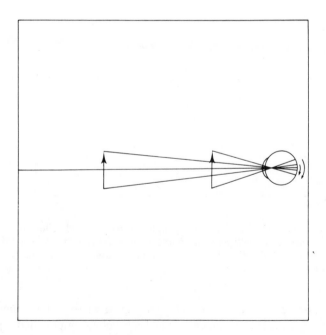

Figure 7.2   The reduction of retinal image size wih distance

ray diagram. Further, not all the light from the source comes directly to the eye: some rays (a few million) may reflect from a wall to the object and then to the eye; others may strike the floor and then the object before entering the eye. Other rays may come to the eye not from the object but from the surface on which the object is standing. The eye is bathed in a sea of radiant energy, of complex interactions between light rays moving in different directions, many of which have been reflected by surfaces. The visual world comprises *surfaces under illumination.*

The next point is so obvious that it is often overlooked: it is *because* light travels in straight lines that it can carry *information* about the environment through which it has travelled and from which it has been reflected. In a mad universe in which the rays swerved erratically, light could not be informative.

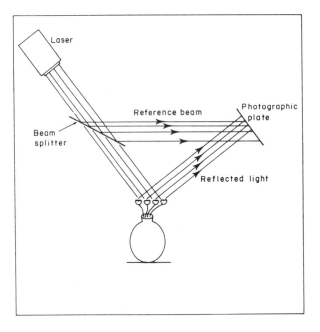

Figure 7.3   The construction of a hologram. The reference and reflected beams from the laser form an interference pattern on the photographic plate. When this plate is developed and illuminated with coherent light from the laser, a three-dimensional image of the original scene is created

It was a happy chance that since Gibson started writing about the richness of light in this way, the development of the laser hologram provided a powerful confirmation of his claim. When laser (that is, very coherent) light is shone onto a real scene, reflected rays can be captured on a photographic plate. If a reference beam is now shone directly onto the plate, the two beams form a complex interference pattern. When the plate is developed photographically and illuminated with laser light, the original scene is recreated in an extraordinary manner: it is in the form of a three-dimensional image or hologram which can be studied as though it were the original (see Figure 7.3). If one object is in front of another one can move one's head and look behind it; one can focus a camera on different objects at different distances in the three-dimensional space. But when one scans the photographic plate used to generate the hologram for an image or picture of the original scene, none is to be found. What is there on the plate is simply the interference pattern. Moreover, the information necessary to create the hologram is stored all over the plate: one can break the plate into small pieces and each piece can then be used to generate the three-dimensional hologram. Light (and interactions between light rays) can be a rich source of information.

To summarize: if we examine light arriving at the eye in real situations we find that it is *structured*. It is highly complex and potentially rich in information. A single momentary retinal image may be impoverished, but this is not true of the arrays of nested solid visual angles through which the head and the eyes sweep during normal perceiving. As we come to understand more and more about these arrays and the potential information contained in their structure, the less frequently will we need to invoke supplementary, indirect processes in explanations of seeing.

## PERCEPTION AND EVOLUTION

Gibson was undoubtedly influenced in his thinking by an important book by Walls (1942). In *The Vertebrate Eye and its Adaptive Radiation* Walls presents a mass of evidence to show how the astonishing variety of vertebrate eyes can be explained by considering the range of habitats or ecological niches which their owners occupy. Any extant animal is, by definition, successful and embodies the results of millions of years of evolution. To understand what an animal's perceptual systems can do we must consider the environment in which they evolved, for it is this environment which shaped the systems. We should consider the animal and its environment as two interacting systems:

> 'The words "animal" and "environment" make an inseparable pair. Each term implies the other. No animal could exist without an environment surrounding it. Equally, though not so obvious, an environment implies an animal (or at least an organism) to be surrounded.'
>
> (Gibson, 1979, p.8)

> 'An animal is what it is given that its niche is what it is; an animal's wings, gills, snout, or hands describe that animal's environment. Likewise, a complete description of a niche describes the animal that occupies it.'
>
> (Michaels and Carello, 1981, p.14)

These statements need elaborating (as Gibson and Michaels and Carello do in their respective books), for they describe an idea which can be a powerful stimulus to the imagination. Consider this very unusual environment: boiling sulphurous mud. This environment can be analysed in detail—its lack of oxygen, its acidity, the ferocious temperature. When these factors are combined we have effectively defined the only creature which could inhabit such a strange niche: it is in fact a rare bacterium. When, on the other hand, the structure of the adult form of a relatively 'simple' multicellular organism, *Taenia saginata* (a tapeworm), is examined it can be seen to lack the muscular capability of mediating rapid movements and thus it cannot move far in its daily existence. It possesses none of the common major sense organs. *Taenia*'s body comprises a long chain of segments, each quite flat in form and sheathed in a membrane which is not destroyed by weak acids but which permits absorption by osmosis. We are close to defining the only environment which could support such a creature: the large intestine of a warm-blooded vertebrate.

## ECOLOGICAL OPTICS

The environmental niche determines the structure of an animal and its senses. In order to understand the animal's perceptual systems it is necessary to consider the environment in which these systems evolved. But what is it exactly that we need to know? Gibson's advice (in the case of vision) would be unhesitating: find out about the patterns of light which arrive at the eye from the environment and the potential information which these patterns carry. This is a first step. Later we can discover whether particular aspects of this information are or are not utilized in perception. But we must begin by examining the lit environment, and to do this we need a new science: ecological optics.

When we draw simple ray diagrams (for example, Figure 7.2) we are using classical optics. As this is a science which is neutral with respect to the viewer, extraction of principal rays is a legitimate simplifying exercise. But, as has been shown, the study of simple ray diagrams makes the problem of size constancy seem a formidable one. Similarly, simple physical measurement leads to puzzlement over the phenomenon of brightness constancy: why, for example, does coal look black on a summer's day when it can be shown that the light which it reflects is many times more intense than that from snow on a winter's evening? How do we continue to perceive the 'true' properties of these stimuli when simple measurement suggests that this should be impossible?

One answer, arising from the ecological approach, is that optical science has overlooked what happens in the real environment. When an object moves further away from the eye its image does indeed get smaller. But this is not the only change in the complex pattern of light arriving at the eye. Most objects are bounded by textured surfaces and the grain of this texture gets finer as the objects recede. Objects obscure a portion of the textured ground against which they are seen. The further away an object is the closer it will be to the horizon, and so on. And although the light reflected from a dark object under strong illumination may be quite intense, it will always be less intense than light from more reflective objects in the same scene. The important point is that objects are not usually judged in complete isolation. The optical array commonly contains far more information than that associated with a single stimulus object. The use of classical optics and an over-concentration upon laboratory experiments may cause us to overlook this important truth. (See Gibson, 1961, for a much fuller discussion of this point.)

## THE ROLE OF INVARIANTS IN PERCEPTION

One of the most important concepts in direct perception theory is the *invariant*. The emphasis on invariants may be Gibson's single most important contribution to psychology, and understanding them is the key to understanding direct perception theory.

Gibson frequently stressed the importance of movement in perceiving (see, for example, Gibson, 1966). Indeed, he insisted that the distinction commonly drawn between sensory and motor aspects of behaviour was an artificial one and leads to false problems, such as the question 'Why doesn't the world move when we move our eyes?' For Gibson, the changes brought about as a result of our motor behaviour should be thought of as an integral part of the process of perceiving. We rarely receive a static, unvarying view of any object or scene. We move our head and eyes, we walk around the environment, things come into and out of view: perception is an *activity*.

Imagine that one was reduced in size to the point that one could get inside an eye. What would it be like, down among the rods and cones of the retina? What one would *not* see would be part of an image, the edge of a static picture. Instead, one would see shimmering patches of light flickering across the retinal cells. At any moment the textures in the environment would project countless points of light into the eye. As the eye moved, fresh patterns would sweep across one's position. The scene would appear kaleidoscopically complex, even chaotic. But this flow of coloured patches of light is not in fact random. Among the patterns of flow are lawful regularities; the movements of adjacent parts are correlated.

An example will serve to illustrate this claim. When one approaches a textured surface the patterns of stimulation from the environment change from moment to moment. But this change, although complex, is non-random. Photographic analysis of the scene (and even informal introspection) reveals that the changes in the textures seen (and thus the changes on the retina) follow patterns of *flow*. That part of the vertical surface with which one will eventually make contact remains stationary, although growing in angular extent. All around that point there is an apparent radial expansion of textures flowing

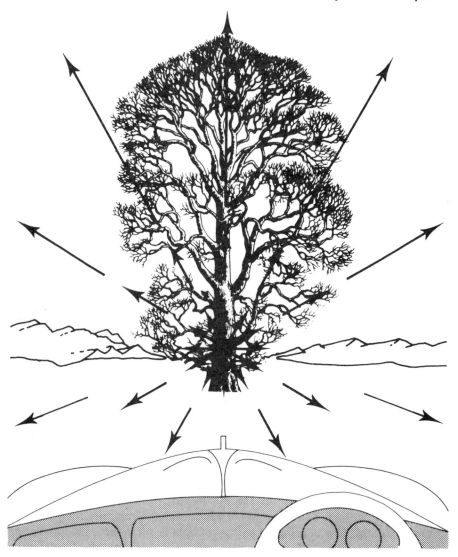

Figure 7.4  Optic flow surrounding the point of collision. Direct perceptionists believe that this is a very important source of information arising from the movement of perceivers in the environment

around one's head (see Figure 7.4) The textures expand as one approaches them and contract as they pass beyond the head. And the situation we have described will be the case *whenever we move towards something*. In other words, over and above the behaviour of each texture element is a higher-order pattern or structure, and this is available as a source of information about the environment. In this case the flow of the texture is *invariant*.

Here is another example of the lawfulness which can be exposed when familiar situations are scrutinized: how do we know that an object which has gone out of sight has not gone out of existence?

> 'Any movement of a point of observation that hides previously unhidden surfaces has an opposite movement that reveals them. This is the law of reversible occlusion, which states that the hidden and unhidden real things in a locale can be interchanged by moving around. Going out of sight is not the same as going out of existence. The perception of persistence does not rely on the persistence of perception, but on tests using reversible occlusion.'
>
> (Reed, 1987, p.107)

The essence of invariants is that they are associated with change. They can be thought of as higher-order properties of patterns of stimulation which remain constant during changes associated with the observer, the environment, or both. Modern theorists distinguish between two types of invariant, Transformational and Structural.

### Transformational invariants

These are patterns of change which can reveal what is happening to an object or objects. For example, when an object moves away from us at constant speed its apparent area (the size of the solid angle subtended at the eye) diminishes lawfully. (In fact, the decrease in area is proportional to the square of the distance.) Whenever this relationship is present it must mean that the distance between us and the object is changing in a regular manner. Departures from this invariant rule can mean only that (i) the rate of movement has slowed or accelerated, or (ii) the object is actually changing in size. Here it is the *style* of change which is a source of information. (Interestingly, because of perceptual constancy we tend not to notice the changes in angular size with distance. To experience the rapidity with which visual angles change as we come close to a surface, reverse a car towards a wall whilst looking through the mirror. Notice how the image swells. This can provide a dramatic demonstration of the Inverse Square Law, and is a stylish way to remove an unwanted wall.)

### Structural invariants

These are higher-order patterns or relationships which remain constant despite changes in stimulation. As an example of a structural invariant, consider a situation in which two objects having the same physical size are at different distances from an observer. Clearly, the visual angles subtended by the objects (and hence the sizes of their retinal images) will be different. How can we know that the objects are in fact the same size? This is of course yet another way of introducing the problem of size constancy.

Analysis of the situation described above reveals that there is indeed an invariant property of the stimulus array which could serve as information specifying that the objects are the same size. The invariant is a subtle one and was overlooked for many years. If the objects are in a natural environment they will usually be viewed in a scene containing a visible horizon. It can be shown that *the ratio of an object's height to the distance between its base and the horizon is invariant across all distances from the viewer* (see Figure 7.5). Analysis of light with reference to the environment has yielded a possible solution to the problem of size constancy. (Interestingly, it looks as though the horizon plays a similar role in the perception of depth in pictures. See Sedgwick, 1980; Rogers and Costall, 1983.)

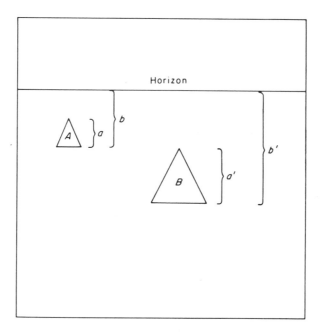

Figure 7.5   A possible invariant underlying size constancy. If $a:b = a':b'$ then $A$ and $B$ are the same size

## AFFORDANCES

In Gibson's later writings (for example Gibson, 1971a, 1977, 1979) an increasing emphasis is placed on the concept of the *affordance*, a concept which has been developed by several of his followers. It is at this point in the theory that the relationship between perceiver and environment becomes vitally important. The environment contains invariant information the detection of which has survival value for a perceiver.

> 'Roughly, the affordances of things are what they furnish, for good or ill, that is, what they *afford* the observer.'
>
> (Gibson, 1971a)

Gibson goes on to list a series of possible affordances. These include, for humans, surfaces that are stand-on-able or sit-on-able, objects that are graspable or throwable, objects that afford hitting, surfaces that afford supporting, substances that afford pouring. A single object may give rise to more than one affordance: an apple, for example, affords eating *and* grasping and throwing.

It is clear that affordances are the *meanings* that an environment has for an animal. As meanings, the affordances guide behaviour: they tell the observer what is or is not possible. The range of possible behaviours in response to affordances has been described as the set of *effectivities* available to the organism, although some theorists believe that the term 'actions' is all that is required. It is clear, too, that this part of his theory reveals the influence of the functionalist tradition in Gibson's thinking and also accords with the views of Koffka and other Gestalt theorists who stressed the meaningfulness of the perceived world.

The originality of Gibson's approach to affordances, these seemingly abstract properties of things and events, lies in his claim that they can be perceived *directly*, without prior synthesis or analysis. Thus the properties of objects which reveal that they are graspable (just consider the vast array of different objects to which this description could be applied) are there to be perceived directly from the pattern of stimulation arising from them. All the information needed to specify graspability is represented in the patterns of reflected light. This is a very bold claim.

Two further aspects of the theory of invariants and affordances should be stressed. First, we must remember that understanding perception requires the joint study of an organism and its environment. This essential relationship must always be borne in mind. To start with a familiar human experience: when a piece of music is transposed to a new key, the new set of notes may be completely different. But something is preserved in this change, namely certain important relationships between successive notes. This identity (or near identity, for the situation is a little more complicated than this) of musical intervals provides a basis for the equivalence of tunes across keys. But this equivalence will be experienced only by a perceiver sensitive to interval information: it will be of little use to the tone-deaf. Similarly, when a rectangle is tilted away from us its projected shape becomes trapezoidal (see Figure 7.6). It is possible, however, to use mathematics to show that the trapezoid is a *transformation* of a rectangle. That is to say, the rectangular shape could be 'recovered' from a trapezoidal projection. There is therefore something invariant in the property of the shape which may allow a viewer to decide that he or she is seeing a tilted rectangle. But whether or not sensitivity to this transformational invariant is the basis of shape constancy is an empirical question which would not be solved simply by defining the *potential* invariant: it is necessary to know whether a particular perceiver can use such information. Gibson's important term here is *attunement*: organisms need to be attuned to affordances before these can shape actions.

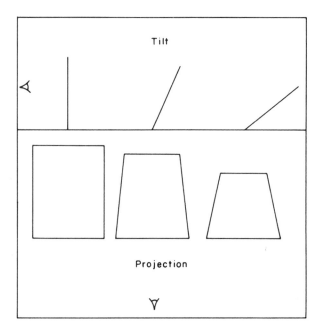

Figure 7.6    The projected shape of a tilted rectangle is trapezoidal

Second, it is important to remember that an invariant or affordance for one species may not be an invariant or affordance for another. Sensitivity to certain odours, to ultraviolet light, or to the earth's magnetic field provides some species of animals with invariant information which is quite outside our own direct experience. Failure to recognize this important fact may lie behind many misunderstandings of the apparent oddities of animal behaviour: our pets are not miniature humans.

**The origins of perception**

We have outlined some of the claims of direct perceptionists: the richness of information in light; the invariant qualities to be found in stimulus arrays; the overlap between the sensory and the motor aspects of behaviour; the closeness of the relation between perceiver and environment; affordances as meanings or guides to action. The question now arises as to *how* the perceiver comes to perceive. Is it necessary to learn which invariant properties of an array are useful? Are we born able to detect affordances? How do we extract the higher-order information contained in optical arrays? Direct perceptionists have addressed these questions, and we shall now attempt to summarize their main conclusions.

Gibson was by no means a crude nativist. But on the question of the origins of perception, he and his followers would remind us that we and other sucessful organisms are the products of millions of years of evolution. The environmental niches in which our sense organs operate have been responsible for the evolution of the organs; as they have shaped their structure, so also must they have shaped their performance. Thus learning *has* occurred in the development of perception, but much of this has been during the history of the species rather than the lifetime of the individual. The same sort of evolutionary pressures which have 'taught' our kidneys to respond correctly from birth could have shaped our visual systems to respond in certain ways to contours or gradients of texture.

There is, however, one certain role for learning during the history of the individual perceiver: humans (and many other 'higher' animals) must surely learn which affordances can be relied upon to satisfy certain goals. That is to say, although the invariant stimulus properties comprising the affordance of 'graspableness' may be perceived immediately, knowing when graspableness is an appropriate property to search for is situationally determined and must presumably be learned. The most important contribution of learning to perception is to educate attention.

## PERCEPTUAL MECHANISMS

If the perception of the real world involves detecting appropriate invariances in the rich and ever-changing sea of stimulus energy, it is natural to ask how these invariants are detected. Is there, for example, a moment in the visual process when the relative motions of different texture elements are extracted, possibly by correlating their directions and speeds in order to detect texture flow? The reply to this question is that it is the wrong way to approach the problem; it leads to the reductionism and the reliance on hypothetical stages within processes which mar the empiricist approach to perception.

A direct perception theorist knows that there are identifiable peripheral processes to be observed in receptor systems (such as the contour sharpening brought about by lateral inhibition in the retina), but the conclusion would still be that the reductionist approach is wrong. Gibson and his supporters argue that the response to stimulation is a response involving the whole organism, and the nature of this response is described by Gibson as follows:

'I suggest that the nervous system operates in circular loops and that information is never conveyed but extracted by the picking up of invariants over time ... a perceptual system does not respond to stimuli (although a receptor does) but extracts invariants.'

(Gibson, 1976)

Once again, the active role of the perceiver in extracting informative, invariant patterns is being stressed. Later, Gibson extended his notion of information pickup by likening perception to a process of *resonance*, which he explained through the analogy with a radio set. The space in any room in a modern city is filled with electromagnetic radiation broadcast from large numbers of transmitters, some close at hand, some many miles away. This radiation is non-random: it can convey information. On switching on a radio all that may be heard is the hissing noise arising from its own circuits. But on tuning the radio speech or music may suddenly emerge: the radio is now set to resonate with the information available in the electro-magnetic radiation. We are witnessing a process of information pickup.

The direct perceptionist can now challenge us with this question: 'In which part of the radio is that particular sound being processed?' The answer must be that it is everywhere, for all parts of the radio's circuit are active during the transduction of the radio waves into audible music. Remove any one part of the circuit and the set will fail. But that part cannot then be said to 'compute' music or speech—these are rendered audible by the behaviour of the whole radio with its components acting together as a single system.

The radio is not a perfect analogy, of course, for it is a passive device—we do the tuning. When perceiving, information is obtained rather than imposed. Thinking along such lines suggests that the nervous system may be better modelled by analogue, rather than digital, devices. Using an old-fashioned slide rule enables one to multiply and divide pairs of numbers without engaging in the process of number manipulation *per se*; one simply adjusts two scales (adding two quantities) and reads off the answer. The trick, of course, is that the markings on the rule are drawn to represent logarithmic quantities. The necessary mathematics *has been built into the structure of the device*. Is this what evolution has done during the development of the senses?

## REALISM

It should be clear from this introduction to direct perception and ecological optics that Gibson and his followers assume a philosophical position, that of Direct Realism. Stated very simply, direct realism is the assumption that there is an external world of objects and that we can become aware of these as a result of our perceptions. This doctrine is contrasted by Gibson with the position that as our senses must intervene between external objects and our experience of them, all that we can be directly aware of must be sensations or sense-data.

That is to say, we can never experience directly a hot object, but must construct this percept from sensations of heat, touch and pain.

Gibson accepted that sensations exist and that we can be made aware of them by training or by adopting certain mental sets. We can be aware of our own physiological states; and no other person can experience that vague presence in our visual field created by our nose.

> 'Physical acoustics tells the man-in-the-street that sensations of loudness, pitch, and pitch mixture are in his head, and only arise because they correspond to the variables of sound waves in the air. He could not possibly *hear* a mechanical event; he can only infer it from the data. But nevertheless he goes on hearing natural events like rubbing, scraping, rolling, and brushing, or vocal events like growling, barking, singing and croaking, or carpenter's events like sawing, pounding, filing, and chopping. Ecological acoustics would tell him that that the vibratory event, the source of the waves, is specified in certain invariant properties of the wave train ... Information about the event is physically present in the air surrounding the event. If the man is within earshot, he hears the event.'
>
> (Gibson, 1967a)

This is as clear a statement of his position as we can find in Gibson's writings. Naturally, the philosophical differences between direct realists and their rivals are debated at greater length than this. The arguments can be quite complicated, as may be seen by consulting some of the references to be given later.

## GIBSON ON THE PERCEPTION OF PICTURES

We leave the discussion of the main body of work in direct perception to discuss, briefly, Gibson's ideas about the perception of pictures. For many years this was a neglected topic in the psychology of perception. Now, thanks in part to Gibson's interest, it is an active area of theory and research.

In a valuable essay, Reed (1987) points out that whereas Gibson held that we can perceive the world directly, using information, rather than indirectly from sensations and mental representations, he accepted that a form of indirect awareness was also possible. Perception can be based upon language and symbols; it can also be based upon pictures. When perceiving (representational) pictures awareness comes from stimulus sources produced by other humans. Reed's essay expands on this point and deserves to be read in full.

Pictures have figured importantly in the psychology of perception. For example, many of the most important demonstrations of Gestalt phenomena take the form of simple line drawings. Most perceptionists have probably, at one time or another, drawn one of the geometric illusions, to wonder why it is perceived as it is. Our culture presents us with so many pictures, some of them extremely life-like, that we tend to forget that these are artificial stimuli, that they are all to some extent abstractions, and that they are flat. When we watch a car chase on television, it is well-nigh impossible to remember that we are 'really' seeing a series of flat images sliding up and down a flat surface: we see objects racing into the far distance. Precisely what happens when we look at a picture or a photograph is something which Gibson speculated upon repeatedly. That this is no easy problem is attested to by the fact that Gibson changed his opinion about the perception of pictures during his career. We shall not attempt to follow these developments in Gibson's thinking, but will attempt a summary of some of his more important ideas.

Gibson saw two main themes in traditional writings on picture perception, and disagreed with both. One approach to the perception of pictures maintains simply that, under the right viewing conditions, a picture can provide the viewer with many of the same stimuli that would arise from the original scene. And in fact there are experimental results showing that viewers can be made to confuse a colour transparency of a scene with the real thing.

In marked contrast with the above is the claim that pictures are conventions. They need to be read, just as language needs to be learned before the arbitrary signs and sounds can convey meaning. On this view, linear perspective is simply a convention to be learned and used by artist and viewer alike. The artist could as easily use a reverse perspective in which parallel lines *diverge* as they recede from the viewer (this is in fact the case in some medieval art).

Gibson raised a number of objections to the first position outlined above, one of the most serious of which is the realism possible in line drawings. Here it is obvious that there can be nothing like a one-to-one correspondence between, say, the brightness levels in the drawing and those in the real scene.

Gibson's response to the second claim, namely that one needs to learn to read pictures and that perspective is merely a convention, is to deny that this is true. An artist is free to use any perspective convention of his or her choice, but the truth is that parallel lines visibly converge as they recede into the distance, and only linear perspective captures this truth. Eastern artists may use reverse (or divergent) perspective in their pictures, but:

'No rule or canon of reverse perspective could possibly be systematic, that is, it could not be consistently applied in the practice of projecting a layout of surfaces on a picture plane. I do not know why Oriental painters (and Medieval painters and sometimes children) often represent the edges of table-tops and floors as diverging upward on the picture surface instead of converging upwards but I know that they do not have a *system*.'

(Gibson, 1971 b)

What is unusual about pictures (apart from their artificial nature) and our perception of them? First we must note some important differences between pictures and three-dimensional scenes. When a picture has been painted using linear perspective, it is as if a piece of glass has been placed between the artist and a scene and the objects in the scene traced in outline on the glass (Leonardo actually recommended this technique, which is illustrated in Figure 7.7). Such a picture, drawn as if on the glass, will faithfully represent the disposition and shapes of three-dimensional objects. But the 'correctness' of the perspective holds only if we view the picture from the single correct vantage (or station) point: why then isn't there considerable distortion of pictures when we view them from oblique angles?

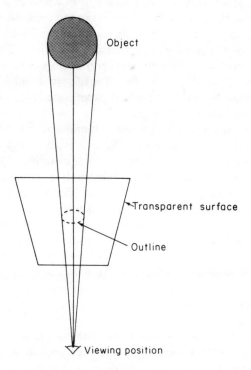

Figure 7.7   Leonardo's window. If the outlines of objects are traced on a screen placed between them and the eye, the tracings will be in 'correct' linear perspective when viewed from the same position

Another theoretical problem is that although such a linear perspective picture is, necessarily, a correct representation of the scene it depicts, there is an infinity of actual scenes which could have given rise to that particular projection. But we tend to see the correct one. How?

Then there is the curious status of the depth in a representational picture. A competent artist (and any photographer) can capture the depth of a depicted scene with great success. Experiments have shown that under special viewing conditions a person may be unable to distinguish between a life-like representation and an actual scene. But, with the exception of special *trompe l'oeil* paintings, although we 'see' the depth in a picture and can often make quite accurate judgements of the distances between different objects portrayed in it, we would never try to reach into the picture and grasp something. We see depth but are not deceived. At such moments our perception has a curious duality.

These are some of the problems which representational pictures pose for perceptionists. A final problem concerns an art form which does not attempt to be representational in the usual sense of the term: the caricature. In this tradition a skilled artist seems able to capture an essential quality of the appearance of a person. Think of the cartoons of Churchill, Reagan or Thatcher. These can seem truer than photographs; their exaggerations heighten the real and significant appearance of an individual. But if a life-sized, solid realization of the caricature appeared before us we would experience real horror. A caricature represents without fully resembling.

Perceptual theorists have made various attempts to deal with these problems using known perceptual mechanisms. The interested reader should consult the account by Haber (1980) which is an excellent example of the traditional approach. Summarized as briefly as possible, such traditional explanations run along the following lines. Looking at a picture involves us in two types of perceiving. First, our binocular vision, the presence of the frame, and details of the texture of the surface are powerful indicators of the flatness of the picture: we know that we are looking at a two-dimensional display. When we move from the correct vantage point two things happen. First, the objects represented as being at different distances in the depth of the picture fail to show the motion parallax which real objects must show whenever we move. But then, as we move away to one side of the picture we compensate for the perspective distortion of the frame with our powerful ability to maintain shape constancy. Thus the image of the frame, although now trapezoidal, is interpreted as rectangular. Our adjustment (the phenomenon of shape constancy) to the frame allows us to perceive the distorted perspective of the picture equally correctly.

Caricature has received less theoretical attention than other artistic phenomena, although attempts have been made to explain its basis in terms of the heightening of salient features and the possible involvement of 'canonical' forms.

Gibson's work in this area reflects the general importance which he placed upon the role of invariants in his theory of the perception of the real, three-dimensional world. But pictures differ from three-dimensional reality. As we have shown, certain important invariants such as those associated with the perceiver's movement are missing. What is it that a picture offers the viewer in order that he or she may see the depth depicted? Gibson's final position on this important question was that pictures capture some of the *information* provided by natural scenes. What we must do if we are to understand the perception of pictures, as in the case of the perception of real scenes, is to overthrow our tendency to think in terms of forms:

'A good picture is not just one out of a vast family of perspectives. It contains graphic information, not forms, and this information is of the same kind as the mathematical invariants that become noticeable during a sequence of perspective transformations.'

(Gibson, 1973)

At first reading this seems a rather strange claim. And the truth is that Gibson's statements on this topic are not as clear and unambiguous as one might wish. In his last statements on pictures Gibson suggested that pictures 'capture' information 'of the same sort' as that arising from a natural array. Pictures (and real scenes) contain *formless invariants*. These

'must consist of features of optical structure that we do not have adequate words to describe... things like the following: alignment or straightness (being "in line" but not necessarily a line as such) as against bentness or curvature; perpendicularity or rectangularity; parallelity as against convergence; intersections; closures and symmetries. These features are present in an unchanging array but they are best revealed in a changing array, one kind of change being transformation.'

(Gibson, 1973)

Commentators such as Costall (1984) and Sedgwick (1980) have helped to flesh out this rather bare idea. Gibson's pictorial invariants, as Sedgwick explains, are structures in the static array from a picture 'that would remain invariant if the optic array were from a real scene and were being transformed by a movement of the observer.' (Sedgwick 1980)

Thus if, in a real scene, one object is nearer to us than another, then certain aspects of the spatial relationship between the two objects will remain unchanged over a wide range of our movements. The nearer object will appear more coarsely grained in its texture; it will probably be lower in the visual field; if it is in line with the further object it will have unbroken contours, whilst the other will show broken contours where portions of it are obscured. The artist can capture each of these invariants to give us rich information as to the positions in space of the objects represented in the painting or drawing. And we can see how this idea can be extended to caricatures. Quite simply, if a person has prominent ears, then this prominence is obvious and invariant over a range of postures and distances. Heighten it in the caricature and one has recorded a pictorial invariant.

## An evaluation of Gibson's work on pictures

After that very brief outline of Gibson's work on the perception of pictures, we shall offer an equally brief evaluation. First, it must be recognized that Gibson's approach has stimulated interesting research. For example, the article by Sedgwick (1980), to which we have already referred, should be read by anyone interested in perception and art. Sedgwick carefully analyses, in considerable detail, the relationships existing between the three-dimensional world and a two-dimensional surface onto which it can be projected. He is able to point to a large number of cases in which these relationships are strictly lawful: paintings or drawings which make use of these relationships can give us precise information as to the positions and sizes of objects in the depicted world.

But although Sedgwick's writing acknowledges its debt to Gibson, it does not seem logically dependent upon Gibson's theory; rather, it is the sort of analysis which could have been carried out by anyone astute and able enough to attempt it, provided such a person knew a lot about perspective and geometry and was interested in the perception of pictures. The analysis is not dissimilar, for example, to those published from a very different theoretical standpoint by Pirenne (1970).

It seems fair to conclude that Gibson's contribution to this area is less impressive than much of his other work. Kennedy expresses this well:

' Gibson's definition of a picture is "promissory". . . .At most, [it] can be used to guide our thinking about pictures, for he can only suggest some properties of light that might be informative.'

(Kennedy, 1974, p.44)

More seriously, Gibson simply got things wrong on occasion. In a passage quoted earlier in this section, he says of artists using 'reversed' perspective that they could not have had a system. They did. In a thorough analysis of perspective systems Hagen (1986) is able to show that the problem of mapping one surface (the world) onto another (the canvas) can be solved in a variety of ways. The system of mapping used (the perspective system adopted) depends upon what the artist wishes to achieve. Aesthetic considerations and the reason for making the representation are all-important. It is true that European art since the Renaissance was preoccupied for centuries with the problem of inducing feelings of reality in the viewer; it attempted to make him or her feel as though they were looking at real scenes. But the perspective used in much Japanese art aims at something else: the pictures typically offer a synoptic view of a story as it takes place—in time as well as in space. And the orthogonal perspective system employed does this superbly. (See Hagen, 1986, for a remarkably interesting account of different geometries and perspective systems.)

Thus there are no grounds whatever for saying that one form of art is inferior to another in terms of the 'rightness' of its perspective. All cultures contain artists who display systematic competence. To think otherwise is chauvinism. These last points may be strengthened by quoting from a distinguished art theorist, one who has consistently opposed the type of approach to the perception of art outlined above.

'optical projection is a physical fact only loosely related to visual perception. Visual experience, strongly influenced by the constancy of size and shape, all but ignores the effects of distance and projection. Pictures are to be understood in their relation to visual experience, not to the physics of retinal projection. Psychologists, of all people should be expected to guard against this elementary mistake.

... What looks like inaccuracy when considered as a duplicate of perception is the perfectly logical and appropriate translation of perceptual qualities into the properties of the medium.'

(Arnheim, 1984)

Probably the most damning criticism of Gibson's ideas on pictures is that they are simply unexciting. It could be argued quite forcibly that all that he said about the invariants available to artists has been known for a long time; after all the invariants used are actually there in paintings for us to see. It is unlikely that any teacher of art could have overlooked them when giving technical instruction; rather, they have been described in detail, but using different names. Similarly, the explanation of caricature which direct perception offers is hardly sufficient to explain this remarkable skill, nor is it a formula by means of which anyone could do it. As many art students and would-be satirists will confirm, caricature is harder than it looks.

It must be conceded, however, that Gibson's theory of the perception of art has had some successes. Among these is the finding that children seem able to recognize the depth in pictures from a very early age (See Kennedy, 1974 for a review ). This would follow, in the theory, from the fact that the children have been responding to many of the invariants used by artists long before they have seen any pictures. One would predict that the children would find the formal, two-dimensional aspects of paintings harder to detect than the depth, and this appears to be true also.

Findings such as this suggest that the real usefulness of Gibson's approach to pictures may be in explaining their verisimilitude rather than in giving us valuable insights into the phenomenon of painting *per se*. This conclusion comes to mind when one considers what seems to be Gibson's basic assumption concerning art: that there is only one type of perfect picture, that based on strict linear perspective, with photographs representing the best (truest) pictures of all. To repeat a point made earlier, a necessary consequence of this view is that pictures departing from strict optical rules are somehow distortions or deviations from ideal standards. But, as Hagen (1986) has shown, this is not even a valid interpretation of perspective. And as artists are usually doing much more than simply depicting things—they work in a social context, they comment on things—it seems highly unlikely that Gibson's work could lead to a successful account of art or our perception of it.

## AN EVALUATION OF THE DIRECT PERCEPTION APPROACH

Here now is a general assessment of the direct perception tradition which Gibson founded. First, we shall list what seem to be the most pertinent criticisms to have been levelled against direct perception, and then we shall summarize some of the achievements of this new approach.

**The meaning of 'Direct'**

A valuable debate on direct perception (Ullman, 1980) begins with an interesting criticism. What does it mean, asks Ullman, to say that any process is direct? Using a simple analogy, Ullman analyses arithmetical addition. The input to the 'process' of addition is a pair of numbers, the output is their sum. Addition would be described as direct if it involved simply looking up the answer in a lookup table containing sums of all pairs of numbers. But as soon as we allow the decomposition of each number into hundreds, tens and units, to be summed separately with right-to-left carry rules, we have an intervening process: this method of addition, whilst more powerful, flexible and economical (at least for large numbers) can no longer be described as 'direct'. Do direct perceptionists mean by 'direct' the procedure used in Ullman's lookup table?

A possible answer to this criticism might be that Ullman has confused levels of analysis. Gibson held that perception is direct in the sense that information is extracted directly from optic arrays and that our awareness of the world is not itself mediated by schemata or representations. He did not deny that mediating processes exist (and he accepted that awareness of the world via words and symbols must be indirect in this sense). But it is the direct relation with information which is important: the fact that it is not necessary to decompose it to sensory elements and sensations. However, direct perceptionists have never been very clear about the nature of the processes which mediate this relationship, apart from suggesting that the nervous system somehow 'resonates' with information. Had direct perceptionists been more explicit about resonance (and said in what way it is direct) then Ullman's remarks could have been debated more fruitfully.

Arithmetical calculation may seem far removed from perceiving. Here is a more psychological example which can be used against direct perception (this was suggested by articles in the Ullman debate, 1980). It is quite easy to make an outline wire model of Necker's reversible cube. The simple device shown in Figure 7.8 should be painted matt black for the best effect, then viewed at arm's length with one eye closed.

Very soon the viewer will experience a reversal of perspective, such that the further sides of the figure suddenly appear nearer than the front ones. If the cube is now slowly twisted it will appear to move the wrong way, that is, against the motion of the hand. But as soon as the figure reverses back to its correct orientation, twisting results in normal movement.

The point of this simple demonstration is that although the stimulus array does not change physically, two distinct motions may result from the rotation of the cube. In order to predict which motion a viewer will experience, one needs to know which of the two possible orientations of the cube is being seen. It is quite clear that in this case the perception of orientation (correct or reversed) comes prior to the perception of motion (correct or reversed). Does this not mean that the perception of the cube's motion is decomposable into stages and hence cannot be direct? How would a direct perceptionist respond to this suggestion?

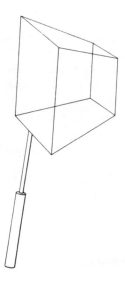

Figure 7.8   A reversible solid. This shape (actually, a truncated pyramid) comprises a large rectangle at the front joined to a smaller rectangle at the rear. When constructed from blackened wire and viewed monocularly the perspective will sometimes reverse. If the handle is then twisted, the shape will appear to move in the wrong direction. (A miniature version of this apparatus is easily assembled from the shaped wire on a champagne cork.)

Faced with such questions, direct perceptionists have replied as follows. The hollow cube has been *designed* to be difficult to perceive; it has been carefully shaped in such a manner that information in light reflected from it specifies an ambiguous object. After all, it might be added, Necker's discovery of the illusion named after him came not from an examination of crystals (his main interest) but from *drawings* of them. Crystals aren't ambiguous, but two- or three-dimensional sketches of them can be, although only rarely—which is why Necker's illusion was a novelty.

### The detection of invariants

The detection of invariants is of central importance in direct perception theory. It is attunement to higher-order patterns within a mass of stimulation which forms the basis of awareness. However:

'Although one can criticize certain shortcomings in the quality of Gibson's analysis, its major and, in my view, fatal shortcoming lies at a deeper level and results from a failure to realize two things. First, the detection of physical invariants, like image surfaces, is exactly and precisely an information-processing problem, in modern terminology. And second, he vastly underrated the sheer difficulty of such detection.'

(Marr, 1982)

These are important criticisms. Gibson and others believe that there are invariant properties in physical events which afford the perception of those events. But workers in the field of Artificial Intelligence (AI), such as Marr, have set themselves explicit goals, one of which is to devise systems which will simulate the process of seeing. When these workers try to create some model which will actually extract invariants, they commonly find that it is a very difficult thing to do. However, it can be argued (as will be seen in Chapter 8) that Marr and other workers in AI have adopted a faulty model of the perceiver: it is true that the contribution of motor activity, which plays a large part in Gibson's theory, is not stressed in Marr's work. But Marr's comments, coming as they do from someone who has tried to simulate seeing, must be taken seriously. This is not to say, of course, that theorists such as Gibson are wrong; rather that asserting that something *must* be the case may delude one into thinking that one understands *how* it is the case. The danger is that a theory may be leading one away from those very problems which it might be fruitful to pursue.

### The nature of affordances

The most subtle forms of invariance are affordances. Reading Gibson and others on affordances is rather like reading Freud on dreams: one is convinced at the time, but reflection brings doubt. It is clear that to know and describe the relatively straightforward invariances used in, say, the perception of space is a formidable task. But if certain objects in the world direcly afford eating, just what is it in the nature of the optic array which can make explicit this affordance? In Gibson's terms the answer (in the visual modality) must be some nested array of solid visual angles; but, as he admitted, we do not really have any idea of the characteristics of such a complex array, and the answer must be many times more complicated than that to the already formidable problem of the spatial invariants. The situation is actually worse than this: even if we could define some affordances for a perceiver, it would still be hard to predict behaviour. This is because, in terms of the theory, organisms may have to learn to attend to particular affordances. Before we can predict behaviour we must know, not only what affordances are available, but the perceiver's current attentional state. This is a formidable requirement.

There is one rather weak response to this criticism. Some modern direct perceptionists would say that their job, at present, is to describe and understand

and not to control. To attempt to predict behaviour from a particular stimulus situation is to ignore the essential fact that affordances are always *relationships* between organisms and their environment. Asking about prediction is to fall into the animal-environment dualism which direct perception wishes to avoid.

A related problem is whether affordances can ever mislead. Gibson changed his position on this point. He held initially that a surface afforded walking, and that was that. But as Costall (1981) points out, 'surfaces are not where all the action is'. They may or may not afford walking: ground covered with a dusting of snow does, but a thinly frozen lake does not. Later Gibson modified his statements on affordances to recognize their probabilistic nature, thus moving much closer to Brunswik's earlier statements (see Chapter 4) concerning the ecological validity of cues.

## Finding new invariants and affordances

This is closely related to the preceding point. Anyone who becomes interested in the concepts of invariants and affordances as developed by Gibson and subsequent workers may wonder how to discover new ones. After all, by doing this one would be finding out some of the most important knowledge one could have about a perceptual system. Here the direct perception literature is not very consistent or helpful.

Much of what we know about human perception has come from what were, originally, casual or accidental observations. Any careful observer, at any time in the past, could have noticed the patterning of optical flow and its relationship to our movements and position in space. Of course, it took an intelligent researcher to explore this phenomenon to the point when it could be embedded in a convincing theory of perception; nevertheless, the phenomenon was there to see, easily controlled and easily manipulated.

But how do we know that infrared radiation affords prey detection by snakes? Simply observing snakes in a natural environment won't do: when the prey moves in the dark there are changes in sound and smell, as well as in the direction and strength of infrared radiation. Only careful experimental studies, in which all variables save infrared are controlled, can convince us that we have isolated the correct invariant. Similarly, to observe that the domestic cat can learn to go to a coloured bowl is not evidence that dominant wavelength is the invariant which the cat has detected: it could be the case (and probably is) that the cat is relatively insensitive to wavelength changes, but responds readily to differences in brightness or saturation. As these variables would be uncontrolled in the original demonstration, there would be a risk of drawing false conclusions from the cat's behaviour. Ethologists have discovered many instances of behaviour being controlled, not by a whole pattern (such as the sight of a conspecific), but by some isolated feature (the red belly of a female, for example).

In such cases, observation of the real-life behaviour may be less successful than performing controlled experiments, despite the inevitable reductionism of the latter.


## RESONANCE

The idea that a nervous system mediating some form of perception behaves in a holistic manner, resonating to invariant properties among stimuli, is initially attractive, particularly to anyone who has waded through innumerable 'stage' models of perception. On reflection, however, it is necessary to conclude that resonance is barely more than an interesting speculation. With stage models of perception it is at least possible to be sure, most of the time, what should be happening in the nervous system if the necessary techniques of observation were available. More importantly for the psychologist, there are hypotheses which predict the temporal and logical ordering of processes. For example, retinal sharpening or filtering ought to occur prior to binocular fusion processes; the recognition of familiar forms should come even later, when meaning has been 'added' to the input, and so on. But how is resonance to be observed? If the answer is, 'Whenever an organism is functioning as though properly in touch with the real world', then this amounts to a tautology: if behaviour were not appropriate or adaptive then resonance would not have been invoked.

Could the process of resonance be observed if remarkable new techniques of anatomical observation became available? Does the nervous system resonate to different modalities simultaneously (it seems that this would have to be the case during bimodal perception), and if so, is there a cost to be paid in terms of capacity? Do all nervous systems resonate in their own particular ways, or has evolution produced only one form of resonance?

The truth is that we are told very little about resonance. The metaphors used (the radio, the slide rule, etc.) are intriguing and stimulating, but they are only metaphors. It could be said that a demand for neurological plausibility is unreasonable at this stage of our knowledge of perception, and sites the problem at the wrong level of discourse. But then we should be given some guidance as to a possible operational definition of the term resonance, or the type of evidence that could convince its proponents that they were wrong.

In response to such objections a direct perceptionist might reply as follows. A criticism which focuses on the nervous system, asking *where* resonance occurs, misses the point: resonance is a *relationship* between the perceiver and the environment. Until there is much more knowledge about the nature of such relationships, and until we can learn to stop thinking about organisms in isolation, it is pointless to look for a place where resonance occurs: resonance is not that sort of concept. It will not be 'observed' in any place in the brain. The important thing now is to develop our ability to use this new conceptual approach and to see whether it proves enlightening.

There is, however, another possible answer to the request for more explicit statements about resonance: this comes from artificial intelligence research. In the next chapter we shall describe a new form of computational system, Parallel Distributed Processing (or Networks). The essence of such systems is that they comprise simple units connected in complex and modifiable ways. Knowledge does not reside in particular places in the networks—they do not have stored memories—and their properties cannot be described in terms of the individual units; what is important is the activity of the network *operating as a whole*. This is not too different from saying that parallel distributed networks resonate with their inputs. Such devices may permit interesting links to be forged between direct perception and modern work in AI.

## GENERAL CRITICISMS

Two final general criticisms of the direct perception approach may be offered. The first of these has to do with the style in which the ideas of Gibson and subsequent theorists are put forward. There is a tendency in writings on direct perception to define problems out of existence. Evidence of this has been given when discussing the extraction of invariants and Marr's appraisal of Gibson's work. We can only repeat our earlier point that to say that something simply is the case may be to lose one's grip on a real problem. In an interesting and provocative section on learning, Michaels and Carello challenge the concept of memory:

> 'And just as we do not need a vessel in which *ancient* history is brought to bear on the present, we do not need a vessel (memory) in which *recent* history is brought to bear. Plainly and simply, experience changes the animal.'
> (Michaels and Carello, 1981, p. 78. Italics in original.)

But if it *is* so plain and simple, why has it been so difficult to discover the laws of learning and forgetting during a century of research?

The response to this criticism would be that the problems of memory, forgetting and so on arose when psychologists adopted the wrong ways of thinking about organisms. However, real research problems remain: it is still desirable to learn *how* 'experience changes the animal', and Gibson's ways of thinking may eventually suggest more appropriate ways of finding this out.

A second general criticism has also been outlined earlier. It is simply that, in our opinion, direct perception theory underestimates the achievements of workers in the rival experimental tradition, probably for polemical reasons. This claim will be supported with a single example drawn from recent work on the perception of motion.

It is a fact, long recognized, that when the perception of an object is difficult and its shape and identity elusive, movement of the object (or moving around it) commonly resolves any ambiguity. We have all had numerous experiences of this kind of thing: the brown patch against the tree becomes an owl as we approach; the two-headed monster in the field is seen to be a pair of cows. How many views, how much movement do we need, in order to see the uniqueness of *any* shape? The answer takes the form of a new theorem, unknown until recently, even among mathematicians: *we need three views of four non-coplanar points* (Ullman, 1979). This is a very important gain in our understanding of the perception of three-dimensional shapes. But the research leading to this discovery consisted of experiments employing highly simplified stimuli, often displayed under very artificial conditions: brief exposures, the casting of shadows onto screens, etc. The result, however, has been an undoubted success.

## IN SUPPORT OF DIRECT PERCEPTION

Here are some more positive comments concerning Gibson's (and his followers') approach to perception, which may balance some of the critical remarks made above. Note first that there is more depth to the theoretical writings of Gibson and others than can possibly be summarized in a short precis, and followers of the direct perception paradigm would respond vigorously to some of the criticisms that have been made in this chapter. Readers are urged to read some of the references given below for a more detailed account of a major theory.

First, direct perceptionists can be said to have restored the environment to its central place in the study of perception. Despite Brunswik's earlier warnings, examination of published work in perception over the past 10 or 20 years reminds us that too little attention has been given to ecologically valid information. The use of artificial stimuli has, as we have tried to show, had many successes. But one feels that there really is something artificial, even risky, about doing research which is tied very closely to laboratory conditions: organisms did not evolve in a world of simple isolated stimuli.

Second, as Gibson and others have reminded us, the human is just one out of a vast range of perceiving animals. If the phrase 'ecological optics' stimulates more research into the perceptual abilities of non-human species it will have rendered an important service. Phrases such as 'perceptions are hypotheses', convincing at the human level, do not seem to carry as much weight when we look at the behaviour of dragonflies or swallows.

Third, the approach begun by Gibson has stimulated some highly interesting empirical research—a good indicator of the quality of a theory. Four examples will serve to support this claim.

(1) When a face ages our perception of the face tells us two interesting things. First, that it is the same face; second, that the face has changed. This

is a complex situation involving simultaneous perception of identity and change. What is the basis of this physiognomic perception? How can we see the continuing identity of a face? A partial answer is that some of the important changes which occur during ageing can be described by a mathematical function, the Cardioidal Strain transformation. The outline of a skull can be fitted by a cardioid. As the skull ages, small changes in the parameters of the cardioid can match the changing shape. And it is changes in the shape of the skull which are partially responsible for changes in our faces as we grow up. Now when a sketch of a face is subjected to controlled distortion by cardioidal strain (see Figure 7.9) it appears to age (Todd, Mark, Shaw and Pittenger, (1980; Pittenger and Shaw, 1975; Pittenger, Shaw and Mark, 1979 ). It seems clear that there is something which persists during the ageing of a face, an invariant which can be recovered from the cardioidal function, and which we seem to be able to perceive. What seemed like a very difficult problem has begun to yield to the application of the concept of the invariant.

(2) Texture flow has been brought under experimental control by Lee and Lishman (1975). The creation of a textured room which can move relative to a standing observer produces interesting and amusing responses: some observers fall down. Measures of optical flow have also provided some understanding of how skilled long-jumpers control their approaches to the take-off position. The analysis of textural flow is proving valuable, as Gibson would have predicted.

(3) When patterns of random dots projected onto a screen are caused to move in certain ways, remarkably complete and confident judgements of objects' behaviour can be made with great rapidity (Johansson, 1964; Cutting, 1982). For example, attaching lights to a person's body and then filming the person in the dark produces a moving picture containing only a few points of light. And yet one can see what the person is doing. Other patterns can induce strong feelings that one is seeing, say, a tree swaying in the wind, or similarly unexpected events. Although this work did not arise directly from a Gibsonian context, it offers great hope that many of the invariant patterns of motion associated with the behaviour of real objects will be discovered.

(4) Direct perception research is part of experimental psychology. Part of the debate concerning the usefulness of the approach involves the interpretation of results from experiments, many of which are too complex to permit brief descriptions of them in this chapter. However, we shall now describe one example of such experimental work which is relevant to the theory of direct perception. This is an investigation of visual masking. Note the extent to which it makes full use of laboratory control and instrumentation, and its use of artificial stimuli.

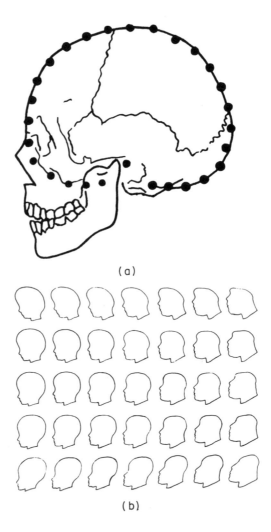

(a)

(b)

Figure 7.9   (a) A cardioid fitted to the profile of a skull; (b) Outline drawings of a face made to age in appearance by subjecting the original outline to a cardioidal strain transformation. ( (a) is from Shaw, McIntyre and Mace, 1974. © 1974 Cornell University. Used by permission of Cornell University Press. (b) From Pittenger and Shaw, 1975. © 1975 American Psychological Association. Reprinted by permission of the publisher.

Turvey (1977) describes some unusual and very interesting results obtained during a visual masking experiment. Such an experiment involves presenting a target stimulus for a very brief duration, often for only a few milliseconds (the eye is effectively stationary during such short exposures). Then, following a controlled interval, a second 'masking' pattern is exposed. Earlier results from numerous studies of this type have shown that when the position of the mask coincides with an area of the original pattern it can effectively obliterate the latter, so that it is not seen. The shorter the time interval between the two exposures, the greater the degree of interference or masking. The experimental paradigm is illustrated in Figure 7.10.

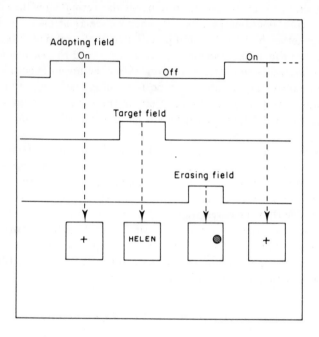

Figure 7.10   Functional diagram of a three-field tachistoscope experiment. All exposure and interval durations may be varied. In the example shown, the erasing pattern will coincide with the letter 'N', unless the eye is moving (see text)

The usual explanation for the fact that stimulation of the eye *after* target exposure can prevent the observer from seeing the target is that somewhere in the retina there is visual persistence—what has been called *iconic storage*—which the masking pattern interferes with or erases. As was shown in Chapter 6, this is precisely the sort of interpretation which led to the stage models of perception which direct perceptionists have criticized.

Turvey points out that in this type of experiment the spatial positions of events in the world (the items in the first pattern and the mask) are made coincident with particular sites on the retina: the eye is effectively stationary.

Thus it is usual to conceive of the first stage of visual perception solely in terms of spatial coordinates on the retina: an area of cells is stimulated, the effects of stimulation persist, but the masking pattern restimulates and somehow disrupts the functioning of the cells.

But suppose the original target (comprising, say, a single line of patterns) and a small post-exposure mask are presented sequentially *as the eye is moving*: which items will be masked? Target and masking stimuli could be seen as occupying positions in real space: they may be referred to *environmental* coordinates. But as they are stimulating particular retinal sites they can also be referred to *retinal* coordinates: after all, when we see an after-image in the dark we can tell whether it is on the right or left side of the retinae. Note, however, that in the experimental arrangement described above *the environmental and retinal coordinate systems do not coincide*. After the target exposure the retina moves to a new position. Therefore, a post-stimulus masking pattern delivered from the same position in the display (having the same environmental coordinates) as part of the original pattern will no longer arrive at the same retinal locus.

This experiment has been performed. The result was that masking was maximal when the target and masking items shared the same *environmental* coordinates and minimal when they shared the same *retinal* coordinates. Theorists such as Turvey rightly claim that this is an important result: 'Tentatively, we may hypothesize that the correlate of stimulation in environmental coordinates does not depend on that in retinal coordinates, although the two may occasionally interact' (Turvey, 1977). This masking experiment has yielded strong evidence against simple stage models of perception. It is an interesting example of how to attack theorists on their own ground.

## THE FUTURE OF DIRECT PERCEPTION

This chapter ends with some remarks on recent trends in the theory of direct perception. First, it seems that the ratio of empirical discovery to philosophical speculation may be falling in recent publications on direct perception. This may be a necessary stage, an attempt to be quite clear about the philosophical underpinnings of the theory before launching into further research. To the outsider it does seem, however, as though the majority of recent papers are more concerned with what Gibson said and when he said it, than with attempts to unearth new and interesting phenomena. This may be an unfair criticism, but the pace of discovery does seem to have slackened. It would be sad if direct perceptionists lost the delight in discovery which Gibson clearly felt.

That was a rather negative comment. However it is also possible to outline some of the ways in which the theory of direct perception appears to be developing, and this may restore the balance.

## Philosophical refinements

Lest this seems an odd heading, given what was said at the outset of this section, we should state that philosophical clarity is vital in the development of any theory. The worry stated above is merely over the ratio of theory to empirical research.

Contemporary direct perceptionists have been rightly concerned over the implications of Gibson's use of the term Realism. Noble (1981), Reed (1982, 1987) and Katz (1987) and Costall (1986) have all contributed towards a better understanding of the issues involved.

Reed (1982) has made a detailed study of the origins of the indirect approach to awareness. He traces it back to Descarte's Corporeal Ideas hypothesis. In essence, Descartes argued that as sensations do not resemble the objects which cause them (as in tickling, for example), there must be two distinct worlds: the Gallilean world of objects, and the world of thinking creatures. What follows from this is the belief that mental processes operate on the 'deliverances' of the senses. This is, as we have shown, the basic form of an argument for indirect awareness and perception. Reed's contribution is to show what a long history this idea has had, and how it has been refined over the years until it has become interwoven into the fabric of psychological thought. What was originally a scientific hypothesis has become dogma, which may explain some of the resistance to the new paradigm represented by direct perception.

Katz (1987) has examined Gibson's interpretation of the term realism. Had Gibson really adhered to a basic form of realism, Katz argues, then his theory could not have taken the form that it did. To assume the existence of an objective world, independent of perceivers, and also perceivers who are in but separate from that world, leads to some serious problems: 'How could one conceive an ultimate structure that applies in all conceivable circumstances, from every imaginable point of view?' Perception, says Katz, is a matter of circumstances, 'determined jointly by subject and by object.' If there is only one world to be perceived, how can perception in one species differ from that of another? And how can we explain errors in perceiving? But Gibson constantly stresses the need to consider affordances (for example) in terms both of the world *and* the perceiver. For this reason, Katz suggests that Gibson's is really a *relativist* rather than a naive realist.

Costall (1986) is concerned with the same issue. Because organisms play an active role in the creation of environments, we must abandon Gibson's distinction between the objective world and perceivers which is implied in his statements on realism.

> 'For organisms do more than merely look and listen and sniff and touch. They also act upon, and transform their surroundings. Yet, when Gibson discusses the question of realism, he too treats the organism as nothing but a perceiver. And

this is very curious since the basic point of his work was to deny this traditional view of the organism, as a mere contemplative spectator.'

(Costall, 1986)

Costall cites modern biologists who also reject the idea of the environment as a 'pre-existing slot within which the organism must "fit" '. Costall makes a strong case for what he describes as *mutualism*. And if we acknowledge that the world has changed since the beginning of life and that organisms indirectly influence their environment, we must concede that 'in an important sense, the world is other organisms'. Costall hopes that a stress on mutualism will provide a much sounder underpinning for the framework of direct perception:

> 'In short, mutualism is neither mentalism nor environmentalism, but embraces both their important half truths. And, unlike realism, it undermines many of the stark dichotomies and dualisms of traditional thought.'

(Costall, 1986)

The papers cited in this section should be consulted by anyone who wishes to learn more about the effort which is now being put into the philosophical refinement of direct perception.

## Developmental studies

The idea that perceivers can become aware of the world directly is a challenging one. An obvious question follows: how do infants perceive the world? Do they respond immediately to the patterns of invariance within change which Gibson held to be the basis of stable perception. And if, for example, evolution has created our capacity to affordances, how long does it take to learn to attend to them?

The study of perception in human infants owes its long history to the fact that it is inherently interesting. Also because it may eventually throw light on the innate/acquired controversy in psychology. However, the following is concerned solely with those parts of infant research which can be related to the ideas of direct perception. A study of the recent literature enables one to conclude that this is a very active area—one of the growth points within direct perception research. A few examples of relevant infant studies will now be outlined.

Eleanor Gibson (1982) has reviewed the concept of the affordance from a developmental point of view. In a convincing argument for the importance of the affordance for theories of development, Gibson takes as a starting point the claim that:

> 'Perceiving an affordance implies perception that is meaningful, unitary, utilitarian, and continuous over time to the extent that environmental events that pertain to the observer may require. To what extent must young creatures (human or otherwise) learn to perceive them? And if they must learn, how is it done?'

(E. J. Gibson, 1982, p. 57)

Eleanor Gibson then reviews some of the research which is relevant to these questions. Work on 'graspability', for example, appears to show that objects of graspable size are responded to differently from non-graspable objects by the age of three months. This discrimination is revealed by patterns of hand and arm movements towards the objects. Other studies have shown that when infants aged about fourteen weeks put their hands out to grasp moving objects they move them to positions *where the objects will be*: they seem able to extract the relevant affordance for prediction.

When three-month old infants are habituated to the sight of objects which have been subjected to certain rigid transformations (rotations around horizontal and vertical axes for example), a non-rigid deformation (squeezing) causes the object to be attended to once more. Infants thus appear capable of distinguishing between these two fundamental ways in which objects can change.

It has been found that by six weeks infants will blink when faced with a looming object, that they are sensitive to optical information concerning impending collision. (Parents reading this should sit down again—these infants never actually get bumped.)

Another reviewer, von Hofsten (1983), describes experiments which have shown that infants can fuse information across modalities by an early age. For example, when viewing two moving films (shown simultaneously, side-by-side) of an object rising and falling, they prefer (they spend a longer time looking at) that film which is synchronized with the appropriate sound of a contact with the ground.

Von Hofsten reasons that the stability of our perceived world is vitally dependent upon our ability to perceive the permanence of objects during changes across space and time. Studies have shown that infants at eight months will attempt to retrieve hidden objects, and that when an object goes behind an occluding surface and a different one emerges on the other side, the infants show signs of surprise.

Butterworth's valuable reviews (1983, 1988) include many infant studies which are directly relevant to the theory of direct perception and should be consulted in full by interested readers. It has been shown, for example, that infants placed in an experimental room which can be moved towards or away from a stationary viewer will fall over in just the same way that adults do when faced with this sudden change in optic flow which their own movements have not caused. This happens to infants who are still too young to stand—they topple from a sitting position. Similarly, when infants are lowered towards the ground they raise their heads just before what would be the moment of impact; this response to information in the expanding optic flow is present by three months.

In another study reviewed by Butterworth (Granrud *et al.* 1984), infants watched computer-generated displays of randomly moving dots. An impression of discontinuity at an edge was created by having part of the texture on the screen continuously deleted by the remaining texture. To adult observers this looked like one moving surface sliding behind another (such occluding effects are referred to frequently by Gibson in his later writings). It is known that infants, faced with a choice, will attempt to grasp the nearer of two objects. In this study, infants aged five months reached and attempted to touch the television screen at a position where one surface appeared to be above the other. It seems therefore as though infants can use dynamic properties of stimulation to acquire knowledge of depth.

His interpretation of studies of this kind leads Butterworth to suggest that the vital distinction which each of us must acquire—that between ourselves and the world—is imposed very early in life by the structure of the optic array, which is what Gibson would have predicted.

The above was not a review of contemporary infant research—there is too much of it to fit into a single chapter—rather, it was an attempt to show the originality of the problems being posed to infants. For the theorist this area of psychology is potentially very important. It may well be that results from infant studies will eventually help us to decide upon the correctness (or otherwise) of key parts of the theory of direct perception. Already, the ability of infants to respond to higher-order invariant properties of stimulation is looking very impressive. Gibson may have been correct in believing that such abilities have been acquired through the course of evolution and do not have to be learned during the development of the individual (although it must be remembered that Gibson was not in any sense a crude nativist). At the very least it can be claimed that the perception of some invariances comes very easily and naturally to the human infant: a fact which supports direct perception but which will have to be accounted for by general theory.

### Cognitive issues

It was stated earlier that Gibson always accepted that there were indirect forms of awareness or knowing. His concern was rather to show that the study of perception reveals many possibilities of direct or unmediated awareness. However, since Gibson's death there has been debate over the differences between these two forms of awareness and over the implications of some of Gibson's claims. The following brief account owes much to ideas contained in reviews by Noble (1981) and Reed (1987).

Gibson published a number of articles on the perception of pictures, which he considered to be forms of indirect or mediated perception. However, Noble (1981) believes that Gibson seriously undervalued the importance of language and social perception. As an example, Noble discusses what he calls 'the muddle of the mailbox'. Gibson would claim that a mailbox affords 'mailing' directly; the necessary information is there in the light reflected from it. But a critic may ask: How would a Bushman perceive the box: surely the affordance could not specify mailing to one who has no concept of mail? It could be said in reply that the mailbox at least affords 'containership'. But imagine being told that there is a mail strike: does the box still afford mailing? Is it not rather that the affordance of mailing is, in Reed's term, 'socially sustained'? And the pieces on a chess board may be seen to be graspable, but this is by no means their most important characteristic: chessmen may be moved only according to certain *rules* which become apparent when the game is observed. In fact, these rules *are* the game.

Noble points out that some of his own thoughts relate to the philosophical tradition of Pragmatism, particularly the writings of the philosopher G. H. Mead, who claimed that our interactions with the environment always contain a social component; we always perceive ourselves as part of our dealings with things in the world. Noble makes a good case for seeking to unite certain pragmatist interpretations of perception and awareness with Gibson's later ideas.

Reed (1987) points out that Gibson's use of the term 'direct perception' refers to knowledge of the environment which is *tacit*, 'It is not formulated in pictures or words, for it is the knowledge that makes the formulation of pictures and words possible.' (Reed, 1987; p.150) Reed's concern is really this: once that portion of perception which is direct has been assessed, what can we say about the remainder, about mediated perception? The answer is quite a lot. From the basis of knowledge of direct perception, one can look afresh at other forms of perceiving.

For example, given that information is available in the environment, it can be picked up by many observers. Two observers cannot stand in the same place at the same time, but they can swap positions. For this reason, direct perception does not have to remain private; we live in a shared environment. It follows that one perceiver can detect affordances for another, provided he or she can communicate the relevant facts. This in turn offers a novel way of interpreting the evolution of gestures, signs, pictures and words. Once pictures exist it becomes possible to make others aware of what they have never seen, or to draw their attention to particular invariants they may meet in the future. In Gibson's (1976) phrase, the role of such representational systems is 'to consolidate the gains of perception by converting tacit knowledge into explicit knowledge.'

Reed then proceeds to apply his analysis to the development of language, the concept of shared awareness (through language and gesture), and the social aspects of perception and knowledge. He strives always to clarify the distinction between direct and indirect forms of awareness, so as to be able to re-evaluate the contribution of the latter to our general psychological functioning.

Enough has now been said to indicate the directions taken in this aspect of modern direct perception theorizing. The reader who consults the references which have been given may find this a new and stimulating way of thinking about language, pictures, gestures and so on. On the other hand, it may seem not too different from more traditional work in these areas. This is perhaps a danger for direct perception theory: the more it acknowledges and attempts to incorporate indirect processes into its general account of awareness, the less distinctive it may become. It will be interesting to see how this aspect of the theory develops.

## Ecological optics and the ecology movement

This last section should be read simply as a piece of speculation. It is a curious fact, however, that the lack of interest shown by many towards traditional politics coexists with a growing concern over the environment. For many people, particularly the young, there seems to be something essentially wrong with the idea, which has been dominant since before the industrial revolution, that nature exists to be tamed and exploited. Many have become worried about the effects of modern agricultural practices, industrial pollution, acid rain and nuclear fallout. There is a growing feeling that the huge modern city may not be the best place to live, that modern buildings are inhuman in scale and the architects crass in their attitudes to people. Things seem to have gone seriously wrong. As evidence in support for these assertions, consider the interest in books with titles such as, *Small is Beautiful*, *The Future of Technics and Civilization*, *The Ecology of Freedom*, *Toward an Ecological Society*.

The ecological movement, in its many forms, is one of the phenomena of our time. Many people, often of no particular political persuasion, are beginning to take a stand on the issue of the environment. In Western Europe the Green candidate is a new electoral phenomenon. And when agents of the French government destroyed the *Rainbow Warrior* in a New Zealand harbour it was time to recognize that the ecological movement is now seen as a threat by some traditional politicians.

When those concerned with the ecology look to the sciences for help or guidance, what can they expect? Expert advice about the environment itself from biologists, of course. But what from psychologists? The answer is, very little. But the essence of the Gibsonian tradition is to ask questions about the relationship between perceivers and their ecology. It is an attempt to overcome the age-old dichotomy between us and the world we inhabit, to overcome habits of thought which treat the world as neutral and essentially meaningless—a concept which encourages the belief that nature is 'there' to be exploited. It would be highly interesting (and this is as much as can be said at the time of writing) were direct perception theory to suggest the basis for a new form of sensitivity towards the environment. A contribution to ecological ethics, perhaps?

This ends our discussion of the work inspired by Gibson's ecological optics and the theory of direct perception. Although we have pointed to what seem to be weaknesses in this work, we have also tried to convey something of the excitement and novelty of this way of thinking about perception. It is likely that the debate over the correctness or otherwise of Gibson's approach will continue for some time to come. It should be an interesting debate.

## NOTES ON CHAPTER 7

The Ullman reference (above) is the start of a debate for and against direct perception. Ullman's critical analysis of direct perception is followed by a series of comments by various researchers arguing for and against the theory. This is an invaluable debate.

The Michaels and Carello reference cited is an excellent introductory text on direct perception. It is clear, well-written and conveys an enthusiasm for the Gibsonian approach which is highly infectious. Its existence has made it difficult to write parts of the present chapter; having read Michaels and Carello, unconscious plagiarism is an ever-present risk. Their book is highly recommended.

Gibson was a good writer. The reader is urged to consult as many of Gibson's original publications as possible. Most of these have been referred to in this chapter.

# Chapter 8

# Marr's computational approach to visual perception

This chapter will outline what many consider to be the most important development in perceptual theory in recent years. To date the emphasis has been on visual perception, although there are good reasons to believe that successful applications will be made in other sensory modalities. We shall illustrate the computational approach to vision through the work of one man, David Marr, whose contribution was made within the context of the new discipline of Artificial Intelligence.

## DAVID MARR

David Marr's first interest was in mathematics which he studied at Cambridge, becoming a Wrangler. After this distinguished start to his career Marr did graduate work in the department of physiology at Cambridge, where he developed a model of the functioning of the cerebellum. He then learnt the techniques of computer modelling at the Massachusetts Institute of Technology, where he spent the last years of his life. David Marr had specialized knowledge of mathematics, physiology, computer science and experimental psychology. His work on artificial intelligence led to numerous papers on perception and, finally, to his book, *Vision*, which was published posthumously. He died of leukaemia in 1980 at the age of 35.

## BACKGROUND

Artificial intelligence research in general, and the computational approach to vision in particular, are part of an important scientific movement. The historical background to this movement can be outlined by describing three important developments: Information Theory, Cybernetics and the construction of large digital computers. These developments might seem somewhat irrelevant to the study of visual perception, but in fact they comprise the theoretical tradition out of which the computational approach crystallized.

*Information theory*, as developed by Shannon (1948), made it possible to quantify the information flowing through any system, whether that system be a telephone cable, a television channel, or a person reading a page of text: the measure was essentially neutral with regard to the content of a message. One obvious application of the new calculus was in neurophysiology: a nerve fibre fires according to an all-or-none principle and at certain rates. This transmission of discrete impulses can be viewed as a code, and the rate at which information can be transmitted by one or many neurons may be assessed. Similarly, when a person reacts at maximum speed to one of several possible signals, information theory can be used to assess that person's information-handling capacity. To be able to compare such apparently different situations using an objective measure of information seemed to many to be a very fruitful development.

*Cybernetics*, which was developed initially by the mathematician Norbert Wiener, is the application of mathematics to various systems, particularly those which show self-regulation. Initially applied to self-regulating machines, certain concepts from cybernetics quickly proved useful in psychology and physiology. A notable example is 'feedback', which describes how part of the output from a machine can be used to regulate and control the input. 'Negative feedback' typically ensures stability by using the difference between a desired level of output and the actual output level to reduce the input to the system; this damping effect is used to maintain homeostasis in living organisms. 'Positive feedback' tends to have the opposite effect, using output to increase gain and drive the system into instability. Thus an after-image (which will form if one stares at a bright light) which is off-centre in the visual field will induce reflex pursuit movements of the eyes which are attempts to centre the image. The movements cause the image to appear to move even further to one side and so the pursuit continues, the apparent speed of the after-image getting faster and faster.

*Digital computers* have exerted an influence upon modern thought which is too familiar to need much elaboration. By the 1950s there were large numbers of these remarkable machines. For many psychologists they became irresistible as a metaphor for the human brain. Computers operate by rapid manipulation of symbols, these operations being controlled by explicit programs. There is an important distinction between the permanent structure or hardware in the computer and the instructions or software controlling the operations of that hardware. Is this very different from the age-old distinction between mind and body? Soon the language of computers had invaded psychology and researchers were talking about buffer stores, problems of retrieval and access, information flow, and information processing. Early successes in teaching computers to mimic human abilities such as problem-solving, chess-playing and language translation led to some extravagant claims:

> 'Intuition, insight, and learning are no longer exclusive possessions of humans: any large high-speed computer can be programmed to exhibit them also.'
>
> (Simon and Newell, 1958)

'the task of a psychologist trying to understand human cognition is analogous to that of a man trying to discover how a computer has been programmed.'
(Neisser, 1967)

The developments listed above created a new discipline, artificial intelligence. This is an engineering approach and it treats organisms as machines, machines controlled by processes. And some of these processes are perceptual. Perception thus offered an obvious challenge to workers in the new discipline.

The research to be described did not arise solely from theoretical considerations. The period when artifical intelligence was being developed was also a time when important empirical discoveries were being made in the study of perception and related areas. We shall summarize some of the most important of these to show what sort of knowledge was available to Marr when he started to build his theory of vision. Four examples will convey the quality of this empirical work.

The first example has been referred to in some detail in Chapter 5. This is the work by Hubel and Wiesel (1962, 1968), who succeeded in recording the electrical responses of living cells in the visual cortex of the cat to various patterns of stimulation. One of the most striking and thought-provoking discoveries was that the visual cortex of the cat contains cells which respond differentially to lines and edges according to the orientation of these stimuli. This was a remarkable finding, for it suggests that the visual system analyses visual inputs into specific components, and that the mechanisms which do this are 'wired into' the nervous system. It is therefore possible that the perception of certain basic features of the world is unlearned (although subsequent research showed that the activity of the cortical cells can be modified by prolonged experience).

Second, Julesz (1960) created *random dot stereograms*. When these are fused in a stereoscope a powerful illusion of depth is seen. The depth arises because the paired stereograms contain central portions which differ slightly, thus capturing the cue which normally triggers stereopsis: disparity of left and right views. The strange and wonderful thing about the Julesz demonstration is that the disparity is not visible when one scrutinizes the individual stereograms: one appears to be looking at two random textures—arrays which contain no hint of form (see Figure 8.1). This proves that the visual system can extract disparity information in the absence of pattern recognition, a remarkable discovery.

Third, Pantle and Sekuler (1968), Campbell and Robson (1968) and other workers studied various visual systems to see how they respond to changes in the spatial frequencies of test gratings—displays containing black and white stripes which a viewer may or may not be able to resolve. The *spatial frequency* of a grating is the number of changes (commonly, the number of black and white stripes) it contains per degree of visual angle. It was found that if an observer stares for a time at a particular grating, sensitivity to that grating is temporarily reduced. That this is not a general loss of visual acuity is shown by the fact that

Figure 8.1   Two random dot stereograms. These are best viewed through a stereoscope; however, if they are fixated either with the eyes crossed, or by staring straight ahead to infinity, the stereograms should fuse. Following fusion a small central diamond will be seen to emerge in depth from the apparently random textures. (From Julesz, 1971. © 1971, Bell Telephone Laboratories, Inc., reprinted by permission.)

sensitivity to other spatial frequencies remains unchanged. A related discovery was that recordings from the visual cortex of the cat reveal the presence of cells which are differentially sensitive to particular spatial frequencies. It began to look as though one could consider the acuity of vertebrate visual systems in terms of *tuned channels*. Thinking about vision in terms of spatial frequencies led in turn to the use of powerful new techniques of analysis, the most successful of which has been Fourier analysis. These have been very fruitful developments.

Fourth, Land and McCann (1971) and Horn (1974) offered a solution to a classic problem in perception: how does the visual system 'know' that the varied appearance of a coloured surface is a feature of that surface rather than the illumination? Their suggestion was that whilst the effects of changes in illumination are usually gradual, changes due to a surface's geometry—its edges, boundaries between facets, and so on—are usually abrupt. If a visual system could somehow ignore or filter out the slow changes, what remained would be information about the characteristics of the surface rather than its illumination; perception could then be veridical. This was not, of course, an *empirical* contribution, although it was inspired by some striking new colour phenomena which Land had discovered and which caused him to challenge the traditional theories of colour vision.

Describing the history of his own ideas, Marr says of the Land and McCann work:

'I do not now believe that this is at all a correct analysis of colour vision or of the retina, but it showed the possible style of a correct analysis ... gone is any explanation *in terms of neurons*—except as a way of implementing a method. And present is a clear understanding of what is to be computed, how it is to be done, the physical assumptions on which the method is based, and some kind of analysis of the algorithms that are capable of carrying it out.'

(Marr 1982, p.18)

As will be shown, the *style* of explanations in perceptual research was something which Marr attempted to change.


## MARR'S THEORY OF VISION

Marr's contribution to the study of visual perception will now be described. One of Marr's acknowledged contributions is his attempt to clarify our thinking about information-processing systems. In what follows the reader should keep the following points in mind: (a) the term 'information' is used here more loosely than in the technical sense defined by Shannon (1948) which is related to reduction of uncertainty, and (b) 'information-processing' is not mere transduction of energy. For example, a telescope changes light by magnification, but magnification is not an informational process—the image is simply a linear transformation of the object. As nothing else is really changed by the magnification we cannot apply informational concepts to this effect. Note, however, that things can be seen through a telescope which are invisible to the naked eye. This is because the eye itself is a non-linear device. So when the eye and the telescope are considered *as a single system*, it becomes appropriate to use informational concepts.


### Representations and descriptions

Marr's definitions of these terms are as follows:

'A representation is a formal system for making explicit certain entities or types of information, together with a specification of how the system does this. And I shall call the result of using a representation to describe a given entity a description of the entity in that representation.'

(Marr, 1982, p.20)

These definitions, which appear quite abstruse at first glance, may be clarified by a simple example. From a satellite photograph of a country an outline map is drawn. Suppose that the satellite has great power and that it can assess the maximum height in each ten square mile area of the terrain, allocating a numerical height value to each area. We can now select and add to the map all points with heights of 200 feet, 400 feet and so on, each represented by a coloured dot. Joining dots of a particular colour (representing a particular height) with straight lines will generate a crude contour map of the country.

Next, data are obtained concerning the distribution of people in the country and a single dot is printed to represent each thousand persons. Lines can be added to represent roads and rivers. Finally, markings are drawn to represent, say, birth rates in various regions.

A map of the country has been created from which certain interesting conclusions might be drawn; for example that more people live in valleys, roads wind round hilly areas, and people living on high ground are relatively more fecund. Now although one conventional map has been described, it is obvious that five distinct *representations* (outline, height, population density, rivers, roads) have been used to arrive at five *descriptions*: one can imagine the final map as formed from five superimposed transparencies.

That was an imperfect explication of Marr's definitions, for the procedures described were not ones that can be done by machines; they would normally be carried out by people wearing knitted pullovers who are called geographers. However, the important point stands: *symbols* have been used to represent things or events.

### The three levels at which a process must be understood

Marr's own example of an information-processing task is one that is definitely carried out by a machine. (From now on all quotations are from Marr, 1982, unless stated otherwise.) Marr describes a cash register. It is at this point that he introduces the distinction between the three levels of explanation which he insists must be kept separate in our thinking about any informational process. This distinction pervades the whole of *Vision* and may well be one of Marr's enduring contributions. The three levels which Marr distinguishes are: (a) the computational theory, (b) the algorithm and (c) the hardware implementation.

### *The computational theory*

Marr asserts that at this level of enquiry the key question is, 'What is the goal of the computation, why is it appropriate, and what is the strategy by which it can be carried out?' In the case of the cash register the function of the machine is clearly to add sums of money. And it is this procedure of addition which brings the machine within the class defined as information-processing devices: several subtotals may be 'compressed' into a final sum from which they cannot be recovered, so the process is not a linear translation or transduction.

In this example the computational theory is simply *the rules of arithmetic*. That is to say, it should not matter in what order data are entered into the cash register; if a zero sum is entered, then the total should be unaffected, and so on. This is describing what the machine achieves and also the *constraints* upon it. These constraints allow the processes within the machine to be defined. It is clear that at this stage there may be complete ignorance as to *how* the machine does its arithmetic.

### The algorithm

'How can the computational theory be implemented? In particular, what is the representation for the input and output, and what is the algorithm for the transformation?' The input to the machine is known (key entries which represent sums of money in decimal notation), as is the output (total sums of money displayed in decimal notation), but what has the machine actually *done*? The machine could have translated keyed entries into electronic or mechanical equivalents of decimal quantities. Or entries might have been translated into binary form (this would be very likely if the cash register was linked to a large computer network). So there is something to discover about the *representation* of the data which the machine will process.

Knowledge of the representation may suggest hypotheses as to the *algorithm* or formula used within the machine. Clearly, the algorithm chosen will depend in part on the nature of the representation. For example, if the machine is operating according to binary arithmetic then the algorithm must include some procedure which will change entries from decimal form prior to adding, and then reconvert before displaying totals.

### Hardware implementation

'How can the representation and algorithm be realized physically?' A machine such as a cash register is not fully understood until the implementation is known. We know the computational theory of the machine (the rules of arithmetic) and can form hypotheses as to how input and output are represented and how the correct answer is attained. But there is still an area of ignorance: how does the machine actually work? It might contain interlocking cogs like an old-fashioned mechanical calculator. Or it might assign voltages to particular numbers using thermionic valves. Or (and most probably) the machine might function by the operation of a series of electronic switches—devices which can represent one of two possible states. The concern is with the hardware of the machine, the nature of its component parts and how they operate.

### A simple application

Many readers, including those with some previous knowledge of perceptual theories, may find these ideas somewhat puzzling. As they are central to Marr's approach, it might be useful to pause at this stage and offer a short summary and another example before proceeding to describe more of his work.

When the computational approach is applied to vision the following considerations will provide the framework for subsequent thinking. Vision must start with the image on the retina. But the end point is our awareness of the world. There seems to be a picture of the world available to us whenever we open our eyes and look around. But the fact is that light stops at the retina. There can be no actual pictures in our heads, only neural activity. It follows that this neural activity is representing the world *symbolically*, and we must therefore strive to understand this symbolic process or processes. Marr argues that symbolic representations of various aspects of the world, initially obtained from the retinal image, are combined into the descriptions which we call seeing.

Marr suggests that the most rigorous way in which to conduct research is to ask a series of systematic questions arising from the computational approach. Using the perception of contours as an example, the appropriate sequence of questions would be:

(1) Why is it important to be able to perceive contours? If the visual system can extract them from the visual image, what use is this to the perceiver? In other words, what of importance in the real world correlates with contours in the visual image? Why should the visual system work to make them explicit? How might contours be represented symbolically in our heads? If a contour is seen is it likely that this has arisen from an edge—a feature which reveals discontinuities between the surfaces of different objects? It is clear that this last question matches Brunswik's concern over the ecological validity of cues. It is equally clear that to answer the questions requires knowledge about (a) the visual system, (b) the purposive aspects of the perceiver's behaviour, and (c) the nature of the real world which sets constraints upon the theory.

(2) When the preceding questions have been answered it becomes possible to consider possible algorithms. In the present example the starting point is the retinal image, which is a set of light intensities spread across part of the retina this is the input. The output must be a symbolic representation of the lines or edges which are experienced. Now the question arises as to *how* a process operating on the retinal image could deliver contour information.

The example chosen is a relatively easy one, for quite a lot is known about contour perception. A successful algorithm would utilize a well-known property of retinal cells, namely the ability of some cells to inhibit the action of others. Developing this idea suggests that it would be useful if contour perception involved processes which did not pass on information to later stages in the visual pathway from areas in which retinal illumination was homogeneous, or even graded in intensity, but which produced outputs in response to rates of change within gradients (the second derivative of intensity). This would 'extract' the relevant contour information. Then it would be necessary to think about possible excitatory and inhibitory fields in the retina to see whether such mechanisms could respond to entire edges. It would also be necessary to suggest plausible rules by which these fields could interact.

It is possible to test algorithms of the sort described above using electronic circuits designed so that the components simulate mutual excitation and inhibition. This can reveal whether the circuits can respond in the hoped-for manner, say to the second derivative of a brightness gradient. This can be done in two ways (a) by actually building assemblies of photo-detectors and electronic components or, (b) by computer simulation. Many ideas in artificial intelligence have been tested in this way.

(3) It is now necessary to think about hardware capable of running the algorithm. In the present example independent evidence strongly suggests that it is the retinal ganglion cells which initiate the process of contour extraction. In fact, inhibitory relationships have actually been demonstrated among these cells. It would be of obvious interest to observe the activities of large groups of such cells, but technical problems render this impossible at present.

This, then, is the way in which Marr believes we should approach the task of understanding vision. Lack of progress in the past has often stemmed from failure to ask the right questions about perceptual systems, or confusion between the three levels to which research attention can be directed. As a test of the reader's understanding of Marr's point, we offer the following challenge (first put to me by my colleague Dave Earle): apply the computational approach to an ordinary lock. What is the computational theory of locking? What would be an appropriate algorithm for the lock? In what way(s) might the algorithm be implemented? Those who find it easy to answer these questions have certainly grasped Marr's distinctions between levels of explanation.

Early in his book Marr describes how his thoughts on vision developed until he reached his most important insight. What was required, he realized, was 'a theory in which the main job of vision was to derive a representation of shape'. Vision can do much more than this, but informing the perceiver about brightness, colour, texture and so on, is secondary to deriving a representation of shape. The problem then is to discover how the visual system is able to derive reliable information concerning the shapes of objects in the real world from information contained in the retinal image. Marr's theory is that vision is organized as an information-processing system and that this system comprises successive *stages*: it is unlikely that reliable or stable conclusions about objective shape could be derived in a single step. Marr also uses his knowledge of computer science to formulate a guiding principle, *Modular Design*. This is simply that in solving computational problems generally, it is wise to break down the computation into component parts which should proceed as independently as possible. The reason for this is that if part of a system goes wrong and this part interacts strongly with others, debugging the complete system becomes a formidable problem. Marr's hunch is that many of the processes of vision are modular, and for good reason.

## The stages of visual perception

### The image

The 'function' of the retinal image can be defined as representing intensity. The image is a spatial distribution of intensity values across the retina and is the starting point of the process of seeing.

### The primal sketch

The function of this stage of vision is to take the raw intensity values of the visual image and make explicit certain forms of information contained therein. The most important information concerns the spatial or geometrical distribution of intensity changes and the manner in which they are organized. The types of information which are becoming explicit at this stage are such as to afford the possibility of detecting surfaces.

### The $2\frac{1}{2}$-D sketch

At this stage of the visual process the orientation and rough depth of visible surfaces are made explicit: it is as if a 'picture' of the world is beginning to emerge. Note, however, that at this level what is emerging is organized with reference only to the viewer, it is not yet linked to a stable, external environment.

### The 3-D model representation

Here shapes and their orientation become explicit as tokens of three-dimensional objects organized in an object-centred framework, that is to say in a manner that is independent of particular positions and orientations on the retina. By this final stage of vision the perceiver has attained a model of the external world.

## THE THEORY IN ACTION

The reader who can see the potential rigour and clarity afforded by Marr's ideas may yet wonder how the approach actually works, how Marr moves from verbal description to a scientific attack on the problem of vision. Selections of Marr's work will now be examined in more detail to convey the style of the computational approach. The first topic is the Primal Sketch.

## The primal sketch

The starting point for this early stage in vision is the array of intensities represented in the retinal image. Marr's theory holds that certain *primitives* or place tokens are derived from the image. These are: zero-crossings (which will be explained below), edges, bars (which can be thought of as pairs of parallel edges), blobs (the ends of bars or small clusters of dots), terminations (of edges or bars), edge segments, virtual lines, groups, curvilinear organization, and boundaries.

The development of the primal sketch begins with the derivation from the spatial retinal array of primitives which can be thought of as *tokens*. The idea of tokens is very important in this approach. To explain this a little more fully consider a recent trend in television commercials, the reverse zoom. A typical advert starts with a shot of a group of individuals. Because these are seen *as* individuals, each must have been assigned a visual token. Now the camera rises and it can be seen that the people form various groupings. When the camera reaches its greatest height the people become letters in a word (the advertised product, etc.). Seeing each letter as a coherent whole implies that it must be represented in the visual system, and thus, in Marr's terms, a new token has been created. (Of course, the tokens formed in the visual system are 'really' neural events. When Marr or other theorists in artificial intelligence use actual visual tokens to illustrate the successive processing of images, this is argument by analogy.)

During the development of the primal sketch groups of adjacent tokens having a common property, such as orientation, are replaced by 'level one' tokens representing this common property. Then, if there are whole groups of similarly orientated level one tokens, these are used to construct boundaries between parts of the full primal sketch. There is nothing mysterious about these notions. Remembering the earlier example of a map, it is obvious that when a sufficient number of concentric contours occupy a given region, they could all be replaced by a single purple patch to indicate a mountainous area: cartographers do this routinely. This patch would form a token, like those formed for the letters and words in the television commercial described above.

A question arises as to *how* the initial primitives of the primal sketch are actually extracted. The attempt to answer this question leads Marr to a most impressive piece of work and demonstrates the advantages of his background in artificial intelligence. We shall concentrate upon the primitive known as the *zero-crossing*.

When a photograph or an actual image (such as that on a television screen) is scrutinized it is obvious that important information about the shape and orientation of objects comes from edges, contours and boundaries: that is, from areas in the image where intensity values are changing rapidly. Clearly then it should be important to represent these portions of the image in the primal sketch. But what sort of process can take intensity values as inputs and deliver tokens representing lines, edges and so on as outputs?

The first step in the required processing is to move from the continuous image to some sort of discrete representation. A process which will do this is *convolution*. One way of convolving an image is to choose a particular position and then apply weighting functions so that the intensity value at the position is enhanced by a certain factor, whilst simultaneously reducing the values of immediately adjacent positions. The process is then repeated at all positions on the image. Convolution is a valuable technique in computer image enhancement and it is quite easy to see how combinations of excitatory and inhibitory cells could perform an equivalent function in the visual system.

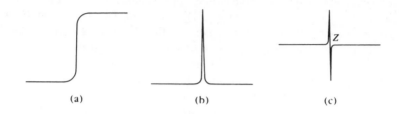

(a)                              (b)                              (c)

Figure 8.2   (a) Represents an intensity change, such as would arise when measuring intensity across a light/dark boundary. (b) Is the first derivative of the intensity distribution and plots the regions in (a) where intensity changes rapidly. (c) Is the second derivative and is a plot of the distribution of changes in (b). Where the lines in (c) cross the horizontal mid point are the zero-crossings referred to in the text. (From *Vision* by David Marr, Copyright © 1982 W. H. Freeman & Company. Reprinted with permission.)

Consider the graphs drawn in Figure 8.2 (adapted from Marr, 1982, p.54). In this figure (a) represents a change in intensity in a portion of an image, this is the input to our hypothetical process. (b) Is a representation of the first derivative of the intensity change. By this is meant simply that the intensity curve is replotted to indicate the rate of change of intensity: this is clearly zero from $w$ to $y$, rising rapidly from $y$ to $z$ and falling to zero again from $z$ onwards. (c) Is the second derivative of (a): by examining curve (b) we can find points when it too is changing rapidly; clearly the curve is initially at zero, then rises positively (upwards) quite rapidly before diminishing (in a negative direction) with equal rapidity. In moving from its positive to its negative peak the graph displays a *zero-crossing* and this, in Marr's theory, is the primitive we require. We have moved from a continuous image (or part of one) to a discrete representation. (In a later part of his theory Marr guesses that the *sign* of the zero-crossing may be represented, this would give additional power to the extraction process.)

The computational theory has suggested the zero-crossing as a primitive. The next stage is to construct an algorithm, a set of rules by means of which zero-crossings may be extracted from images. Marr's suggestion takes the form of an *Operator* or mathematical equation: $\nabla^2 G$, where $\nabla^2$ is the Laplacian operator ( $\nabla^2 = \delta^2/\delta x^2 + \delta^2/\delta y^2$ ) and $G$ is the two-dimensional Gaussian distribution ($G(x,y) = e^{-(x^2+y^2)/2\pi\sigma^2}$ ). The reader for whom this sort of equation is very unfamiliar should not feel discouraged: Marr is simply describing a mathematical process which will convert intensity changes in a two-dimensional image into zero-crossings, rather as in the one-dimensional case illustrated in Figure 8.2

It is mathematically certain that the above equations will do the required extraction, but, of course, these are ideal, abstract formulae. There is, however, an actual engineering device which closely approximates the $\nabla^2 G$ operator: this is a particular type of filter known as a Difference of Two Gaussians (DOG). The performance of DOG filters is known and they have certain advantages for the present purpose, the most important of which being that they can be tuned to different scales. The necessity of tuning can be demonstrated very easily. The reader should stare at this page with partly closed eyes. Then the page will be seen as an area of brightness which differs from the surface on which it is lying. Similarly, the paragraphs on the page can be seen as blocks of dark grey against the white page. But on opening the eyes again it can be seen that there are discontinuities in brightness operating at a much finer scale: one is aware of lines of black print and spaces between words and letters. This shows why a successful filtering process attempting to capture zero-crossings should be capable of operating at more than one scale. More importantly, by using spatial frequency filters tuned to different scales and comparing their outputs, the chance of detecting an actual edge—one that is present in the external world—is greatly increased. In fact, Marr and Hildreth (1980) have proved that if several different spatial filters agree on the position of a contour in the image, then there must be an edge in the world which is giving rise to these outputs. Here knowledge of the real world is being used to shape a theory.

An important advantage of the artificial intelligence/engineering approach to vision is that it is possible at this stage to make a powerful indirect test of the theory so far. One can substitute photographs of real scenes for retinal images and process them through actual filters. Then, by examining the outputs of these filters, one can see to what extent lines, edges and so on, have been made explicit and whether the shapes in the photographs have been separated. It is also a simple matter to assess filters other than DOGs to compare their performances. Marr's book contains numerous illustrations of such tests. We must point out, however, that it is not yet *proved* that zero-crossings are computed by the visual system, but this is not Marr's main concern at this stage.

After finding an appropriate computational theory and related algorithms it becomes necessary to consider the hardware implementation; to look for neural devices which will extract zero-crossings and other primitives. From what is known about the neurophysiology of the retina, it is obvious that this search should concentrate upon systems or cells having inhibitory capabilities.

There are in fact cells in the retina and the lateral geniculate nucleus (a subcortical structure between the retina and the visual cortex) which exhibit receptive field properties. By this is meant that the activity of the cells can be shown to reflect patterns of stimulation of groups of retinal cells sending their outputs to them (see the discussion of receptive fields in Chapter 5). Receptive fields can be organized in various ways and have various shapes. Marr's guess concerning the cells delivering information about zero-crossings is that they are the retinal ganglion and lateral geniculate cells known as X-cells: in particular those having On-Centre/Off-Surround organization (firing when the centre of the receptive field is stimulated, inhibited when the surrounding portion of the field is stimulated), and the Off-Centre/On-Surround cells (having the opposite type of organization). In a striking demonstration of the probable truth of this part of the theory, Marr displays, simultaneously, the outputs of DOG filters to lines and edges and the outputs of actual X-cells responding to the same stimuli. The similarity between these outputs is remarkably close.

### An application of the computational approach to stereopsis

Marr's theorizing on the early stages of vision has now been described. The rigour and power of the approach can be underlined by describing the computational attack on a second problem. We shall now give an outline of a possible solution to the problem of stereopsis. The reader who wishes to experience at first hand the high quality of Marr's work should consult the relevant chapters of *Vision*, or the original research paper by Marr and his collaborator, T.Poggio (Marr and Poggio, 1979). Beware though, this is very difficult material and it can take several readings before one feels confident that the arguments have been mastered. It is, however, well worth the effort.

*Stereopsis* is a term having two meanings. First, it refers to that extra sense of solidity and depth which is experienced when using two eyes rather than one, an experience which is confirmed by the superiority of binocular depth judgements. Second, stereopsis is triggered when two slightly different views of a scene are viewed in a stereoscope. In this case the two flat stimuli are inducing an illusion of depth which can be used to gain an understanding of normal stereopsis.

Classical work showed that the basis of stereopsis must lie in the difference between the left- and right-eye images. Providing these fall onto corresponding areas of the two retinae, disparate images will induce an illusion of depth in a stereoscope. That this *disparity* is a necessary and sufficient cue for stereopsis is demonstrated by the ability of random-dot textures to induce depth when the actual disparity is hidden, as it is in Figure 8.1. This figure shows that the problem of stereopsis is a formidable one: how is depth assigned to such stimuli? And how is this possible in the absence of all the familiar monocular cues to depth such as size, perspective and shading?

The value of the computational approach becomes evident at the start. Simply to state, as many have, that disparity is the basis of stereopsis, begs important questions. Marr wishes to take our understanding much further, and begins by asking two questions: how is disparity *measured* by the visual system, and how is it *used*?

We shall outline Marr's attempt to deal with the first of these questions, the Measurement of Disparity. Marr's analysis of the situation at the two eyes during binocular viewing leads him to recognize two major related problems (he was by no means the first person to describe them). Although the problems are easy to describe, it has taken over a 100 years to find plausible solutions.

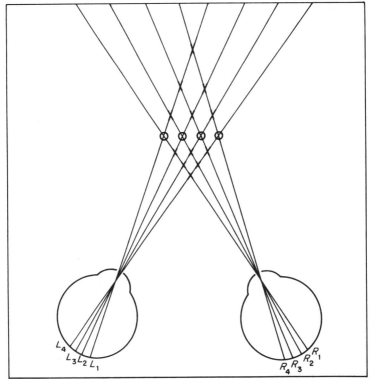

Figure 8.3    The false location problem in stereopsis. The circles represent four coplanar objects viewed by the two eyes. $L_1-L_4$ and $R_1-R_4$ are corresponding positions on the left and right retinae. Crossings represent false locations: positions from which patterns of stimulation at the eyes could arise which are identical with those arising from the four objects. The problem is to account for the fact that the visual system can solve this problem and avoid false locations

Figure 8.3 shows the situation when a person looks at a row of lights at a fixed distance from the two eyes. Given that the process of vision starts at the retinae, stereopsis must take the inputs there as the vital information concerning the location of the lights. Further, the solution as to where the lights are must be found in the relationships (or matches) between the two retinal patterns. But examine the situation closely: drawing rays from each light to the two eyes creates the crossover pattern shown in Figure 8.3. This figure is important because it reveals that *the patterns falling upon the left and right retinae are not uniquely determined by the configuration of the lights, but could have been caused by any of a number of alternative configurations: those represented by the various crossover positions in the diagram.* We have used a small number of stimuli in this illustration; the number of *false locations*, as they are known, grows exponentially with the number of stimuli and would be huge in many actual situations.

The two problems then are (i) how are parts of one image correctly matched with parts of the other whilst (ii) avoiding those matches arising from false locations? In other words, how is the truth obtained from the ambiguous information in the two visual inputs?

Marr realized that if he could account for the stereoscopic depth induced by random dot displays, which are meaningless and contain no other depth information, then an account of 'normal' stereopsis would follow quite easily. The dot displays contain, in a sense, 'pure' disparity. A world sprayed with dots is also simpler to consider.

As would be expected, the computational approach to stereopsis involves three levels of discourse, the first of which is the computational theory.

## The computational theory of stereopsis

We are considering the perception of a three-dimensional world containing only dotted surfaces, and have discovered a fundamental problem: how is a dot seen by one eye correctly matched by the other whilst avoiding false matches? Marr starts by adopting two constraints set by the nature of the world in which the visual system evolved.

(1) A given point has a fixed position at any moment in time.
(2) Matter is cohesive. Surfaces are not arranged in ways that can trick us. They cannot, for instance, suddenly bend or change their curvatures without yielding clues to such changes.

The formal computational theory begins with three matching rules applied to a textured surface which is in binocular view.

(1) Black dots can match only black dots. We are considering surfaces which contain only black dots and white spaces, and the rule is simply stating that a point on a surface seen by one eye stays the same when seen by the other.
(2) A black dot in one image can (truly) match only one dot in the other.
(3) Disparity, the magnitude of the difference between the left and right eye matches, varies smoothly. Once again it is being assumed that the world does not (cannot) play tricks.

We now have the beginnings of a computational theory. Can a combination of the matching rules and the constraints suggest a solution to the problem of stereopsis?

Marr now presents an interesting analysis of the situation at the eyes when both are looking at the same scene (this was first described by Marr and Poggio, 1979). This analysis is illustrated in Figure 8.4. In this figure the positions of 'descriptive elements' in the left and right images are plotted along the two axes. Horizontal and vertical lines represent lines of sight from the left and right eyes respectively. Where these lines intersect are possible disparities, that is, positions of matches and false locations as shown in Figure 8.3. The dotted diagonal lines are lines of constant disparity, or positions along which the differences in left- and right-eye views of a surface have the same magnitude.

This deceptively simple diagram is an important component of the proposed solution of the problem of stereopsis. The aspect of the diagram to note is that *the distribution of matches and false locations is not chaotic: both are spatially distributed among the two images in an orderly manner*. A regularity such as this, existing in the physical world, suggests that here is a source of information. This in turn implies that there should be a solution to the problem of correct matching.

Support for this optimistic conclusion comes when the simple matching rules described above are combined with an equally simple logical analysis of the situation. Let the density of dots in each image be, say, 20 per cent. In other words, there is a one in five chance that a dot will be present at any location. Now consider the correct plane in Figure 8.4. What can be said about the density of possible matches—of dots which can signify by their disparity that a surface is present? Clearly this too must equal 20 per cent. But what is the density of possible matches on the incorrect planes in the figure? A little reflection shows that as these planes are the wrong ones, dots will match only by chance. This gives us the same probability of matching which would occur if two transparent sheets, each with a (random) dot density of 20 per cent, were superimposed. This probability is calculable and is simply the product of the two individual densities (more simply, their probabilities, which are the inverse of the densities): $p = 0.2$ squared equals 0.04. Hence, provided that the difference between the density (or probability) value in the 'true' situation is

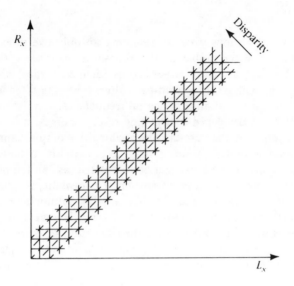

Figure 8.4   The Marr–Poggio analyis of stereopsis. The vertical and horizontal axes plot the distribution of stimuli at the two eyes. Continuous horizontal and vertical lines in the figure are lines of sight from the two eyes: where these meet are possible positions giving rise to disparities of view of the same object. The dotted diagonal lines are lines of constant disparity. Rule three of the Marr–Poggio algorithm requires correct matches across the two eyes to cluster along the diagonal lines. This limits the set of possible solutions and thus a potentially chaotic situation becomes a manageable problem: there are noticeable regularities that could be the basis of the true matching of left and right stimuli during stereopsis. See the text for a fuller account of the stereo-matching algorithm. (From Marr and Poggio, 1976 © Reprinted with permission from *Science* © American Association for the Advancement of Science.)

detectably different from those in all remaining situations, the matching rules will yield a unique solution.

The question now is whether the visual system (or a mathematical algorithm) can profit from the orderliness which has been demonstrated. With this in mind, Marr continues by asking what could be the input to the stereo-matching process required by the computational theory. He suggests that it must take the form of zero-crossings from filtered images. Evidence outlined earlier suggests that the visual system has various tuned spatial frequency channels. If the first attempt to find stereo-matches uses inputs from the larger (lower spatial frequency) channels, this will have two benefits. First, the number of possible matches (and false matches) is reduced because the search through the arrays is coarser. Second, finding some evidence of corresponding matches in an array can direct eye movements so that finer and finer spatial channels can be used for further searches.

## The algorithm

Marr now considers various ways of designing an objective procedure which will yield a solution of the problem. His proposal is that the $\nabla^2 G$ operator is applied to each image and the zero-crossings (defined earlier) are extracted. The $\nabla^2 G$ operator will act as a band-pass filter, that is, a filter which allows through it only a restricted range of spatial frequencies.

As the algorithm is developed a surprising result emerges. It is of the nature of band-pass filters that the zero-crossings which are output cannot occur at less than known spatial separations. Thus the probability of finding a match between zero-crossings in each eye can be calculated, as can the probability of finding false correspondences. Marr shows, in a plausibility argument, that in a variety of situations the desired matches will far outnumber false matches when a particular disparity value close to the truth is being evaluated. If a new disparity value is assessed, and is false, then the ratio of correct to incorrect matches will fall dramatically. All that one needs to add to the algorithm is the ability to know a good situation, in terms of successful matches, from a poorer one.

Although the let-out phrase, 'It can be shown', has been avoided, the reader may feel a sense of unease at this point. Does this technical claim that something will work dodge a real explanation as to *how* it might work? Two additional points may help convince the sceptic.

First, it is important to remember the *constraints* which the computational theory made explicit. Think about the two eyes looking at a flat surface. The two views must be slightly different. The size of this difference (the disparity between the two images) contains the information as to where the surface is in depth, and this is what the visual system is trying to calculate. But remember that in normal viewing there really is a surface there in front of the eyes. An element of the surface seen by one eye is actually present to the other— it cannot suddenly move or disappear. And if the selected disparity value is correct, it will be correct over a major portion of the display, for a physical surface does not move away or change in an instant (this is one of the constraints adopted above). If the visual system makes a wrong calulation as to the disparity value for part of the surface, then not only are the matches at that point wrong, they will be generally wrong all over the image. In other words, it is because of plausible assumptions which can be made concerning the real world that certain procedures can be guaranteed to have a high rate of success.

There is a further reason for thinking that Marr's algorithm might be correct: it works. A computer programmed with the algorithm which has been outlined can solve the Julesz stereogram displayed in Figure 8.1. It is not necessary to take this part of Marr's work on trust; it can be seen to work in practice. The algorithm is sufficiently explicit and powerful to allow the computer to find the hidden disparity in random-dot displays. This is an impressive and convincing demonstration.

### The neural implementation

The final stage of what Marr considers to be a satisfactory explanation (or model) of stereopsis is the implementation. What sort of neural hardware could carry out the operations contained in the algorithm? Marr admits that the search for a plausible neural implementation of his theory may be premature, given our rather hazy knowledge of the neurology of some parts of the visual system. He does, however, offer some hypotheses as to how his model could be implemented.

The ways in which cells in the visual system could mimic the operations of the $\nabla^2 G$ filter have been dealt with earlier. The detection of zero-crossings can be achieved by simple logical gates which neural cells can mimic by suitable interactions between excitatory and inhibitory processes. In stereopsis it is necessary to combine binocular information about zero-crossings and their signs (positive-going/negative-going) in order to match, say, black dots to black dots. Once again logical devices (in this case AND gates, which fire when both possible inputs are active) are capable of doing the required work, with each gate having as one of its inputs the difference between the left and right eye inputs at the position of whichever zero-crossing (left eye or right eye) is chosen as the starting point for the comparison; the zero-crossing forms the other input to the gate.

Exactly where in the visual system these AND gates will be found is uncertain. Marr guesses, on the basis of published micro-electrode studies, that the proposed disparity detectors may lie in Area 18 of the visual cortex (this is an area of the brain in which it is believed that visual information may be integrated with that from other senses and with memory). The fine resolution of depth which is possible at the limit of stereo acuity may be based, at least in part, on the activities of granular cells in layer IVc Beta in Area 17 of the visual cortex (this is a region of the brain onto which retinal outputs are mapped in an orderly spatial projection). These would use inputs from the high resolution spatial outputs from the $\nabla^2 G$ filtered images.

## FURTHER ASPECTS OF MARR'S THEORY

The understanding gained from the attack on the problem of stereopsis allows Marr to extend the computational approach to other areas of perception. Further chapters in *Vision* contain interesting discussions of directional sensitivity, the perception of motion, shape and contour, lightness and brightness, shape from shading, and, finally, the perception of three-dimensional objects when perception moves from viewer-centred to object-centred frames of reference. In terms of the model of vision, the processes have finally arrived at a description of the objective world.

Some of the later parts of *Vision* are extremely provocative and informative. In a discussion of the recovery of shape from silhouettes, for example, Marr's careful analysis of the stimulus situation allows him to predict when a silhouette is a reliable guide to shape and when not: it is reliable when the portions of a surface generating the silhouette are in the same plane, not otherwise. Reading these sections one feels that few can ever have thought so analytically and deeply about the nature of the three-dimensional world and the ways in which it gives rise to visual images.

Towards the end of his book Marr attempts to outline how we perceive three-dimensional shapes. An important part of this work concerns the ways in which the visual system uses *canonical* forms in a *modular* organization (that is, split into different parts). As an example, consider the attainment of the three-dimensional representation of a human being. One possible canonical form which would be useful here is the cylinder. Following the principle of modular organization, an initial cylinder could be constructed to represent a person, provided the visual system could first decide upon the direction of the principal axis: in this case, from head to feet. This would be a self-contained unit in the shape description. It is possible to enrich the description, using the same canonical form to represent the head, the torso, the arms and legs by smaller cylinders. Next the arm could be represented by a set of cylinders, one of which is the hand. Finally, the hand cylinder could be elaborated into a set of cylinders representing the wrist and the fingers. The same canonical form—the cylinder—has been used throughout, but successive applications at different scales yield descriptions which are increasingly 'lifelike'. In terms of the computational approach, a three-dimensional model of a human being has been attained.

It is clearly impossible to attempt a detailed description of the whole of Marr's work. We shall, however, state an opinion, which is that, despite the ingenuity of his reasoning, Marr's ideas on the perception of objects are less impressive and convincing than the earlier chapters of *Vision*. This is hardly surprising: the problems are much more formidable. Thus, for example, the account just given of Marr's approach to the perception of three-dimensional shape gives one the impression (and this is not true in other parts of Marr's work) that whilst his ideas seem quite plausible in terms of machine recognition of objects, the evidence that this is how a living visual system might function is not at all compelling. This assertion gains some support from the fact that, to date, the only occasions when machine systems do recognize objects is when they are operating in artificially constrained worlds—worlds typically comprising only blocks or prisms.

## A GENERAL APPRAISAL OF THE COMPUTATIONAL APPROACH

It would be unwise to offer too confident an evaluation of the computational approach to perception. The work of Marr and his colleagues was carried out in laboratories specializing in artificial intelligence research. It has taken some time for the ideas of these workers to become widespread in psychology and physiology. As we have been able to demonstrate, many of the concepts and mechanisms invoked to explain perceptual phenomena are complicated. The language is not one which is familiar to many who work in other disciplines. The mathematics is occasionally difficult, and lacking the facilities to use the various operators and filters described by Marr means that some readers have to take his findings on trust. This state of affairs will undoubtedly change. But it will be some time before every worker in perception will be able to demonstrate computer-filtered images as easily as they can generate, for example, Mach bands, random dot stereograms or rotating shadows. Support for this claim comes from the relative paucity, to date, of critical tests of Marr's predictions, or replications of his major findings.

There are, however, two studies which are worth reporting here as they throw some doubts upon the adequacy of one important part of Marr's computational model.

Mayhew and Frisby (1981), who work within the computational framework, present psychophysical evidence from experiments using stereograms. It will be remembered that in Marr's model the raw primal sketch makes explicit intensity changes in the image using primitives such as bars, blobs, terminators, etc. These in turn are replaced by more abstract tokens which lead to the achievement of the full primal sketch. In the full primal sketch only two-dimensional projections of objects are represented. The system is not concerned with the extraction of three-dimensional disparity information until the later stage of the $2\frac{1}{2}$-D sketch. Mayhew and Frisby used sawtooth patterns as stereograms. They found that the depth which results is not predictable from knowledge of zero-crossings—the primitive which Marr adopts as the input to a stereo-matching process. Mayhew and Frisby have published examples in which the positions of zero-crossings are identical in two stereograms (and hence cannot signal disparity) and yet the stereograms can induce depth. Thus in Marr's model one would have to include other sources of information, for example the peaks obtained from the convolutions, in order for stereopsis to be achieved. More importantly, Mayhew and Frisby present convincing arguments in favour of a model of stereopsis in which disparity is computed much earlier than the $2\frac{1}{2}$-D sketch: probably at the level of the raw primal sketch.

My colleague Dave Earle has also published evidence which suggests that part of Marr's thinking may be wrong. This is highly technical research and is difficult to describe briefly and lucidly. It is included here to illustrate the level of precision required to test detailed parts of Marr's theory. Earle used Glass patterns (Glass, 1969; Stevens, 1978) which Marr cites as important evidence in favour of part of his model. A Glass pattern forms when two patterns of dots or other simple shapes are superimposed. The first pattern is typically a random array, the second is some transformation of the first—an expansion or a rotation, for example. Depending upon the transformation, merging the two displays gives rise to an organized pattern having a strong radial or circular appearance. Typical patterns are shown in Figure 8.5.

Marr cites work by Stevens (1978) on Glass patterns as evidence for the ways in which an early stage of visual processing is organized. For Marr, the important point is that the process that enables structure to be perceived in Glass patterns (as in Figure 8.5) occurs at the level of the primal sketch. Remember that in Marr's model the primal sketch is not concerned with the three-dimensional information in the image, but only with the two-dimensional information. Therefore, Glass patterns should form even when the two component patterns are separated in depth. In an elegant series of demonstrations, Earle (1985) has created stereograms in which Glass pattern structure is in fact destroyed by apparent depth; more importantly, he has also designed stereograms in which novel *three-dimensional* Glass patterns arise when no structure is visible in the two-dimensional components. Combining Earle's findings with those of Mayhew and Frisby cited above we are forced to the conclusion that some of Marr's ideas on what happens during the process of seeing may require revision.

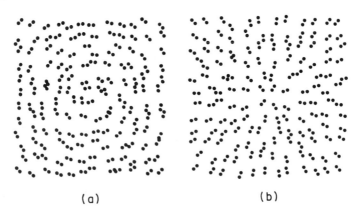

(a)                                                      (b)

Figure 8.5   Glass patterns (a) is formed by superimposition of a random array and its rotation, (b) is formed by superimposition of an array and an expanded version of the same array. (Prepared for the author by Dr. D. C. Earle)

We shall now offer some general comments on the computational approach to visual perception as exemplified by Marr's writings. Workers in artificial intelligence distinguish between bottom-up and top-down processes. Bottom-up processes involve lower-level, more peripheral systems which are relatively autonomous. Their outputs can be fed into higher levels of the system. Top-down processes are well described by their name. To use one of Marr's own examples, it might have been the case that the visual system solves the problem of stereopsis in a top-down manner. A major portion of the image in the left eye (say the representation of a tree) would be chosen and the right-eye view of the object compared. Then the branches could be scanned, then the twigs, and finally the leaves. This process would profit from, and be guided by, the perceiver's knowledge of trees. It would be a top-down process. (In fact, our ability to see depth in meaningless random dot stereograms tells us that stereopsis must make considerable use of bottom-up processes.)

When this distinction is applied to Marr's model it is clear that he was guided by many top-down considerations. The basic idea that the *goal* sought by a perceptual process should feature large in any explanation of that process is obviously a form of top-down modelling. However, much of Marr's detailed work concentrates upon what are clearly bottom-up processes, such as, for example, those involved in contour extraction and texture discrimination.

Marr is often most convincing when he speculates about bottom-up processes. We are told what is required to achieve some desired result, what the inputs and outputs to the necessary computations must be, and which neural mechanisms could do the necessary work. It is always satisfying to work through expositions of this kind. They contribute importantly to the high quality of *Vision*.

It is when Marr speculates about processes involving knowledge of the world and acting in a top-down manner that his work becomes less convincing. For example, do we carry in our heads those canonical shapes such as generalized cones and cylinders which he postulates as the primitives for three-dimensional shape perception? How could we test this possibility?

## Computer models of psychological processes

The computational approach arose from within artificial intelligence research. Fundamental criticisms of AI have been made by those who doubt whether it is in principle possible for machines to simulate human processes such as thinking and perceiving. Is Marr's approach inherently flawed?

Dreyfus (1972) marshals a number of arguments against computer simulations, some of which will be mentioned. If he is correct then the computational approach could be doomed to eventual failure.

Dreyfus maintains that any system which can be said to equal human performance must be able, like a human, to do the following:

(1) Distinguish between the essential and inessential features of patterns. In solving a problem (and perceiving frequently does require problem-solving) the solver must acquire knowledge of what is and is not relevant to the solution. But it is a characteristic of many of the problems which humans can solve that the essentials are not known ahead of time. There are no simple rules for us, nor any for the computer. Where computers have in fact solved problems, it has been the programmers who have stipulated what is and is not relevant.

(2) Use cues which remain on the fringe of consciousness. In a famous experiment on problem-solving the task was to join together the ends of two pieces of string suspended in a room, but too far apart to be grasped simultaneously. Lying on the floor were some unusual 'aids' to the solution of this problem. If a subject was unable to solve the problem, the experimenter could often help in a most subtle manner: by brushing against one of the strings so that it swung gently to and fro. At this point several subjects suddenly saw how to solve the problem: use the hammer (one of the 'aids') to make a pendulum of one of the strings, swing the string, get hold of the other string and wait for the first to swing within reach. Notice the obviousness of this solution once one knows it; but how would one instruct a computer to make use of the hammer? Programmed to notice such apparently irrelevant information, what information could the computer safely ignore? Wouldn't it have to consider each and every discriminable object in its field of view as potentially relevant? But this comes close to saying that everything in the world would have to be considered. This is a nonsense, practically and theoretically, and cannot even resemble the ways in which humans solve such problems.

(3) Take account of context. In Wittgenstein's phrase, a mouth smiles only in a face. The expression is not *deducible* from a simple list of all the features of the face; the organization of the features *is* the expression. How could this principle be built into a computer program?

(4) Perceive the individual as typical or atypical. One of the impressive things which we do in perceiving is to notice family resemblance. But we can often do this without being able to describe any particular traits which two patterns have in common. The basis of this ability is unknown in humans: could it be programmed into a computer?

Dreyfus's book is an example of aggressively polemical writing. Additional criticisms of artificial intelligence arise in his discussion of the role of the body in perception—could a computer perceive without one?—and certain phenomenological experiences: for example when we perceive, say, a house, we are simultaneously aware of the front which we can see, and the volume, which we cannot. We are always aware of the world continuing behind us, even when it is beyond peripheral vision. There is, then, much in Dreyfus to make us cautious about accepting too uncritically the claims of artificial intelligence within which the computational approach arose. There is however one development in computing which could revive the status of the computer as a model: the Parallel Distributed Process or *Connectionist* model.

### New models of the brain: parallel distributed processes

This is one of the most exciting ideas to have entered psychology in a long time. What follows is an introduction to the topic. It has direct relevance to some of Marr's work, and is certainly relevant to some of the general criticisms which have been levelled against the artificial intelligence approach. Placing this section here interrupts the discussion of Marr's contribution, but the importance of this new approach is such that it must be mentioned, if only briefly.

Remember that the model of the mind (or brain) which Dreyfus and others have criticized is that derived from the modern digital computer. In the early years of artificial intelligence research and theory, computer models shared the following characteristics:

(1) An important distinction is made between the permanent structure of the system—the hardware—and the set of programmed instructions—the software.
(2) The models are rule-governed; that is to say, they operate via explicit instructions.
(3) The operation of the models is sequential.
(4) Knowledge or information within the system is stored in specific memory addresses and retrieved by means of these addresses.
(5) Most real or hypothetical digital computing systems are essentially 'top-down' devices, in that their behaviour is under the control of parts of the system labelled as 'Central Processing Units' and so on.

The listing above is a partial description both of the modern digital computer and of the human being seen from the point of view of many workers in AI. We now break away from the main topic in order to outline an alternative model to the traditional one criticized by Dreyfus and others. This too has arisen within the framework of AI research and is attracting the interest of a growing number of workers. The possible alternative is the idea of Parallel Distributed Processing (PDP).

### *Some antecedents of PDP theory*

During the 1930s and 40s the distinguished neuropsychologist Karl Lashley set out to discover the sites in the brain where learning and memory occurred. He failed. In a famous monograph entitled, '*In search of the engram*' (1950), Lashley described a series of experiments on the rat's brain in which experimental damage was caused to different regions before and after learning. The results of these experiments showed that the precise site of an experimental lesion is less important in its effects on the rat's memory or learning ability than the amount of cortical tissue which has been damaged: the greater the damage the greater the impairment in performance, with complex skills suffering more than simple ones. Lashley elevated these results into the self-explanatory Principles of Equipotentiality and Mass Action.

Hebb, a contemporary of Lashley's, took a discovery from neurophysiological research and developed it into a mechanism for perceptual learning (Hebb, 1949). The discovery was that groups of interconnected neurons continue to show increased activity after the termination of the event which originally disturbed them. Hebb proposed that clusters of neurons displaying this *reverberating* activity acted as functional units and that modifications to such an interacting network could be the basis of both short-term and long-term learning. Hebb called these networks 'cell assemblies'.

As a final antecedent to the development of the theory of parallel distributed processing we may cite the first description of Rosenblatt's Perceptron (Rosenblatt, 1959).

The perceptron was a device (in fact, like most devices to be described, it was simulated on a computer) comprising an input layer or 'retina', a decision layer, and between these a set of predicates. The retina can be interpreted as a simple array generating binary outputs when stimulated in some manner. The predicate layer comprised a set of threshold units, each connected to a subset of the retinal units and capable of computing some simple function from their outputs. The decision units were joined to the predicate layer by a number of modifiable connections. The task set for the perceptron was to see to what extent it could adjust its outputs to match a given input: could it act as a primitive pattern recognizer?

The perceptron was a 'one layer' computing device (it had only a single modifiable layer). And it contained vital flaws which were subsequently exposed by Minsky and Papert (1969). Nevertheless, it will become apparent that the perceptron was an important forerunner of subsequent developments in this area.

There were, in addition to these technical and theoretical antecedents to PDP theory, other reasons why some AI workers felt the need for alternatives to the then accepted computer models of human processes such as memory, learning, language, perception, and thinking. These essentially psychological considerations may be described quite briefly:

(1) Two men are facing a firing squad. When asked if they have any final request, one of the men steps foward and asks for a blindfold. The other

says, as he pulls him back, 'Don't offend them'.

To 'see' a joke like that is to solve a problem. It requires one to bring together, in a novel manner, very different kinds of information, such as a knowledge of etiquette and what is and is not likely to happen in desperate situations. The same combination of different parts of one's knowledge enables one to appreciate the wit and force of James Joyce's 'Lawn Tennyson'. Could one visualize a traditional computer model, with its fixed memories and sequential operations, ever 'getting' such a pun? And this elusive, 'lateral' aspect of thought is manifest not only in the appreciation of jokes and puns: Kekulé hit upon the ring structure of the benzene molecule after he had visualized a snake biting its tail; what could be more different than an animal and a molecule, except for this bit of geometry?

(2) Human memory is content-addressable. In most computers each stored item is kept at a particular labelled address. Lose this address and it is impossible to recover the contents it has stored within it. But is human memory like this? Here is a description of someone: male, fictional, a Central European, an aristocrat, a night prowler, a drinker of blood. The recognition in this case is easy and quick. But how many times has the reader thought of Count Dracula during the past year? (If the answer is, 'frequently', then this book may not be for you.)

(3) Humans can generalize. The author's daughter, then a little girl, once looked up at a rose window in a church and said, 'It's a telephone dial'. His son used to see large farm silos as 'squeezy' plastic bottles. We see such similarities with ease: clouds can look like faces; penguins like waiters. And when we know a symbol such as the letter 'A', we can recognize it in any typeface, at any size, and in any orientation.

Humans use context to complete percepts in ways which are often complicated and sometimes circular. Consider the middle symbol in the words CAT and THE in Figure 8.6. The resolution of the ambiguous central shape must depend in part upon the context supplied by the two familiar words; but the words themselves are formed using the ambiguous symbol. The effortless manner in which we solve this and other perceptual problems seems very mysterious and complex and not the sort of process to be easily modelled by traditional computer simulations.

Such doubts and speculations led to the search for a new type of computer model. An additional motive was the discovery of formidable problems in

Figure 8.6

robotics, where, for instance, it may be desirable to design a machine to do a complex task involving coordinated movements of several component parts, but without being able to give the machine a set of explicit rules guaranteed to be successful in all situtations. This is a real problem in applied research, for as the number of functional units in such a machine is increased, the total number of combinations or patterns of possible movements grows explosively. Consider, by analogy, a chess-playing machine attempting to consider all possible outcomes following an early move in a game: the total of such moves is greater than the number of atoms in the universe. To understand or even mimic the performance of actual chess players clearly requires a procedure that is more subtle than a mere sequential analysis of all possibilities.

*Parallel distributed processing models*

So far we have not yet said what a PDP model actually is, other than to describe the perceptron as a forerunner. Rumelhart, Hinton and McClelland (in Rumelhart and McClelland, 1986) provide an excellent description of PDP models which forms the basis of the following account. Interested readers should certainly consult this invaluable exposition.

Rumelhart *et al.* state that there are eight major components of any PDP model.

(1) A set of processing units. The units 'represent' (in the sense defined earlier in the account of Marr's theory) some aspect of the real or hypothetical world against which the model will be tested. The representation may be *discrete*, in which case the units will represent particular parts of a display: shapes, letters, or words. Or the representation may be *distributed*, in which case each unit will represent some small feature-like entity, whilst the *pattern* existing among the set of units represents some more abstract aspect of the display or world. Each unit has but one function: to accept inputs from other units, compute some value, and then pass this on to neighbouring units. The computations may occur simultaneously and so this part of the PDP model has marked degree of *parallelism*. There are three possible types of unit: input units which we have been describing; output units, sending signals from the system; and 'hidden' units whose only interactions are with other units within the system.

(2) The state of activation of the system. Different models use different possible values for the activation of units. These may be discrete, binary (0 or 1), or they may have a range of possible numerical values.

(3) Outputs from units. Signals from units to neighbouring units affect the latter. The strength of these effects depends in part upon the activation level of the sending units.

(4) The pattern of connectivity. According to the particular model under consideration, one unit may affect its neighbours in different ways: for example, the effect may be additive or subtractive. Or some inputs from units may be given weightings to increase or decrease their influence in the network. (Note the resemblance between this aspect of the PDP model and a network of interacting neurons.) The points to remember are that units interact, and that the strengths of these interactions may be altered by various weighting functions.

(5) The rule of propagation. In simple terms, this is simply the rule governing interaction or competition between two or more inputs to a unit. If, for example, positive (excitatory) and negative (inhibitory) inputs are allowed to interact in a straightforward manner, then they will cancel when their strengths (or weights) are equal. And so on.

(6) This is an addition to rule 5 above. To decide what will result from an interaction between units we must consider not just the interactions between inputs, as in rule 5, but how their sum or product interacts with the current state of the unit onto which they impinge.

(7) Modifying patterns of connectivity as a function of experience. By this Rumelhart *et al.* mean that there are different ways of changing the structure, activity, or 'knowledge' of a PDP network. Thus for example, new connections may form and old connections may be lost. Or the strengths of connections may be changed through experience. We are now at the core of PDP theory.

(8) Representation of the environment. The environment in which the PDP model must operate is represented across the input units. Typically, the environment is characterized as a set of labelled probabilities.

As stated earlier, the above description has been abstracted from an account by Rumelhart *et al.*, who are pioneers in this field. Their account is much more precise and powerful, but this precision is achieved through the use of mathematical concepts which we have tried to avoid. It must be said, however, that a really full description of PDP models is probably impossible without some recourse to mathematical terminology. Nevertheless, readers who ponder over the definitions listed above should achieve an intuitive understanding of PDP models.

In essence then, a PDP model comprises sets of simple units joined together in a complex network and interacting according to rules of weighting which vary the strengths of their connections. The PDP network can be set a problem in the form of an input pattern. A sucessful solution to the problem comprises a matching or otherwise acceptable output pattern. Obviously, the first 'run' through the PDP model is unlikely to yield the required match or solution; rather, only parts of the output pattern will match the input. How does the model move towards the correct solution? The answer is that the discrepancy between input and output is fed back into the hidden layer of the model. This is done in ways which selectively change the connections to those output units which are correct (or nearly correct) by strengthening (or reinforcing) them according to some predetermined rule. Other connections may be left unchanged or even weakened. In practice this is a more complicated process than we have outlined, and the assessment of the degree of mismatch between the desired and actual outputs may be in terms of large groups of numbers grouped as vectors. Those readers possessing the relevant mathematical knowledge can find an explanation of how vector sums and products can be made to operate on a network in the required manner in Rumelhart and McClelland (1986). (Consult the chapter on the use of the Delta rule.)

There is no supervisory control of the network, no central executive guiding the overall flow of information. And the common distinction between hardware and software vanishes: all units and their connections are essentially 'hardwired', but the connections can be changed, like software. Further, knowledge is held briefly in the units and for longer terms in the connections: there is no special set of places equivalent to the memory addresses of orthodox computers. Knowledge and memory are not explicit, rather they are implicit within each pattern of connections.

It must be pointed out that very few PDP models exist as machines. Generally, they are simulated on digital computers, and it is the designer who typically sets the initial weightings in the connections and gives a model its initial problem or input and its target output. The number of trials to solution forms a measure of the performance of the model.

## The achievements of PDP models

The reader has in fact been presented with an outline of a PDP model earlier in this chapter. In the Marr and Poggio account of stereopsis, the search for corresponding elements in the right- and left-eye images was done by simple processing units joined via excitatory and inhibitory connections. When developed into a distributed network this model successfully avoids false locations, detects true correspondences, and is thus capable of extracting the depth from Julesz stereograms. The model works.

To date, the performance of PDP models has been only modest, but it has been good enough to trigger insights of considerable theoretical importance. PDP models have successfully solved problems in robotics; they have learned to complete patterns; they have formed concepts from sets of features; they have extracted meanings from letter inputs; they have learned to discriminate between pairs of letters irrespective of their orientation; they have learned rules governing the past tense of verbs.

It would not be wise to describe these achievements as simulating successful behaviour; rather, they represent only pieces of behaviour. Equally, if not more significant, however, are the *emergent properties* which PDP models have revealed:

First, PDP models have shown *spontaneous generalization*. A model described by McClelland *et al.* (1986) was set a classification task. It proved capable of selecting a subset of exemplars, all of which were similar, but none of which had all the formal qualities required for category membership. The model had done something like human thinking under conditions of incomplete or imprecise information.

Second, PDP models exhibit *graceful degradation*. When given incomplete or slightly faulty inputs, PDP models need not go wildly astray. They may come close to the correct solution to a problem. They get things approximately right. And when subjected to experimental damage (by removing some units or inter-connections) they do not suddenly fail; rather they show a general coarsening of performance, a gradual deterioration which is strikingly similar to types of brain damage. In fact, the resemblance between 'damaged' networks and neurological syndromes may be even closer than this. One 'damaged' PDP model actually responded to word probes with words which were unlike the targets in form but similar in meaning, a behaviour which in humans is known as Deep Dyslexia.

Third, some PDP models exhibit *default assignment*. Suppose that a model finds a partial solution to a problem by locating one of the correct target items. The pattern of activity which led to this solution will raise the strength of certain units and their connections. At the same time, however, the strengths of *similar* target items will also receive some increments. In this manner, the model can go from what it knows to fill in properties of less well-known but similar target items.

> 'generally speaking, the more similar two things are in respects that we know about, the more likely they are to be similar in respects that we do not, and the [PDP] model implements this heuristic.'
> (McClelland, Rumelhart and Hinton 1986, Chapter 1)

This of course is what humans do all the time. To know that a person votes on the right and is in favour of capital punishment gives one a fair idea of his or her views on blood sports. But how interesting that a PDP model should show hints of similar behaviour as an unexpected, emergent property.

It is of some interest that there are certain characteristics of PDP models which may ultimately throw some light on the neural systems which inspired their creation. For example, the long controversy over whether perception and other forms of behaviour are innate or acquired may disappear if the PDP approach becomes an accepted model of the brain. The reason is that it is not at all difficult to see how certain weighting functions in a network could be present at birth, but with the possibility that they could be modified by later experience. If so, there would still be an interesting set of empirical questions to ask concerning what is in fact present at birth, but the argument between two extreme theoretical positions would be expected to fade away.

PDP models stress the role of interactions between simple units against the idea of specialized centres located in certain parts of the network. Is this why certain parts of the brain, outside the major sensory and motor centres, have no easily demonstrated functions? Damage to the frontal lobes, for example, produces no single clear-cut deficit in performance. More commonly, what is observed is a general coarsening of behaviour, an erosion of general ability. This is very different from what happens when an orthodox computer is damaged, but very similar to the behaviour of damaged PDP networks.

To summarize this short description of PDP models. A network comprising input and output layers joined via a 'hidden' layer of simple interconnected units with alterable strengths of connections can learn to do many highly interesting things. With their marked degree of parallelism PDP models share some of the characteristics of the brain, and can mimic some of its more interesting properties. The implicit nature of the knowledge within such models—what is represented exists as patterns or relationships between units, rather than as explicitly stored rules—together with the interesting emergent properties of the models in action, suggests that the parallel distributed network may replace the orthodox computer as a model of the brain or mind. The one major insight which designers of PDP models have led us to is that *systems using simple components can do very complicated things, provided these components are allowed to compete and interact*. Might this be the way the brain uses *its* simple components?

Not surprisingly, objections have been raised against the PDP approach. Those readers who wish to go further into this debate should consult the papers by Broadbent (1985) and Fodor and Pylyshyn (1988) cited in the reference section.

### Final remarks on Mar's approach

The material above has been included in this chapter in an attempt to counter some of the arguments against the general enterprise of artificial intelligence marshalled by writers such as Dreyfus. Future developments in PDP may well provide us with the right kind of models required by computational theorists. This would go far to vindicate Marr's approach to the problems of visual perception.

We have described Marr's thinking about the nature of explanation in the study of perception. Then his theory of vision was outlined. Some successful applications of the theory were then described in detail to illustrate the style of Marr's work. Next, places where the theory has been shown to be faulty were mentioned. A list was then given of some of the criticisms of the computer model which has typified the AI approach, and from which Marr's work arose, followed by a possible alternative, the arallel distributed processing model (which, of course, Marr knew about and actually used in some of his own work, that on stereopsis for example).

This chapter on Marr's work ends on a note of appreciation. There seems little doubt that whatever the eventual fate of the computational approach generally, or of Marr's contributions in particular, readers of *Vision* have been in contact with a fine mind. The quality of Marr's work should exert a permanent influence upon theorizing in perception. The idea of different levels of explanation of processes is a powerful one. Realizing that a newly discovered neural mechanism can never provide a sufficient explanation of any aspect of perceiving until one has added the computational question, What *function* does the mechanism subserve? is a definite gain in theoretical sophistication. So too is the idea that the real world exerts constraints upon possible solutions by the nervous system to perceptual problems, because this means that theorists will avoid adopting algorithms simply because they work. If Marr's rigorous approach to perception is widely adopted, then some of the mistakes of the past will be avoided. *Vision* is a landmark in the history of perceptual theory.

## NOTES ON CHAPTER 8

The reader should now acquire a copy of Marr's book, *Vision*. This is quite hard going in places but it is hoped that the present chapter will have helped the reader to feel able to tackle Marr in the original: there really is no substitute.

Frisby (1979) is an enjoyable, clear, and extremely well-illustrated exposition of some of the themes within the computational approach. Written by an obvious admirer of Marr, it conveys much of the enthusiasm of workers in this field.

For a critical but balanced evaluation of *Vision* read Morgan's excellent review (1984).

Marr's obituary appeared in *The Times* in December 1980.

# Chapter 9

# Overview and conclusions

Seven very different approaches to theorizing in perception have been discussed. At this point a brief evaluative summary will be given of each approach. This will be followed by a general discussion of the problems facing theorists in the general area of visual perception.

*Psychophysics* (Chapter 2) brought rigour to the study of perception. It is what first brought perceptual research and theory under the general heading of science. The merits of psychophysics are obvious. This is the source of much of the existing knowledge of perception. Psychophysics showed that experimentation is an appropriate way in which to study perception , and that the use of calibrated stimuli, presented under controlled laboratory conditions, can yield important insights into the workings of the visual system. Theories in this area have been based on impressively reliable data, and there has been a steady development of theoretical sophistication and power over the years.

There are, however, drawbacks to the experimental method in general and psychophysics in particular. First, the approach assumes a mechanistic model of the perceiver: stimuli cause responses. The approach has typically ignored those aspects of perception in which perceivers seek out stimulation, in which they actively sample the world. The stimuli used in psychophysics have tended to be artificially simple ones, so that the situation facing the subject or observer is unlikely to match that in which he or she operates most of the time, where stimulation is rich and changing and in which stimuli commonly interact in complex ways.

*The Gestalt theory* (Chapter 3) was based upon the numerous discoveries made by proponents of this approach. A powerful case was made for the dynamic nature of perceiving, the tendency for perception to tend towards coherent, meaningful, simple solutions. The Gestalt demonstrations of the emergent properties of stimulus interactions present an important challenge to all future theories of visual perception. The decision of the Gestalt theorists to concentrate upon strong, reliable effects may provide a lesson for others who wish to make discoveries about perceptual systems. Finally, the emphasis upon the phenomenological aspects of perception, which was such an important part of the Gestalt approach, is something which is still worthy of debate among contemporary theorists: what is it that theories of perception are trying to explain?

The weaknesses of the Gestalt movement lie mainly in the naive approach to theory and explanation. As was shown in Chapter 3, the Gestaltists often mistook description for explanation. Gestalt theory is, for the most part, not predictive. And when the Gestalt theorists attempted some sort of explanation of the effects they had discovered, they made an unfortunate decision in their choice of a brain model and an equally serious mistake over the selected level of explanation.

*Brunswik's probabilistic functionalism* (Chapter 4) properly drew attention to a number of hitherto neglected aspects of visual perception: that the cues upon which organisms depend are not certain but only statistical; that much of behaviour reveals vicarious functioning; that a careful analysis of the environment from a functionalist viewpoint can sometimes suggest answers to apparently intractable problems. Brunswik's arguments against the classical reductionist approach to experimentation are still relevant, and whilst his own suggestions concerning the correlational analysis of representatively designed experiments have not been widely adopted, this too seems to be a fruitful idea: one which modern researchers, armed with better methods of statistical analysis, might well attempt.

The weaknesses of Brunswik's approach are first that he did not give due recognition to the gains which have been made using the orthodox classical methods which he attacked, methods which uncovered phenomena quite as important and interesting as those which he described. Second, the disappointing outcomes to some of Brunswik's own experiments suggest that the superior approach he claimed to have designed may not be as easy to apply as he believed: Brunswik did not appear to learn from his own failures. Finally, Brunswik's many stimulating ideas were not communicated in a manner guaranteed to cause others to give them serious consideration.

*The neurophysiological approach* (Chapter 5) has demonstrated the benefits of combining disciplines. Discovering the neural mechanisms underlying certain perceptual phenomena has been an impressive achievement, one which has confirmed the essential correctness of a number of psychological theories. Knowledge of actual mechanisms has helped some theorists in their work and has also provided a useful constraint upon subsequent speculation. Generally, the work described in Chapter 5 was of the highest scientific and intellectual calibre.

The main drawbacks to the neurophysiological approach to vision are that it tends always towards reductionism and that the language used must remain 'within' the organism. These two drawbacks mean that such an approach can never, of itself, pay proper consideration to the nature of the environment from which stimuli arise—it would be difficult for it to deal with the probabilistic nature of stimuli, for example. Nor can explanations at the level of neurophysiology deal with the subjective nature of seeing, with the phenomenological experiences which reveal the existence of perceptual problems in the first place. Finally, knowing that neural systems have certain properties, revealed during experimental research, does not mean that the usual functions of these systems have been discovered. As Marr demonstrated, knowing that a neural system does something does not tell us why it does it.

*Empiricism* (Chapter 6). A good case can be made for the claim that this has been the most successful approach to the study of perception to date. The contents of almost any general text on perception, or any lecture course, comprise in large part the data, the explanations and the problems unearthed by workers in the empiricist tradition. Empiricism has dominated experimental psychology for a century.

The doubts about the empiricist approach were described in Chapters 6 and 7. Is perception always a constructive process? Are stimuli (or sensations) really so impoverished that the information associated with them needs to be supplemented by memory, reasoning and so on? Do the problems studied under simplified laboratory conditions accurately reflect the situation facing perceivers in the real world? Does perception procede essentially in stages? Can the dualism between the organism and the objective world be defended? Is the digital computer an appropriate model of the perceiver?

*The theory of direct perception* (Chapter 7) arose in part as a reaction against empiricism. One of the chief merits of this relatively new approach is the emphasis it places upon the study of the environment and the richness of light received by the eye of an active perceiver. Another merit has been the attempt to counter the distinction between the organism and its ecology, between what happens 'inside' and 'outside' the perceiver. There is a freshness about the direct perception approach which will sharpen traditional thinking and which may ultimately force some major revisions upon empiricist theories.

The theory of direct perception has its weaknesses. It shows a tendency to underestimate the challenge posed to the visual system by the need to extract invariants. Some problems have been simply defined out of existence. The resonance model has not been developed with sufficient thoroughness and does not seem plausible in neural terms. The centrally important concept of the invariance is often vague and affordances are not easy to predict. Finally, the provocative differences between this approach and more traditional theories of perception are becoming blurred as direct perceptionists turn their attention to the various indirect modes of perceiving which they acknowledge to occur.

*The computational approach* to visual perception (Chapter 8) has produced theories which are at present quite narrow (for example the theory of stereopsis outlined in Chapter 8). These are amongst the most rigorous theories to have emerged in the study of vision. However, where theories arising from within the artificial intelligence paradigm differ from earlier scientific accounts is in the fact that their success points the way towards even more general accounts. To develop this point: consider the successful emergence of a scientific account of colour vision (described in Chapter 5). The combination of evidence from psychology and neurophysiology led to an explanation of both the trichromatic and opponent-process aspects of colour perception. But this successful explanation does not of itself suggest how to tackle, for example, the problems of shape or movement perception. By contrast, the success of one application of Marr's approach does genuinely encourage the belief that this approach may be equally powerful when applied to a new range of phenomena. It is for this reason that it has been important to maintain our distinction between Marr's theories and the artificial intelligence paradigm from which they arose.

There are two reasons why Marr attained a high level of rigour in his work. First are the careful distinctions he drew between the appropriate levels at which a process may be understood: the computational theory, the algorithm and the implementation. Marr argued, convincingly, that many confusions over vision in the past arose because of misunderstandings about which level of explanation was appropriate in a particular context. The second reason why the computational approach has been so rigorous has been the form in which theories about vision advanced by Marr and other workers have been presented. To see whether an idea actually works when written into a computer program is a powerful check against vagueness and imprecision: it is no longer possible to define problems out of existence, nor is it acceptable to explain things by appealing to concepts which (a) remain undefined, such as Prägnanz, or (b) are descriptions rather than explanations, such as perceptual constancy. Everything must be explicit.

One of the arguments against the computational approach has been that it represents a new mentalism; that the computer is an inappropriate model of the perceiver; and that by omitting the phenomenological aspects of perception the theory cannot ever do full justice to its subject matter. As was shown in Chapter 8, the new form of computer modelling represented by the parallel distributed network may be able to meet some of these criticisms, although the mechanistic approach and the inadequate treatment of phenomenology will remain as weaknesses in the computational approach.

To conclude this section it can be asserted that there is as yet no satisfactory general theory of visual perception. No theory adequately handles all possible transactions between the regions of the orientating model described in Chapter 1. For example no theory has adequately united a full analysis of the environment *and* the cognitive aspects of seeing. No general theory has thoroughly incorporated and explained the motor aspects of seeing. The direction of the interactions between the regions is not yet clear: the extent to which perception is determined by stimulation (involving bottom-up processes) or knowledge (bottom-down processes) has not been agreed upon.

It has not been possible in an undergraduate text to attempt to describe all theories of visual perception, although many others have been mentioned in passing. And it must be remembered that some of the issues raised in this book are themselves worthy of book-length treatment. However, in each of the earlier chapters an attempt was made to provide enough references for the interested reader to pursue topics to greater depth. Further reading will quickly reveal the existence of other theories, other styles of explaining visual phenomena. It is hoped that readers will now be sufficiently prepared to classify and evaluate these for themselves.

At this point a few general remarks will be offered concerning the theoretical approaches described in previous sections. What, if anything, can be distilled from them? The first obvious point is that there are too many irreconcilables between the various theorists to permit any general fusion of ideas. The differences, for example, between empiricist views of perception and those of the Gestalt theorists, or between Gibson and Marr, are such that they cannot all be right. Nor does it seem reasonable to suppose that the truth must lie between the rival views: they are too different for that. It is, however, possible to hope that each of the approaches described has merit and that for this reason there may be implications for future theorists. Here are what seem to us to be the best aspects of each approach.

(1) Laboratory studies of the highest quality are now possible. Psychophysics continues to provide psychologists and others with powerful means of obtaining precise data from perceptual experiments. The challenge will be to extend this work to perception under real-world conditions.

(2) The power of neurophysiology will enable certain new models of the brain to be tested, particularly those of the type proposed in parallel distributed processing models. Neurophysiology will provide knowledge useful for those who work at what Marr described as the stage of implementation of a theory.

(3) Brunswik's emphasis on the probabilistic nature of cues should be remembered in future theorizing, together with his pleas for more representative design of psychological experiments.

(4) All subsequent theories will have to recognize and explain those dynamic aspects of perception discovered by Gestalt theorists, in particular the tendency towards Prägnanz and the fact that stimulus interactions produce new emergent properties.

(5) Gibson's work has shown (a) that perceivers are active, not passive, and that sensory and motor systems should be viewed together as integral components of perception; (b) that light may be (usually is) rich in information and that the study of any perceiver should therefore begin with an exhaustive examination of the ecological niche occupied by the perceiver; (c) that the dualism implicit in the animal/environment dichotomy may actually impede our understanding of the nature of perception.

(6) The role of central factors in perception has been most brilliantly demonstrated by workers in the empiricist tradition. The question now is to

discover whether or not all perceiving is like this, or whether there are indeed situations where stimulation can specify objects and events without recourse to additional constructive processes.

(7) To the extent that future theories of visual perception will be self-consciously scientific, they may be guided by the clarity and power of Marr's analysis of what it takes to understand any process. The standards Marr set for clarity and explicitness should serve as a model for theorists in the future.

Those seem to be the safest and best conclusions arising from any comparison of the selection of theoretical approaches outlined in this book. We shall return to some of these conclusions during the following sections which contain some further general remarks on theorizing.

The remainder of this chapter is in four sections. First, an attempt will be made to show the challenge offered by visual perception; why it can be expected to continue to fascinate researchers and theorists. Then a list will be given of some of the achievements to date—the gains which have been made because some theorists have attempted to develop general theories of the type described in previous chapters. We shall then repeat the claim that there has not yet been a satisfactory theory of vision, and, in the third section will attempt to explain this by describing some of the problems facing theorists in this area. Finally, some speculations will be offered concerning the next generation of theories of visual perception.

## THE CHALLENGE OF VISION

The theme of this book is seeing and attempts to explain it. But seeing is part of the daily life of anyone who can read this book. We are as familiar with seeing as with anything; so familiar that it is easy to overlook what an achievement seeing represents. Underlying this awareness of a solid, coherent world are the activities of many neurons—saline-filled tubes—and that is all. How do they do it? That is the ultimate question, but it is unlikely to be answered for a very long time.

There are of course many other important problems facing contemporary theorists and fortunately these are of a rather more tractable nature. They are, however, so difficult that they will probably occupy the attentions of researchers for many years to come. Four examples will prove this point.

### What is meant by 'seeing'?

In December 1959, a fifty-two year old man, described as the patient S.B., underwent a corneal graft operation to restore his vision. What is important about this event is that S.B. had been blind for more than 50 years. He had some sight as an infant (how much is not known with certainty) then, following a neglected eye infection at around the age of ten months, he was admitted to an institution for the blind, where he received the whole of his academic and technical education. Shortly after the successful operation S.B. was examined by two psychologists (Gregory and Wallace, 1963), who later took him on a visit to the London Science Museum where he was shown a lathe:

> 'We led him to the glass case, which was closed, and asked him to tell us what was in it. He was quite unable to say anything about it, except that he thought the nearest part was a handle. (He pointed to the handle of the transverse feed.) He complained that he could not see the cutting edge or the metal being worked, or anything else about it, and appeared rather agitated. We then asked a Museum Attendant for the case to be opened, and S.B. was allowed to touch the lathe. The result was startling; he ran his hands deftly over the the machine, touching first the transverse feed handle and confidently naming it as "a handle", and then on to the saddle, the bed and the head-stock of the lathe. He ran his hands eagerly over the lathe, with his eyes shut. Then he stood back a little and opened his eyes and said: "Now that I've felt it I can see".'
>
> (Gregory and Wallace, 1963, p.33)

What did S.B. mean by 'see'? The visual image of the lathe remained the same, but something must have changed in S.B.'s head. What was it? In what way could he *not* see before using his sense of touch? Was the change in S.B.'s visual perception akin to Fodor and Pylyshyn's (1981) distinction between *merely* seeing the Pole Star and seeing it *as* the Pole Star? Questions surely for a general theory of visual perception.

## The different aspects of vision

The term vision embraces many aspects of experience. For example, we can see shape, size, colour, texture, depth, and movement. As has been shown in previous chapters, there are specific theories attempting to explain each of these. But vision is, after all, one single sense. All seeing begins at the retina and continues in the brain. To go blind is to lose all aspects of sight. Here is another major challenge for theorists: to subsume all aspects of seeing under a single general theory.

## Different eyes

Reference has been made throughout this book to 'the eye' and 'the visual system'. In fact, apart from a few references to vision in monkeys and cats, all the main discussions have been about the human eye and the human visual system. But there are millions of different eyes. Vision in insects, for example, is based upon a different set of structures from those of any vertebrate, and visual information goes to a very different form of central nervous system. At present, we can only make a few educated guesses at what it must be like to see as a fish, a bird, or a flea. Even the lives of our pets remain deeply mysterious. It will be a major task to discover what it is that all visual systems have in common.

## Building seeing machines

There is one activity that makes visual research different from that in other sensory areas, and almost unique in science generally. One of the goals of a growing number of researchers is to understand vision and then build a seeing machine. To date, this has inspired some highly original and interesting work. And it has also provided a valuable check upon loose speculation and the imprecise analyis of problems.

> 'The first great revelation was that the problems are difficult. Of course, these days this fact is a commonplace. But in the 1960s almost no one realized that machine vision was difficult. The field had to go through the same experience as the machine translation field did in its fiascos of the 1950s before it was at last realized that here were some problems that had to be taken seriously. The reason for this misperception is that we humans are ourselves so good at vision.'
>
> (Marr, 1982, p.16)

In other words, building a seeing machine is going to be hard work, not least because there are some formidable philosophical problems associated with this whole enterprise which raise doubts as to its feasibility. These will be mentioned later. For now, it is sufficient to say that here is a real goal for general theorists. But if it can be attained and a machine becomes able to do enough to make us say that it can see, then the builders may be in the unique position of knowing with certainty that some of their ideas on vision are correct. The reader will not be surprised to learn that this is a research area of vast commercial potential. Robots able to discriminate quickly and accurately between objects in the environment would have immense value. The implications of machine vision are so important that this is one area where researchers are unlikely ever to be short of funds.

Of course, no existing theory has come close to meeting any of these challenges. They were included at the start simply to show what fascinating challenges they are, fascinating enough, surely, to continue to attract ingenious and creative people into visual research.

## SOME OF THE GAINS MADE DURING THE SEARCH FOR GENERAL THEORIES

General theories of visual perception have done two of the things expected of all scientific theories: they have often converted masses of data into manageable forms; and they have attempted to explain things. In Chapter 2 on psychophysics, for example, it was shown how early work on thresholds led to Weber's Law. Anyone who knows this law has an overall view of several hundred sensory threshold results, and this is invaluable. In the same area, the theory of signal detection explains the pattern of above-chance guessing which is commonly found in threshold tasks. Here are two instances of real gains arising as a result of forming general theories, and numerous other examples are contained in earlier chapters of this book. Here now are some more specific achievements.

**Many general properties of vision have been discovered**

For example, it is one thing to know that subjects tend to see objects as the same size irrespective of distance, and to be able to measure the magnitude of this effect. It became even more interesting when it was realized that shape perception also tends to veridicality. But when the same effect became apparent in colour perception it was clear that here was a general characteristic of visual perception. (The realization that a comparable effect can occur with loudness suggests that the effect is even more general.) However, to recognize the fact that perceptual constancy is a general characteristic of vision requires a theory, for data from different experiments are merely data: something more is required before their more general significance can be recognized, and that something is a theory (in this case it was the Gestalt theory).

Similarly, once the finding that vision can close gaps in sensory inputs has been erected into a theoretical principle, it is but a short step to the assertion that vision is knowledge-based. This in turn opens up many possibilities for new research and the reinterpretation of existing data.

All the theories described in this book have become broader with time. They have sought to embrace increasingly varied sets of phenomena. For example, Gibson's demonstration of the role of invariants in the perception of simple geometric shapes has been extended to include the match between the cardioidal strain transformation and the ageing of the human face. Even further from the original demonstration is the discovery of invariants in sound patterns which can specify the likelihood of collision. But would sound patterns have been examined for this property prior to Gibson's theory?

**The range of application of theories has broadened**

For example, the theory of signal detection arose as a way of thinking about the behaviour of an observer attempting to detect weak signals against a noisy background. It was a new theory in psychophysics. But within a few years of the announcement of the theory of signal detection, the theory had been used to explain the role of acupuncture in the treatment of pain: whether the technique changes the subjective intensity of pain, or only willingness to to report it. This is more than a clever extension of an idea: TSD offered a different way of looking at pain behaviour, a new way of measuring pain responsiveness, and techniques for analysing the psychophysical data. It was a genuine extrapolation from a theory.

In a similar manner, the empiricist/constructivist approach convinced many that here was a theory which could account for many of the dynamic aspects of perception, for example the ability of perceivers to go beyond the sensory evidence—the closing of gaps, the correct identification of ambiguous stimuli through the use of context, and many other tendencies which have been described in Chapter 6. But then an extrapolation of the same theory to the geometric illusions allowed Gregory to suggest 'inappropriate constancy scaling' as a possible explanation of these strange phenomena.

## Theories have led to improvements in technique

Here the influences may operate in two directions: techniques can also influence theory. Typically, however, when a new theory appears it will often popularize new techniques of experimentation and/or data analyis. Consider the history of psychophysical theories. Fechner and all psychophysicists since him knew that subjects make errors when detecting faint signals. As was shown in Chapter 2, these errors can be simple misses, when the subject simply fails to report the signal, or they can be 'false positives' when the subject says that a signal is present when it is not. But how to allow for these false positives during threshold measurement? One answer is to encourage subjects to maintain a low false positive rate and then adjust their scores whenever false positives appear in the data: the classical correction for guessing.

The theory of signal detection changed all that. By distinguishing between signal present/signal absent trials and between hits, misses and false positives, data could be collected in a much more revealing way. Add to this the subject's assessment of his or her confidence in any judgement and one achieves some very informative data. But the analysis of these data requires the use of tables of the ordinates of the normal curve, together with two new measures: $d'$, a measure of sensitivity, and beta, a measure of the position of the subject's criterion stated in units based on ordinates of the normal curve. None of this was available to Fechner. In fact, $d'$ and beta were created as quantifying statistics within the new theory. Once available, however, they started to be widely used by psychologists in a variety of situations. The theory of signal detection came to exert a powerful influence upon research in the 1960s and 70s, partly as a result of the new techniques conceived within this theoretical framework.

## Theories have become more precise and scientific

Two of the hallmarks of any scientific theory are that its terms are precisely defined and that the theory is testable and therefore falsifiable. Of course not everyone agrees that the best solution to problems in psychology will always be scientific ones, a point which will be returned to later. For the moment we shall assume that it is in fact desirable for theories of perception to be as scientific as possible.

If this assumption is agreed upon then it can be claimed that there has been real progress in theorizing. Consider, for example, the Gestalt theory (Chapter 3). Certain key terms within the theory lacked precise operational definition. For example, the concept of Prägnanz was described in a manner which made it seem very interesting and important, with many convincing illustrations. But how did one measure it? How could one be sure that some novel stimulus array would show high or low Prägnanz? Was Prägnanz a descriptive shorthand for such factors as balance, simplicity and symmetry, or was it an explanatory concept: things being seen as coherent wholes *because* they had high Prägnanz?

In another part of Gestalt theory dynamic brain forces were stated to be the underlying causes of the Gestalt laws. But how could these forces ever be measured or assessed by *psychological* methods? Köhler had moved the central explanatory part of a psychological theory beyond the reach of experimental psychologists. (Tests were eventually made, and are described in Chapter 3, but these required techniques from another discipline.)

Brunswik wrote of the 'stupidity of the senses', by which he meant the inability to compensate for visual illusions once one knows the details of their construction. But to what extent did he claim this as a general principle? There are, after all, numerous examples (some of which would have been known to Brunswik) showing that perceivers can be very flexible in their behaviour: the recovery from mild sensory distortion, the ability to reinterpret ambiguous patterns, or to extract meaning from corrupted or noisy displays. Where does 'stupidity' begin and end?

In contrast more modern theories of visual perception are much more precise. Gibson made important use of the term 'optic flow' in his theory. More recent work has shown possible constraints upon what optic flow can in fact specify (it doesn't indicate the point of collision if a surface is approached with the head slightly averted, for example). And Gibson seriously underestimated the difficulty of extracting the higher-order invariants from optic flow (see Marr, 1982, p.212). Nevertheless, there was never any doubt over what Gibson actually meant by the term 'optic flow', it was well-defined.

By the time Marr's computational theory of vision was published, even higher standards of precision had been reached. One of Marr's enduring contributions will probably be the rigour which he introduced into the activity of theory construction. We have already described Marr's distinctions between the computational theory, the algorithm, and the implementation. But the whole of *Vision* is an object lesson in precision and clarity, attributes which owe much to the discipline required when converting ideas into working computer programs.

## OBSTACLES TO GENERAL THEORIES OF VISUAL PERCEPTIONS

Those four examples serve to support the claim that real progress has been made. Nevertheless, there is still no good general theory of vision. We shall now attempt to explain why this is so by describing some of the important obstacles to explanation in this area.

First, it must be accepted that vision must be very complicated indeed. Recognizing this fact will make the next section seem less negative and pessimistic. Think of the things which vision can do. Reflect on the last time you drove or were driven down a motorway on a wet night. That you are alive to tell the tale says a lot about vision: it provides the basis for judgements of speed and distance under difficult conditions, for moving in and out of lanes, steering half a ton of steel between and around hazards. All this whilst thinking about the depth induced by random-dot stereograms. Or think of being forced to sit at the end of a row in a crowded cinema: how distorted the screen seems at first, but how quickly it comes to appear normal. Then think about walking down the cinema steps without consciously looking at them.

All the phenomena described in this book reinforce the conclusion that vision is remarkable. And it has defeated some of the best thinkers of their time. There have been few better scientists than Helmholtz, and he left many problems unsolved. The Gestaltists were clever and creative researchers, but their theory is flawed. Marr has been described as a genius, and yet some aspects of his work have been shown to be wrong. Three of the formidable problems facing any who search for general theories of visual perception will now be described.

### Three major problems for visual theories

#### The definition of a stimulus

It is manifestly true that the job of vision is to inform us of things and events in the external world. The medium by which information is carried to the eye is, of course, light. Sometimes light is informative, sometimes not. When it is informative the term 'stimulus' tends to be applied. It is therefore clearly desirable, when constructing theories, to be able to define, measure and, where necessary, control stimuli. But what *is* a stimulus?

This is one of those problems which gets harder the more one thinks about it. And there is a noticeable lack of agreement between theorists over this basic issue which has also exercised many philosophers.

A sensible aim would be to try to describe any stimulus in terms of its physical characteristics—this would seem to be a natural starting point for any scientific endeavour. After all, part of the success of chemistry and physics, at least in the early days of those subjects, lay in the ability to define and measure such basic entities as atoms and molecules. Is it likely that a comparable degree of objectivity and precision over stimuli will eventually be achieved ? The answer is, probably not. Here are some reasons why.

Imagine that one is a subject in a psycho-physiological experiment. Electrodes have been attached to the back of the head in order to monitor some of the activity of the visual cortex. Every half second a flash of light is delivered to the eye. Then, without warning, the sequence is broken by omitting one of the flashes. What happens? Well, one would notice the gap—it would capture the attention as a novel *event*. And the subsequent renewal of vigour in the electrical responding of the visual cortex would confirm this introspection. Now, was the missing flash a stimulus? It surely possesses many of the characteristics we would wish to assign to stimuli on commonsense grounds. But can it be measured? No, of course not, for the missing light has no physical existence: it is something which might have occurred but did not—the dog that failed to bark in the night.

An equally important phenomenon has been described in the account of Gestalt theory (Chapter 2): sources of stimulation interact to yield novel perceptions. In the phi-phenomenon, for example, the seen movement cannot be explained or predicted from a description of either of the pair of inducing lights—it depends upon their spatial and temporal *relationships*. At the heart of the Gestalt theory is the axiom that wholes are more than the sum of their parts, and Gestalt publications bristle with demonstrations of this effect, although the Gestaltists were never able to offer quantitative data on this point.

Thus it seems certain that any description of a stimulus in isolation will be prove to be inadequate and that it will usually be necessary to consider other stimuli which (a) might have been present, or (b) are present and capable of interacting with the original stimulus.

Another difficulty arises from the fact that stimulus definition is theory-dependent. Psychophysicists would not describe patterns in terms of their Fourier transforms unless they believed that the visual system also performed such analyses. If it is assumed that perceptions are hypotheses, then a stimulus is something which can stand as evidence against which these can be tested: we have described the danger of infinite regress in this way of thinking. In the theory of signal detection, purely internal events can be responded to as if they arose from external causes, so that the final definition of a stimulus becomes some above-criterion subjective event. Gibson objected to any definition of a stimulus as a momentary happening, something frozen in time. Instead, he considered that that which endured or was invariant over change was the basis for a given percept. Gibson also emphasized that activity on the part of the perceiver was a source of stimulation, although it is not always easy to see how such stimulation could be measured. Marr's focus is upon changes in the visual image. Although he acknowledges that Gestalt-type interactions occur, his theory nevertheless concentrates upon the analysis and processing of separate parts of the image: none of his algorithms deals specifically with whole/part effects, nor is it easy to see how any could. The differences between these theoretical approaches go some way towards explaining why there is no single definition of a stimulus.

## The appropriate level of explanation

At issue here is the level at which visual phenomena should be described and explained. It was pointed out in Chapter 5 that there have always been those who prefer to explain perceptual phenomena in terms of neural mechanisms rather than psychological constructs. This form of reductionism has yielded important insights into the nature of perception and the interaction between the disciplines of experimental psychology and neurophysiology has been a fruitful one. But, as was argued in Chapter 5, there is a fundamental flaw in the idea that the eventual explanation of perception will be physiological: namely that neurophysiology remains 'inside' the organism, whilst perception involves the external world. Neural events may be isolated entities, but stimuli arise from within a context, a context which shapes our conscious experience. A general theory of vision will have to respect this fact, and this means that the language of such a theory is more likely to be psychological than physiological.

However, even if the emphasis in the future is away from physiological reductionism, there will still be a problem over the best level at which to write a theory. Assumptions of similarity between humans and computers led to computational theories. Recognition of certain dynamic properties of vision encouraged thinking in terms of vectors and fields. Those who claim that phenomenal experience must be accounted for by theories will write in the appropriate language. And anyone wishing to theorize only at the most formal and abstract level will adopt the language of mathematics. It is a sobering thought that, years from now, a general theory of vision may indeed be so abstract and complex that few workers now alive would be able to understand it. But it is as yet unclear what level of explanation will be adopted in such a theory.

## The place of subjective experience in perceptual theory

Suppose that there was a respected general theory of visual perception, a theory which sucessfully handled the main phemonena of colour, shape, depth, motion, and so on. Would the theory be limited to human perception? Many theorists have clearly believed that their work could embrace non-human species: the Gestalt theorists demonstrated some of their effects in apes and chickens; Brunswik studied probability matching in rats; direct perceptionists talk about different species in different ecological niches; Marr speculates about the landing behaviour of the house fly; cortical edge detectors were first demonstrated in cats. However, although much is known about vision in a few non-human species, we have no way of understanding the quality of their conscious experiences, if any. We cannot know what it must be like to see as a fly.

We are, however, intimately aware of our own consciousness, of what seeing is like 'from the inside'. In actual research it is possible to adopt a tough-minded, behaviourist approach to perception, measuring human and animal performance in similar ways. There is then no place for introspection, only controlled, measurable responses. But where do the researchers' ideas come from, if not from their own subjective experiences? The Purkinje shift—changes in the relative brightness of blue objects with changing illumination—can be demonstrated via the objective operant behaviour of humans or animals. But why should anyone think to do so, unless they had *noticed* the effect (Purkinje was lying in bed when he noticed it, off colour perhaps)? And should perceptionists deliberately omit from their theories that which is part of their daily experience?

Discussions such as this may be dismissed as relevant only to the origins of scientific theories, not to the logic of the theories themselves. After all, it could be argued, much has been learned about the behaviour of honey bees without anyone knowing what it is like to use the sun's position in a signalling dance. And one of the most powerful binocular illusions—Pulfrich's Pendulum—was discovered by a one-eyed man. But, for example, would a purely objective research into colour vision ever have discovered that certain colour combinations are very unpleasant, or that some colours appear warm, others cold, or that some people hear coloured sounds?

It is equally important that experience also tells us what does *not* happen during perception. For instance, our noses are constantly in view but not seen: no formal account of a visual experiment ever includes the nose in a description of the stimulus array—it doesn't need to, for noses are not important in seeing, *and it is subjective experience which tells us this*. We can learn to see that objects occupy less of the visual field when they recede from us (and artists must be able to do this), but phenomenally they remain the same size. Which of these two ways of perceiving the objects should the theorist be concerned with?

The strongest claims for the inclusion of subjective experience in accounts of perception have been made by modern phenomenologists. Some of these claims were listed in the descriptions of Dreyfus's attacks on the classical computer model of the mind (Chapter 6). To recapitulate: modern phenomenologists insist that our perception of, say, a house, transcends any limited vantage point: we 'see' the volume of the house, its solidity, even when the only visible aspect is the front. Our phenomenal experience includes the knowledge that we are 'inside' our bodies. We know what things would look like from alternative vantage points.

The problem of conscious experience has now been alluded to several times in this book. It is, however, so important that one final example must be presented. We have all had the experience of perceiving some thing or event with unusual clarity. At its most dramatic this happens when we witness a violent, sudden accident. But there are other times when one simply feels calm or quiet and yet strangely attentive. It is as if one has achieved a new sharpness of focus in which things are seen as if for the first time.

Developing a scientific account of seeing is very different from the creation of an original work of art; the two activities attract different personalities motivated by different goals. But when it comes to describing the more elusive aspects of experience, who is to say that the artist is not the better analyst? Here is a short sequence from a twentieth-century novel. After reading it do you not agree that it is reminding us of what it is like to perceive something intensely; that the description is as interesting in its way as anything to be found in more scientific accounts?

Two men are making a coffin:

'The lantern sits on a stump. Rusted, grease-fouled, its cracked chimney smeared on one side with a soaring smudge of soot, it sheds a feeble and sultry glare upon the trestles and the boards and the adjacent earth. Upon the dark ground the chips look like random smears of soft pale paint on a black canvas. The boards look like long smooth tatters torn from the flat darkness and turned backside out.

Cash labours about the trestles, moving back and forth, lifting and placing the planks with long clattering reverberations in the dead air as though he were lifting and dropping them at the bottom of an invisible well, the sounds ceasing without departing, as if any movement might dislodge them from the immediate air in reverberant repetition. He saws again, his elbow flashing slowly, a thin thread of fire running along the edge of the saw, lost and recovered at the top and bottom of each stroke in unbroken elongation, so that the saw appears to be six feet long, into and out of pa's shabby and aimless silhouette ...

The air smells like sulphur. Upon the impalpable plane of it their shadows fall as upon a wall, as though like sound they had not gone very far away in falling but had merely congealed for a moment, immediate and musing'

(William Faulkner, *As I Lay Dying*)

Faulkner has used his formidable powers of description to put into words something of the essence of perceiving. In a sense, we are there with him, watching this strange scene. And the ways in which he has noticed things—the muffled sounds, the subtle gradations of light and shade—remind us that there is lot to the business of perceiving, and a long way to go before it is understood. Will computer simulations ever do justice to these aspects of awareness? Can they be captured in scientific accounts of perception? It will be fascinating to see how these formidable problems are approached in the future.

## The evolutionary background to human vision

About six million years ago the earliest humanoids split from the apes. Within another million years our ancestors had become fully bipedal. Then, in the last two million years, the human brain developed more rapidly than any other organ in evolutionary history. It was during these last two million years that the human visual system attained its present form and, presumably, its remarkable range of functions.

But the environment which exerted the selective pressures that shaped the evolution of perception was very different from that which most of us inhabit today. Now our daily lives bring us into regular contact with signs and symbols. We live in a built environment—a place of sharp edges, flat surfaces and artificial lighting. Our bodies have a natural speed across two-dimensional surfaces of four or five miles per hour but are frequently moved passively through three dimensions at speeds one hundred times greater than this. There are many highly unnatural environments.

Although this question has been raised earlier, it is worth just one last mention: can we expect a single theory to explain perception of the natural *and* the artificial world? That is to say, there may be one set of mechanisms (describable by one set of laws) which will ensure that, for example singleness of vision and stereoscopic fusion are achieved in the lit environment; but there can be no such inbuilt mechanism to allow us to fly in clouds. That is something which we can learn to do, provided we have access to the right instruments. Instrument flying undoubtedly involves perception as well as skill, but is it the same sort of perception as, say, normal stereopsis? If not, where is the dividing line to be drawn?

As has been shown in previous chapters, the extent to which a perceptual theorist remains aware of the evolutionary background to vision determines, in part, those things which are emphasized in his or her theory. R. L. Gregory is much more concerned to explain illusions than is J. J. Gibson, who regards these as arising from essentially unnatural patterns of stimulation. It is almost a truism that the more cognitive a theorist is, the greater will be the emphasis upon those things over which we cognate: pictures, puzzles, words, lists. But is seeing a word the same as seeing a face? Do we 'read' these two types of pattern in the same manner? This leads naturally to a much larger question as to which sets of phenomena—the natural or the artificial and symbolic—should be researched. Which offers the greater chance of success? This is clearly an issue over which there will continue to be much controversy.

## THEORIES AND THE FUTURE

Futurology is not to everyone's taste. It is certainly not to the author's. And yet the reader who has come this far has a right to some sort of personal statement; after such a lengthy attempt to be dispassionate and fair, it seems only right to offer some views on theories of visual perception. This should not be read as a prediction concerning 'the' final theory of vision—nobody can be expected to know what form such a theory will take—rather, it is a guess concerning the next important general accounts of visual perception, the future equivalents of something as important in their way as was the Gestalt theory. Here are eight assertions. They should be read with an appropriate degree of scepticism.

### Rivalry will continue between theories

This claim is reinforced by many of the points listed below. It is going to be very difficult, if not impossible, to reconcile a scientific account of perception (possibly based on a computer model) with the claims of phenomenologists. The need to describe and explain human awareness can be expected to form the ground for much future debate among theorists.

### The phenomenological component of theories will grow

This is predicted simply on the basis of a probable future swing away from the reductionist, mechanist approach that has dominated Western psychology this century.

### General theories will be mainly concerned to explain human perception

It will be possible to explain some aspects of perception in other species, of course. Much is already known about, say, vision in insects. But most species are simply too different from us in structure and life-style for their perceptions ever to be predicted from a human theory. We know how bats navigate, but cannot imagine their phenomenal world.

### Future theories will include more thorough analyses of the environment

It seems certain that the successes of direct perception and the computational approach, both of which owe much to precise analysis of the nature of the physical world, will inspire others to extend this type of work.

### Theories will have a functional bias

To repeat Jung's phrase, 'We are of an immense age'. As an increasing effort is made to plot the evolutionary background from which humans emerged, rapid gains in knowledge seem almost inevitable. Recent advances in evolutionary theory have explained such apparently baffling problems as the Panda's sixth finger (see Gould, 1980, to experience the excitement of this type of research). Can we not expect similar researches to uncover the functional significance of, for example, the human tendency to see vertical lines as longer than physically equal horizontal ones; why faces with large pupils strike us as more attractive; or why the human visual system is modifiable only during the first few months of life?

**Perceptionists will continue to be influenced by technical developments**

Those who have not experienced the effects of some major new technique in perceptual research may find it hard to believe what an impact these can have on ways of thinking. For example, it was customary until recently to describe the performance of the eye in terms of (a) its acuity, (b) its responses to intensity. The advent of visual gratings and the associated idea of spatial frequency analyis, tuned spatial frequency channels and the contrast sensitivity function changed our ideas about these aspects of vision completely. This is a very familiar story in psychological research and could be illustrated by many more examples. The point is that psychologists and physiologists are not the only people who are thinking about problems of seeing: engineers, physicists, zoologists and mathematicians, can all claim a legitimate interest in the problem. As more and more of their techniques are adopted, the impact of these other disciplines on perceptual theory and research can be expected to become increasingly dramatic.

**Models in perceptual theory**

This relates to the last point and is too obvious to need stressing. We have already shown how available models determine psychological thinking. As new and more powerful computer systems emerge, these will inevitably be used as models of the brain by many psychologists.

**Simulation will become increasingly common**

Thirty years ago very few perceptionists had access to computers; now they are to be found in every laboratory. It would be hard to exaggerate the impact of these remarkable machines in experimental psychology. That they have provided a very seductive model of the perceiver has been discussed at some length in earlier chapters. Computers have also changed the ways in which actual experiments are conducted. For example, it is no longer necessary always to specify the ordering of stimulus presentations at the start of an experiment. Because the computer can react much faster than any experimenter, the subject's performance can be assessed from trial to trial, and subsequent presentations can be modified accordingly. As an example of the possibilities afforded by this speed and power, consider the dynamic 'staircase' tracking procedures now used in the determination of sensory thresholds (Chapter 2). Or those experiments (described in Chapter 7) in which stimulus presentations are made at precise intervals following the initiation of eye movements. Such work would have been impossible prior to the advent of computer-controlled displays.

There is, however, another way in which computers are having an impact on perceptual research and theorizing, and this is their ability to simulate processes. In the past, a typical sequence would be along these lines: someone has an idea—a possible explanation of some perceptual phenomenon, a critical test of a controversial theory, or simply a hunch about how something comes about. An experiment is designed, equipment built, subjects recruited. Some weeks or months later the data are ready for analysis. Interesting results may or may not be found and the experiment repeated with certain modifications, and so on. This is slow, inefficient, and often frustrating work—ask any experimenter. It is often realized, half way through an experiment, that something is wrong, that things could have been done in a different way, but the rules of experimentation and the demands of statistical analysis mean that the experiment must be run to the end. These are the major problems: the minor ones are that subjects don't turn up, mothers of young infants change their minds, animal research is discouraged.

But some ideas about perception can be tested, at least in the first place, without using subjects at all: a computer will suffice. What is required of course is complete clarity of thought. Each and every part of the hypothetical process which it is desired to simulate must be programmed. But this can be a valuable discipline: it is no longer possible to be vague, to employ undefined terms; everything must be made explicit for the computer. Once started, the simulation will be run at high speed, and the input variables can be modified at will. In this way, several thousand hours of possible experimentation can be compressed into a few days. We have described one famous use of simulation to test a perceptual hypothesis in Chapter 8, when the Marr–Poggio model of stereopsis was outlined. The success of this and other recent simulations is a clear pointer to the future.

That is the last speculation. One thing is certain, however, and that is that vision will always fascinate. The visual sense is, above all, the channel through which curiosity becomes manifest. Think for example of the crowds which gather to see the rare artefacts of other civilizations: Tutenkhanem's mask, the horses of ancient China. Watch people at sporting events, in the cinema, in front of television sets. Ask why it is that every well-known beauty spot has a continual stream of visitors, gazing out across the view.

There has as yet been no satisfactory general theory to explain how we see the world, none that has been able to satisfy all demands of breadth, precision and falsifiability which are required of good theories. Perhaps this chapter has helped to explain why. But we should not be disheartened: visual perception utilizes not only the eye—which is a structure of formidable complexity—but the brain: ten thousand million cells interacting in ways as yet not understood. Underlying our experience of seeing is the most complicated system ever known. Explaining vision will not happen tomorrow, but there are many interesting things to do in the meantime.

## NOTES ON CHAPTER 9

Some of the issues addressed in this chapter are clearly philosophical. Readers wishing to know more about theory, explanation and the philosophical problems associated with reductionism and the computer metaphor of the mind should start by reading the following: Chalmers (1982), Dreyfus (1972), and Russell (1984). For somewhat more advanced discussions of Artificial Intelligence and the computer metaphor see Dreyfus and Dreyfus (1985) and Winograd and Flores (1986).

Contemporary editions of the journal *Behavioural and Brain Sciences* should be watched for interesting debates on some of the issues raised in this chapter.

# Chapter 10

# Some problems

This book has been about explanation in the history of visual research; its subject matter is theory. Throughout the book every effort has been made to relate theoretical material to some of the phenomena of visual perception. There were three reasons for this. First, by relating a theory to the phenomena which it was designed to handle, it should have been easier for the reader to arrive at an independent judgement of its plausibility. Second, this is a good way of keeping one's feet on the ground: no matter how elegant the ideas in a theory, the real test is how well it deals with the facts. Finally, by describing phenomena as clearly and simply as possible it was hoped that this would assist those who have not undertaken a formal course of study in perception. If this last attempt has been successful, then such readers will now know something about the most important discoveries in vision research of the past hundred years.

This is the place to admit that something has been omitted from the previous chapters. Few researchers in perception sit down calmly and decide that they are about to write a new theory. It just isn't like this. Much of the best perceptual research has arisen out of feelings of curiosity. For the truth about vision is that the phenomena have a compelling fascination. The author has shown the classic illusions to thousands of students over the years, and yet these strange effects are as compelling to him now as on the day he first saw them. And there are few experiences to rival that of being totally mystified by some powerful, reliable, but entirely baffling phenomenon. And those (admittedly rare) occasions when one has oneself arrived at a satisfying explanation or has even stumbled onto something quite new, are worth a long wait.

To appreciate how hard it is to theorize in perception, tackle a good problem. Knowing what one doesn't know is itself valuable knowledge. In this last chapter the reader will be presented with some puzzles, any of which would be well worth solving. Some of the investigations to be outlined will require apparatus, but this can usually be extremely simple (well within the capabilities of the average do-it-yourself enthusiast, for example). Most of the problems to be described have attracted some research interest, but none has been adequately solved. Where possible, references will be given to one or more publications to facilitate a search of the relevant literature. Thinking about these problems may add a new dimension to the reader's understanding of the theories outlined in this text. Just as importantly, it should convey some of the excitement that comes from hunting for explanations of perceptual phenomena.

## PERSISTENT AFTER-EFFECTS

The relevant phenomenon can be induced in two ways. First, using two colour displays, one of red and black stripes, the other green and black. Load each of a pair of slide projectors with a black and white striped transparency, one with the stripes horizontal, the other vertical. Ten pairs of stripes per slide is a good number to use. Then place a red filter over the front end of one projector and a green one over the other. On the first trial, act as your own subject. Switch on one of the projectors, say the one showing vertical green stripes, and look at the display (in a dimly lit room) for one minute. Then change to the other display and look at the horizontal red stripes for a minute. Keep doing this for about six trials per slide.

When the inducing trials are over take off the colour filters and notice what happens when looking first at vertical black and white stripes and then at horizontal black and white stripes. If the inducing trials were correctly arranged two after-effects will be seen: the vertical and horizontal displays will each take on a coloured appearance, the colour being the complementary of the original inducing colour. Note, however, that *the colour effects are orientation-specific*: until stripes in the correct orientation are displayed the relevant after-effect is not experienced. This effect has become a famous problem in psychology and it is named the McCollough effect after its discoverer, Celeste McCollough.

Next, for those who lack the projection system required for the McCollough effect, here is an important alternative. Cut out a white cardboard or plastic disc at least 30 cm (12 in) in diameter. Draw on it a black spiral, starting at the centre and spreading outward (Figure 10.1). Mount this on an old record player held vertically. Now spin the disc at 33 rpm and stare at the centre for about a minute. Stop the rotation and look at the spiral. It will appear to move in the opposite direction to the original rotation.

Those were two ways of inducing well-known after-effects. Here is the research problem. If the inducing periods are dramatically increased, to about thirty minutes for the McCollough effect and fifteen minutes for the Spiral after-effect, then the effects can persist for *hours, or even days*. One can trigger them simply by looking at black and white stripes in the relevant orientations, or by looking again at a stationary spiral. But during the interval between the induction and the test many hours later, one's perceptions are quite normal— there are no hints of after-effects when looking at every-day objects. What is happening? How is the visual system able to store these biases without them appearing in consciousness until the moment of re-induction? Why are they so situation-specific? Anyone who can solve these problems will have made a contribution to perceptual theory.

*References*: McCollough (1965), Skowbo, Timney, Gentry and Morant (1975).

Figure 10.1   An Archimedes spiral

## INTER-OCULAR ERASURE

The apparatus required is a simple stereoscope. Look into the instrument and estimate, roughly, the size of each eye's field of view. Cut a piece of white graph paper of a size which fills the left eye field of view in the stereoscope. In front of the other eye place a small pattern in the centre of a piece of white card: a postage stamp is ideal.

Look into the stereoscope. The stamp will appear to be floating in the middle of the graph paper. Now take a pencil or pen and hold it horizontally above the graph paper. Keep looking into the stereoscope, concentrating upon the stamp as the pen is moved slowly across the graph paper. You will find that *the moving image of the pen in one eye erases the image of the pattern in the other*. But can this be due to simple retinal inhibition if the erasure is coming from the other eye? What is happening?

*Reference*: Grindley and Townsend (1965).

## CONTOURS FROM RANDOM DOT PATTERNS

Look at the pair of Julesz random-dot stereograms shown in Chapter 7 in a stereoscope (or view them with crossed eyes) and wait for the smaller shape to emerge in depth. This is formed from two subsets of the random dot textures, but it has sharp edges. Why do these arise?

## REVERSED STEREOSCOPIC DEPTH

Once again, a simple stereoscope is required (notice the extemely interesting things one can observe using such simple apparatus). Take (or purchase) two stereoscopic photographs of a real scene. If doing your own photography simply take a picture, move the camera 12 cm (5 in) laterally, and take a second picture. When viewed in a stereoscope the pictures will induce the familiar illusion of stereoscopic depth. Now swap the pictures round. What is the nature of the depth you now see? Why doesn't the depth in real scenes ever reverse in this curious manner? How would you describe the nature of the stereoscopic depth reversal?

*References*: Shimojo and Nakajima (1981), Kalaugher (1987).

## SUBJECTIVE CONTOURS

First, a warning: very many researchers have tried to solve this one; none has yet succeeded. Look at Figure 10.2. Under the right conditions one becomes aware of lines joining the solid parts of the figures. It would be of great interest to know: (a) how these differ from real lines (lines which are objectively present), (b) what causes them, (c) why we don't experience more illusions of this sort in real life.

*Reference*: Kanizsa (1979).

## SILVER AND LUSTRE

What colour is silver? Is it anything other than a grey? If not, why doesn't it *look* grey? Using a gelatine filter, opaque masking tape, and an empty colour transparency, produce a display which will shine a blue circle of light onto a projection screen; the higher the intensity the better. Now attach a piece of blue paper to the screen and flood it with the blue light. What do you notice? Is this effect related to the appearance of silver objects?

*Reference*: any good text on colour vision, for example, Hurvich (1981).

Figure 10.2   Cognitive or subjective contours

## MOONLIGHT

Moonlight is supposed to be too weak to engage the cone mechanisms of the retina. Objects seen in moonlight should therefore seem achromatic. But watch a thin cloud pass in front of a full moon. Does there not seem to be some orange-brown tinting? How does this arise? This *mesopic* region of visual sensitivity has received relatively little research interest and might be worth further investigation.

*Reference*: look up *Photopic, Scotopic and Mesopic Vision* in any major text on vision.

## REVERSED FACES

Obtain a hollow mask of a face and place it so that the 'wrong' side is showing (that is, so that the face is concave). After a few moments a normally orientated face will be seen. That there is something not quite right about the display is revealed by swaying from side to side when the face's nose will appear to move the wrong way.

Think about the claim that perceptions are 'hypotheses' and then find a way of using other, less familiar, objects in an analogous manner to the reversed face display, to test this claim.

*Reference*: Gregory (1970).

THE DUCK-RABBIT FIGURE

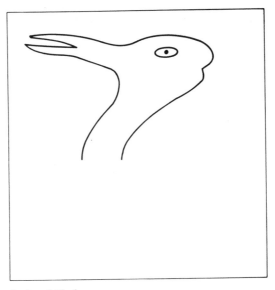

Figure 10.3    The duck–rabbit figure

This, by its nature, is more of a 'thought experiment' than the rest, as many readers will not have access to experimental animals. (Remember that there are strict rules governing the use of animals in research: if you tackle this problem experimentally, make sure that a licensed animal researcher is willing to supervise the work.) It is a tantalizing problem, however. My colleague Bob Brown first challenged me with it; no success to date, alas.

Figure 10.3 is the well-known duck–rabbit picture. It is of interest for several reasons, one being that a single stimulus array can induce two such clearly different percepts. Many people, on first exposure to the figure, see only one of the patterns. (Interestingly, if they are asked to memorize the figure they can do so and many can then draw an accurate version from memory. However, whilst the figure is in memory, it is almost impossible to spot its ambiguity, which may be saying something about the nature of mental representations.) For now though the challenge is a different one: how to demonstrate, with the greatest possible certainty, which of the two possible representations in the duck-rabbit figure is currently being seen *by an experimental animal*?

*Reference*: Neisser (1967).

All the effects so far can be induced quite easily in the laboratory, even the moonlight effect. The next three belong more closely to the real world.

## RESEMBLANCE AND STYLE

Things which are not identical can nevertheless look alike. It is often possible to see a distinct facial resemblance between a grandfather and his granddaughter. But just think of how many *differences* there must be between these two objects. How do we perform the extraordinary feat of seeing, at the same moment that the faces are (a) different, but (b) similar?

A related problem concerns the question of style. How is it that so many things from a particular era seem to have something in common: the period style? The cars, buildings, dresses and factories of the 1920s all seem to cohere in a subtle but unmistakable manner. Is this just because we have seen the artefacts of any period in conjunction; or is it that there is, truly, a zeitgeist which influences designs across such a range of different things. What *is* style?

*Reference*: O'Hare (1981)

## CONTRAST IN PAINTINGS

This is a topic which has received a lot of attention so that quite a lot is known about it. Nevertheless, the power of good paintings, in particular their ability to induce the feeling of looking into a real world, is not fully understood.

The problem is this. On a summer's day the differences in the brightnesses of objects may be enormous. White paper in direct sunlight may be reflecting over seven hundred times more light to the eye than a black or brown object in deep shade. Anyone who doubts this should spend an hour outdoors with a suitable light meter, preferably a photometer. But when one applies the same technique of measurement to the lightest and darkest regions of a picture, it will be found that the greatest possible range of reflectances is only about twenty to one. There is then a great discrepancy between the ratio of brightnesses one can be exposed to in the world and that which is available to artists. And yet artists can capture the experience of seeing bright sunlit scenes. The question is, how?

*References*: Pirenne (1970), Mills (1978).

## SYMBOLS

We live in a world of signs and symbols: patterns which indicate objects, events, and functions, often without actually resembling them. There is only a small direct link between red and danger (fire, blood) and yet red is universally adopted as a warning colour: 'do not' or 'take care' is what it is taken to mean. And we obey. In contrast, an arrow *does* seem to have a close resemblance to what it depicts: it would be hard to train ourselves to reverse it as a symbol and take the direction indicated to be that of the feathered end. International symbols for men and women (on lavatory doors, for example) have a naturalness which presumably springs from our familiarity with customary modes of dress in the Western world; it is however very difficult to understand why the motorway sign for Road Clear should consist of a rectangle and a single diagonal line.

The reader is invited to design a pair of new and compelling symbols. These should indicate, as unambiguously as possible, *whether a door should be pushed or pulled open*. Try to do this without using miniature representations of open doors.

*References*: modern texts on graphics for architectural use; texts on ergonomics; Arnheim (1969). The reader who becomes drawn into this sort of problem may wish to read more philosophical accounts in the field of *Semiology*. See Barthes (1984).

The next problem may not be solvable, but it is a good one to ponder.

## INSECTS' EYES

The typical insect eye is a multifaceted, compound structure. Much is known about the optics of these eyes, and the general conclusion is that they are just about as good as they could be, given the limitations imposed by their basic structure. That is to say, the performance of the eyes reaches limits set by the nature of light, just as in the case of the human eye (Chapter 2). But a compound eye must always be inferior to the simple, single lens eye found in vertebrates.

The problem, or rather the puzzle, is this: many insects live through a larval stage in which they have *simple* eyes of the form typically found in vertebrates. Why should evolution have led them to the adoption of the compound eye in their adult forms?

*Reference*: Land (1981).

The final group of problems involve modalities other than (or in addition to) vision. No apology is offered for this departure from the main topic of the book. The decision to restrict discussion to theories of visual perception was a logistic one; there are many fascinating problems and explanations associated with the other senses.

## WHEN IS SOMETHING UPSIDE DOWN?

Many years ago, as part of the nativist-empiricist debate, some investigators, notably Stratton (1897) attempted to see whether they could adapt to inverted vision. The (logically absurd) argument was that as the image on the retina is inverted, one must have learned to see this 'the right way up'. If this was so, then it might be possible to repeat this process of learning and thereby come to see an experimentally inverted world correctly. These dogged pioneers therefore wore inverting lens and mirror systems throughout their waking lives for periods of up to two weeks. Certainly they adapted: there is a famous film (having some of the charm of the early Laurel and Hardy) of one such pioneer, I. Kohler, actually riding a bicycle whilst wearing his cumbrous lens system. But did this demonstrate anything other than the ability to cope with unusual visual input? If we ask, did the world right itself then the observers' records are curiously vague.

But suppose the world *did* reinvert, would someone be able to describe what this was like? This is a more difficult problem than it first appears. It is analysed by Howard and Templeton (1966) who first suggested this intriguing experiment. Find a picture which is strongly 'mono-orientated'. That is, depicting an object which is normally seen only in one direction relative to gravity: for example, a church with a steeple, or a tree. Mount the picture upside-down on a vertical surface and lock the door. Now put your head between your legs and look at the picture. Does it look right way up?

Thinking about this will bring home with great clarity the whole problem of subjective reporting. It will induce the strange feeling of being on the edge of a problem which is both psychological and philosophical.

*Reference*: Howard and Templeton (1966)

## SALIVA

Does saliva have a taste?

## SMELL

Why do some metals smell?

There are enough problems in this chapter to last a lifetime. Many more will be suggested by the experimenting and by reading about the phenomema in the references cited. I shall be delighted to hear from any reader who thinks that he or she has found a solution to any problem. It will be touching to receive a small mention during the Nobel Prize ceremony. Good luck.

# References

Adrian, E.D. (1928). *The Basis of Sensation*. London: Christophers.

Ames, A. (1949). *The nature and origins of perceptions* (preliminary laboratory manual). Hanover, New Hampshire.: The Hanover Institute.

Arnheim, R. (1949). The Gestalt theory of expression. *Psychological Review*, **56**, 66–171.

Arnheim, R. (1956). *Art and Visual Perception*. London: Faber.

Arnheim, R. (1969). *Visual Thinking*. Berkeley: University of California Press.

Arnheim, R. (1984). Review of Deregowski, J.B., *Distortion in Art: the Eye and the Mind*. *Leonardo*, **4**, 302.

Bahnson, P. (1928). Eine Untersuchung über Symmetrie und Asymmetrie bei visuellen Wahrnehmungen. *Zeitschrift für Psychologie*, **108**, 129–154.

Barlow, H.B. (1953). Summation and inhibition in the frog's retina. *Journal of Physiology*. **119**, 69–88

Barlow, H.B. (1961). Comment on neural quanta. In W.A. Rosenblith (ed.), *Sensory Communication*. New York: Wiley.

Barthes, R. (1984). *Mythologies*. London: Paladin.

Bartlett, F.C. (1932). *Remembering*. Cambridge: Cambridge University Press.

Békèsy, G. von. (1930). Über das Fechner'sche Gesetz und seine Bedeutung für die Theorie der akustischen Beobachtungsfehler und die Theorie des Hörens. *Annalen für Physik*, **7**, 329–350.

Blackwell, H.R. (1953). Psychophysical thresholds: experimental studies of methods of measurement. *Bulletin of the Engineering Research Institute of the University of Michigan*, No. 6.

Blakemore, C. (1974).Developmental factors in the formation of feature extracting neurons. In F.G. Worden and F.O. Smith (eds), *The Neurosciences, 3rd study program*. Cambridge, Mass:M.I.T. Press.

Blakemore, C. and Campbell, F.W. (1969). On the existence of neurons in the human visual system sensitive to the orientation and size of retinal images. *Journal of Physiology*, **203**, 237–260.

Blakemore, C., and Cooper, G.F. (1970). Development of the brain depends on visual environment. *Science*, **228**, 287–478.

Blakemore, C. and Sutton, P. (1969). Size adaptation: A new after effect. *Science*, **166**, 245–247.

Boring, E.H. (1950). *A History of Experimental Psychology*. New York: Appleton-Century-Crofts.

Bornstein, M.H., Kessen, W. and Weiskopf, S. (1976). The categories of hue in infancy. *Science*, **191**, 201–202.

Bowmaker, J.K. and Dartnall, H.J.A. (1980). Visual pigments of rods and cones in a human retina. *Journal of Physiology* **398**, 501–511.

Broadbent, D.E. (1958). *Perception and Communication*. London: Pergamon.

Broadbent, D.E. (1985). A question of levels: comments on McClelland and Rumelhart. *Journal of Experimental Psychology: General*, **114**, 189–192.

Brown, R.W. and McNeill, D. (1966). The 'tip of the tongue' phenomenon. *Journal of Verbal Learning and Verbal Behaviour*, **5**, 55–337.

Brown, S.C. (ed.), (1974). *Philosophy of Psychology*, London: Macmillan.

Bruner, J.S. (1957). On perceptual readiness. *Psychological Review*, **64**, 123–152.

Bruner, J.S. and Goodman, C.C. (1947). Value and need as organizing factors in perception. *Journal of Abnormal and Social Psychology*, **42**, 33–44.

Bruner, J.S., Goodnow, J.J. and Austin, G.A. (1956). *A Study of Thinking*, New York: Wiley.

Bruner, J.S., Postman, L. and Rodrigues, J. (1951). Expectations and the perception of colour. *American Journal of Psychology*, **64**, 216–227.

Brunswik, E. (1938). Psychology as a science of objective relations. *Philosophy of Science*, **4**, 227–260.

Brunswik, E. (1939). Probability as a determiner of rat behavior. *Journal of Experimental Psychology*, **25**, 175–197.

Brunswik, E. (1944). Distal focussing of perception: size constancy in a representative sample of situations. *Psychological Monographs*, **254** (Whole number)

Brunswik, E. (1948). Statistical separation of perception, thinking and attitudes. *American Psychologist*, **3**, 342.

Brunswik, E. (1952). The conceptual framework of psychology. In *The International Encyclopaedia of Unified Science*, **1**, 10. Chicago: University of Chicago Press.

Brunswik, E. (1955). Representative design and probabilistic theory in a functional psychology. *Psychological Review*, **62**, 193–217.

Brunswik, E. (1956). *Perception and the Representative Design of Psychological Experiments*. Berkeley: University of California Press.

Brunswick, E. and Kamiya, J. (1953). Ecological cue-validity of 'proximity' and other Gestalt factors. *American Journal of Psychology*, **66**, 20–32.

Brunswik, E. and Reiter, L. (1938). Eindrucks-Charaktäre schematisierter Gesichter. *Zeitschrift für Psychologie*, **142**, 67–134.

Butterworth, G. (1983). Structure of the mind in human infancy. In Lipsitt, L.P. and Rovee-Collier, C.K. (eds), *Advances in Infancy Research*, Vol. 2. Norwood, New Jersey: Ablex.

Butterworth, G. (1988). Events and encounters in infancy. In Slater, A. and Bremner, G. (eds), *Infant Development*. London: Lawrence Erlbaum.

Campbell, F.W. and Robson, J.G.(1968). Application of Fourier analysis to the visibility of gratings. *Journal of Physiology*, **197**, 551–566.

Chalmers, A.F. (1982). *What is this thing called Science?* (2nd edition). London: Open University Press.

Chapman, C.R., Chen, A.C. and Bonica, J.J. (1977). Effects of intrasegmental electrical acupuncture on dental pain: an evaluation by threshold determination and sensory decision theory. *Pain*, **3**, 213–227.

Cherry, E.C. (1953). Some experiments on the recognition of speech with one and with two ears. *Journal of the Acoustical Society of America*, **25**, 975–979.

Chomsky, N. (1965). *Aspects of the Theory of Syntax*. Cambridge, Mass.: M.I.T. Press.

Churchland, P. (1984). *Matter and Consciousness*. Cambridge, Mass.: M.I.T. Press.

Clark, W.C. and Yang, J.C. (1974). Acupunctural analgesia? Evaluation by signal detection theory. *Science*, **184**, 1096–1098.

Clarke, F.R. (1960). Confidence ratings, second choice responses and confusion matrices in intelligibility tests. *Journal of the Acoustical Society of America*, **32**, 35–46.

Corso, J.F. (1970). *The Experimental Psychology of Sensory Behavior*. London: Holt, Rinehart & Winston.

Costall, A. (1981). On how so much information controls so much behaviour: James Gibson's theory of direct perception. In G. Butterworth (ed.), *Infancy and Epistemology*. Brighton: Harvester Press.

Costall, A. (1984). How meaning covers the traces. In N.H.Freeman and M. Cox (eds), *The Creation of Visual Order: Studies in the Development of Representational Skills*. Cambridge: University Press.

Costall, A. (1986). 'The Psychologis Fallacy' in ecocological realism. Teorie e Modelli, 3, 37–46.

Costall, A. and Still, A. (eds) (1987). *Cognitive Psychology in Question*. Brighton: Harvester Press.

Creelman, C.D. (1962). Human discrimination of auditory duration. *Journal of the Acoustical Society of America*, 34, 582–593.

Cutting, J. (1982). Blowing in the wind: perceiving structure in trees and bushes. *Cognition*, 12, 25–44.

Dartnall, H.J.A., Bowmaker, J.K. and Mollon, J.D. (1983). Human visual pigments: results from microspectroscopic results from the eyes of seven persons. *Proceedings of the Royal Society of London, Series B*, 220, 115–130.

Day, R.H. and Power, R.P. (1965). Apparent reversal (oscillation) of rotary motion in depth: an investigation and a general theory. *Psychological Review*, 72, 117–127.

DeCasper, A.J. and Fifer, W.P. (1980). Of human bonding: newborns prefer their mother's voices. *Science*, 208, 1174–1176.

DeCillis, O.E. (1944). Absolute thresholds for the perception of tactual movement. *Archives of Psychology*, 294, 1–52.

DeValois, R.L. (1960). Color vision mechanisms in monkey. *Journal of General Physiology*, 43, 115–128.

Dixon, N.F. (1981). *Preconscious Processing*. Chichester: Wiley.

Dreyfus, H.L. (1972). *What Computers Can't Do: a Critique of Artificial Reason*. New York: Harper and Row.

Dreyfus, H.L. and Dreyfus, S.E. (1985). *Mind Over Machine*. New York: Macmillan.

Dziurawiec, S. and Ellis, H.D. (1986). Neonates' attention to face-like stimuli: Goren, Sarty and Wu (1975) revisited. Paper presented at the Annual Conference of the Developmental Section of the British Psychological Society, University of Exeter, September 1986.

Earle, D. (1985). Perception of Glass pattern structure with stereopsis. *Perception*, 14, 545–552.

Ehrenfels, von C. (1890). Über Gestaltqualitäten. *Vierteljahresschr. für Philosophie*, 14.

Eijkman, E. and Vendrik, A.J.H. (1963). Detection theory applied to the absolute sensitivity of sensory systems. *Biophysics Journal*, 3, 65–77.

Ekman, P. (1971). Universals and cultural differences in facial expressions of emotion. *Nebraska symposium on Motivation*, 207–283.

Ekman, P. and Friesen, W.V. (1967). Origin, usage and coding: the basis for five categories of nonverbal behavior. Paper presented at the Symposium on Communication Theory and Linguistic Models. Buenos Aires: Nueva Vision.

Ekman, P. and Friesen, W.V. (1971). Constants across cultures in the face and emotion. *Journal of Personality and Social Psychology*, 17, 124–129.

Ellis, W.D. (ed). (1938). *A Source Book of Gestalt Psychology*. London: Routledge & Kegan Paul.

Engen, T. (1971). Psychophysics 2. In J.W. Kling and L.A.Riggs (eds), *Woodworth and Schlosberg's Experimental Psychology*. London: Methuen.

Fechner, G.T. (1860). *Elemente der Psychophysik*. Leipzig: Breitkopf and Hartel.

English translation of volume 1 by H.E.Adler (1966). New York: Holt, Rinehart & Winston.

Fodor, J.A. and Pylyshyn, Z.W. (1988). Connectionism and Cognitive Architecture: a critical analysis. *Cognition* (to appear).

Frisby, J.P. (1979). *Seeing*. Oxford: Oxford University Press.

Galanter, E.H. (1962). Contemporary Psychophysics. In *New Directions in Psychology*. New York: Holt, Rinehart & Winston.

Gibson, E.J. (1982). The concept of affordances in development: the renascence of functionalism. In Collins, W.A. (ed.), *The Concept of Development. The Minnesota Symposia on Child Psychology*, **15**, 55–81.

Gibson, J.J. (1979). *The Ecological Approach to Visual Perception*. Boston: Houghton Mifflin.

Gibson, J.J. (1950). *The Perception of the Visual World*. Boston: Houghton Mifflin.

Gibson, J.J. (1951). What is a form? *Psychological Review*, **58**, 403–412.

Gibson, J.J.(1961). Ecological Optics. *Vision Research*, **1**, 253–262.

Gibson, J.J. (1966). *The Senses Considered as Perceptual Systems*. Boston: Houghton Mifflin.

Gibson, J.J. (1967a). New reasons for Realism. *Syntheses*, **17**, 162–172.

Gibson, J.J. (1967b). Autobiography. In Boring, E.G. and Lindzey, G. (eds), *History of Psychology in Autobiography*. New York: Irvington.

Gibson, J.J. (1971a). A preliminary description and classification of Affordances. Unpublished manuscript reproduced in E. Reed and R. Jones (eds), (1982) *Reasons for Realism*. Hillsdale, New Jersey: Lawrence Earlbaum Associates.

Gibson, J.J. (1971b). The information available in pictures. *Leonardo*, **4**, 27–35.

Gibson, J.J. (1973). On the concept of 'formless invariants' in visual perception. *Leonardo*, **6**, 43–45.

Gibson, J.J. (1976). The myth of passive perception: a reply to Richards. *Philosophy and Phenomenological Research*, **37**, 234–238.

Gibson, J.J. (1977). *The theory of affordances*. In R.E. Shaw and J. Bransford (eds), *Perceiving, Acting and Knowing*. Hillsdale, New Jersey: Lawrence Erlbaum Associates.

Gibson, J.J. (1979). *The Ecological Approach to Visual Perception*. Boston: Houghton-Mifflin.

Gilchrist, A.L. and Jacobsen, A. (1983). Lightness constancy through a veiling luminance. *Journal of Experimental Psychology: Human Perception and Performance*, **9**, 936–944.

Glass, L. (1969). Moiré effect from random dots. *Nature*, **223**, 578–580.

Gordon, I.E., Zukas, M. and Chan, J. (1982). Responses to schematic faces: a cross-cultural study. *Perceptual and Motor Skills*, **54**, 201–202.

Goren, C.C., Sarty, M. and Wu, P.Y.K. (1975). Visual following and pattern discrimination of face-like stimuli by newborn infants. *Pediatrics*, **59**, 544–549.

Gould, S.J. (1980). *The Panda's Thumb*. London: Penguin.

Granrund, C.E., Yonas, A., Smith, I.M., Arterberry, M.E., Glicksmman, M.L. and Sorkness, A.C. (1984). Infants' sensitivity to accretion and deletion of texture as information for depth at an edge. *Child Development*, **55**, 1630–1636.

Gregory, R.L. (1961). The brain as an engineering problem. In Thorpe, W.H. and Zangwill, O.L., *Current Problems in Animal Behaviour*. Cambridge: Cambridge University Press.

Gregory, R.L. (1963). Distortions of space as inappropriate constancy scaling. *Nature*, **199**, 678–680.

Gregory, R.L. (1970). *The Intelligent Eye*. New York: McGraw-Hill.

Gregory, R.L. (1974). Perceptions as hypotheses. Chapter 9 in S.C. Brown (ed.), (1974). *Philosopy of Psychology*. London: Macmillan.

Gregory, R.L. (1980a). Perceptions as hypotheses. *Philosophical Transactions of the Royal Society of London*, **B. 290**, 181–197.

Gregory, R.L. (1980b). Choosing a paradigm for perception. In E.C. Carterette and M.P. Friedman (eds), *Handbook of Perception*. Vol 1. New York: Academic Press.

Gregory, R.L. and Wallace, J.G. (1963). *Recovery From Early Blindness: a Case Study*. Experimental Psychology Society Monograph Number 2. Cambridge: W. Heffer & Son.

Grindley, C.G. and Townsend, V. (1965). Binocular masking induced by a moving object. *Quarterly Journal of Experimental Psychology*, **117**, 97–109.

Gross, C.G., Rocha-Miranda, C.E. and Bender, D.B. (1972). Visual properties of neurons in inferotemporal cortex of the macaque. *Journal of Neurophysiology*, **35**, 96–111.

Grossberg, G.M. and Grant, B.F. (1978). Classical psychophysics: applications of ratio scaling and signal detection methods to research on pain, fear, drugs, and medical decision making. *Psychological Bulletin*, **85**, 1154–1176.

Haber, R.N. (1980). In M.A. Hagen (ed.), *The Perception of Pictures* (2 vols). New York: Academic Press.

Haber, R.N. and Hershenson, M. (1980). *The Psychology of Visual Perception*. New York: Holt, Reinhart & Winston.

Hagen, M.A. (1986) *Varieties of Realism*. New York: Cambridge University Press.

Hammond, K.R. (ed.) (1966). *The Psychology of Egon Brunswik*. New York: Holt, Reinhart & Winston.

Hartline, H.K. (1938). The response of single optic nerve fibres of the vertebrate eye to illumination of the retina. *American Journal of Physiology*, **121**, 400–415.

Hartline, H.K. (1940). The receptive field of the optic nerve fibres. *American Journal of Physiology*, **130**, 690–699.

Hearnshaw, L.S. (1984) *A Short History of British Psychology 1840–1940*. London: Methuen.

Hebb, D.O. (1949). *The Organization of Behaviour*. New York: Wiley.

Helmholtz, H. von (1924–1925). *Helmholtz's Physiological Optics*. Translated from the third edition (1909–1911) by J.P.Southwell (ed.), Rochester, New York: Optical Society of America.

Helson, H. and Kosaki, A. (1968). Anchor effects using numerical estimates of simple dot patterns. *Perception and Psychophysics*, **4**, 163–164.

Henle, M. (1984). Isomorphism: setting the record straight. *Psychological Research*, **46**, 317–327.

Hering, E. (1890). Beitrag zur Lehre vom Simultankontrast. *Zeitschrift für Psychologie und Physiologie der Sinnesorgane*, **1**, 18–28.

Hess, E.H. (1965). Attitude and pupil size. *Scientific American*, **212**, 46–54.

Hess, E.H. (1975). The role of pupil size in communication. *Scientific American*, **222**, 110–119.

Hochberg, J.E. (1968). In the mind's eye. In R.N. Haber (ed.), *Contemporary Theory and Research in Visual Perception*. New York: Holt, Rinehart & Winston.

Hochberg, J.E. (1973). Organization and the Gestalt tradition. In Carterette, E. and Friedman, M. (eds), *Handbook of Perception*, Vol. 1. New York: Academic Press.

Hochberg, J. E. (1971). Perception. In L.A. Riggs and J.W. Kling, (eds), *Woodworth and Schlosberg's Experimental Psychology*, 3rd edition, New York: Holt, Rinehart & Winston.

Hofsten, C. von (1983). Foundations for perceptual development. In Lipsitt, L.P. and

Rovee-Collier, C.K. (eds), *Advances in Infancy Research, Vol.2*, Norwood, New Jersey: Ablex.

Horn, B.K.P.(1974). Determining lightness from an image. *Computer Graphics and Image Processing*, **3**, 277–299.

Howard, I. and Templeton, W.B. (1966). *Human Spatial Orientation*, Chichester: Wiley.

Hubel, D.H. and Wiesel, T.N. (1962). Receptive fields, binocular interaction and functional architecture in the cat's visual cortex. *Journal of Physiology*, **166**, 106–154.

Hubel, D.H. and Wiesel, T.N. (1968). Receptive fields and functional architecture of the monkey striate cortex. *Journal of Physiology*, **195**, 215–243.

Hubel, D.H. and Wiesel, T.W. (1977). Functional architecture of macaque monkey visual cortex. *Proceedings of the Royal Society of London*, **198**, 1–59.

Hurvich, L.M. (1981). *Color Vision*. Sunderland, Ma: Sinauer.

James, W. (1890). *Principles of Psychology*. New York: Holt.

Jerome, E.A. (1942). Olfactory thresholds measured in terms of stimulus pressure and volume. *Archives of Psychology*, **274**, 1–44.

Johansson, G. (1950). *Configurations in Event Perception.* Stockholm: Almqvist & Wiksell.

Johansson, G. (1964). Perception of motion and changing form. *Scandinavian Journal of Psychology*, **5**, 181–208.

Johansson, G. (1977). Spatial constancy and motion in visual perception. In W.Epstein (ed.), *Stability and Constancy in Visual Perception*. New York: Wiley.

Judd, D.B. (1951). Basic correlates of the visual stimulus. Chapter 22 in Stevens, S.S., *Handbook of Experimental Psychology*. New York: Wiley.

Julesz, B. (1960). Binocular depth perception of computer generated patterns. *Bell System technical journal*, **39**, 1125–1162.

Julesz, B. (1971). *Foundations of Cyclopean Perception*. Chicago: Univeristy of Chicago Press.

Julesz, B. (1981). Textons, the elements of of texture perception and their interactions. *Nature*, **290**, 91–97.

Kalaugher, P. (1987). Pseudoscopic viewing: transfer and persistence of reversed depth relations from the viewing of photographs to the real scene. *Perception*, **16**, 359–374.

Kanizsa, G. (1979). *Organization in Vision: Essays on Gestalt Perception*, New York: Praeger.

Katz, S. (1987) Is Gibson a Realist? In Costall, A. and Still, A. (d) *Cognition Psychology in Question*. Brighton: Harvester Press.

Katz, D. (1951). *Gestalt Psychology*. London: Methuen.

Kaufman, L. (1974). *Sight and Mind: an Introduction to Visual Perception*. New York: Oxford University Press.

Kelley, G.A. (1955). *The Psychology of Personal Constructs*. New York: Norton.

Kennedy, J.M. (1974). *A Psychology of Picture Perception*. San Francisco: Jossey-Bass.

Koffka, K. (1915). Reply to Benussi. Reprinted in W.D. Ellis (ed.) (1929). *A Source Book of Gestalt Psychology*. New York: Humanities Press.

Koffka, K. (1924). *The Growth of the Mind*. London: Routledge & Kegan Paul.

Koffka, K. (1935). *Principles of Gestalt Psychology*. New York: Harcourt Brace.

Kohler, I. (1955) Experiments with prolonged optical distortion. *Acta Psychologica*, **11**, 176–178.

Köhler, W. (1920). *Physical Gestalten*. Reprinted in W.D. Ellis (ed.) (1929). *A Source Book of Gestalt Psychology*. New York: Humanities Press.

Köhler,W. (1925). Reply to G.E.Müller. Reprinted in W.D.Ellis (ed.) (1929). *A Source Book of Gestalt Psychology*. New York: Humanities Press.

Köhler, W. (1940). *Dynamics in Psychology*. New York: Liveright.

Köhler, W. (1947). *Gestalt Psychology*. New York: Liveright.

Kuffler, S.W. (1953). Discharge patterns and functional organization of mammalian retina. *Journal of Neurophysiology*, 16, 37–68.

Kuhn, T.S. (1970). *The Nature of Scientific Revolution*. (2nd ed). Chicago: University of Chicago Press.

Külpe, O. (1904). Versuche über Abstraktion. *Berlin International Congress of Experimental Psychology*, 56–68.

Land, E.H. (1985). Recent advances in Retinex theory. *Vision Research*, 26, 7–21.

Land, E.H. and McCann, J.J. (1971). Lightness and retinex theory. *Journal of the Optical Society of America*, 61, 1–11.

Land, M.F. (1981). *Optics and vision in invertebrates*. In Autram, H. (ed.), *Handbook of Sensory Physiology*. Vol.7/6B. New York: Springer.

Lashley, K.S. (1950). In search of the engram. *Symposium of the Society of Experimental Biology*, 4, 454–482.

Lazarus, R.S. and McCleary, R.A. (1951). Autonomic discrimination without awareness: a study in subception. *Psychological Review*, 58, 113–122.

Lee, D.N. and Lishman, J.R. (1975). Visual proprioceptive control of stance. *Journal of Human Movement Studies*, 1, 87–95.

Leeper, R.W. (1966) A critical consideration of Egon Brunswik's Probabilistic Functionalism. In Hammond, K.R. (ed.) New York: Holt, Rinehart & Winston.

Lettvin, J.Y., Maturana, H.R., McCulloch, W.S. and Pitts, W.H. (1959). What the frog's eye tells the frog's brain. *Proceedings of the Institute of Radio Engineering*, 47, 1940–1951.

Lipsitt, L.P. and Rovee-Collier, C.K. (eds) (1983). *Advances in Infancy Research*, Vol.2, Norwood, New Jersey: Ablex.

Luce, R.D. (1960). Detection thresholds: a problem reconsidered. *Science*, 132, 1495.

Ludel, J. (1978). *Introduction to Sensory Processes*. San Francisco: W.H. Freeman.

MacLeod, R.B. and Pick, H.L. (eds) (1974). *Perception: Essays in Honour of James J. Gibson*. Ithaca, N.Y.: Cornell University Press.

MacNichol, E. (1964). Three-pigment color vision. *Scientific American*, 211, 48–56.

Marr, D. (1982). *Vision* San Francisco: W.H.Freeman.

Marr, D. and Hildreth, E. (1980). Theory of edge detection. *Proceedings of the Royal Society of London*, B 207, 187–217.

Marr, D. and Poggio, T. (1976). Cooperation computation of stereo disparity. *Science*, 194, 283–287.

Marr, D. and Poggio, T. (1979). A computational theory of human stereo vision. *Proceedings of the Royal Society of London*, B 204, 301–328).

Maturana, H.R., Lettvin, J.Y., McCulloch, W.S. and Pitts, W.H. (1960). Anatomy and physiology of vision in the frog (Rana pipens). *Journal of General Physiology*, 43, 129–176.

Mayhew, J.E.W. and Frisby, J.P (1981). Psychophysical and computational studies towards a theory of human stereopsis. *Artificial Intelligence*, 17, 349–385.

McClelland, J.L., Rumelhart, D.E. and Hinton, G.E. (1986). The appeal of Parallel Distributed Processing. In Rumelhart, D.E. and McClelland, J.L. (eds), *Parallel Distributed Processing*. Cambridge, Mass.: M.I.T. Press.

McCollough, C. (1965). Color adaptation of edge detectors in the human visual system. *Science*, 149, 1115–1116.

McGinnies, E. (1949). Emotionality and perceptual defense. *Psychological Review*, 56, 244–251.

Mehler, J. and Fox, R. (1985). *Neonate Cognition: Beyond the Blooming Buzzing Con-*

*fusion*. Hillsdale, New Jersey: Lawrence Erlbaum.

Michaels, C.F. and Carello, C. (1981). *Direct Perception*. Englewood Cliffs, New Jersey: Prentice-Hall.

Michotte, A. (1946). *La Perception de la Causalité*. Louvain: Institut Supérieur de Philosophie.

Miller, G.A. (1964). *Psychology, the Science of Mental Life*. London: Hutchinson.

Mills, A.A. (1978). Intensity-modulated illumination of paintings and an unexpected 3-dimensional effect. *Leonardo*, **11**, 213.

Minsky, M. and Papert, S. (1969). *Perceptrons*. Cambridge, Mass.: M.I.T. Press.

Morgan, M.J. (1977). *Molyneux's question: vision, touch and the philosophy of perception*. Cambridge: Cambridge University Press.

— Morgan, M.J. (1984). Computational Theories of Vision. (Review of Marr) *Quarterly Journal of Experimental Psychology*, **36A**, 157–165.

Neisser, U. (1967). *Cognitive Psychology*. New York: Appleton-Century-Crofts.

Neisser, U. (1976). *Cognition and Reality*. San Francisco: W.H. Freeman.

Noble, W.G. (1981) Gibsonian theory and the Pragmatist perspective. *Journal for the Theory of Social Behaviour*, **11**, 65–85.

O'Hare, D. (1981). *Psychology and the Arts*. Brighton: Harvester Press.

Pantle, A. and Sekuler, R.W. (1968). Contrast response of human visual mechanisms to orientation and detection of velocity. *Vision Research*, **9**, 397–406.

Penrose, L.S. and Penrose, R. (1958). Impossible figures: a special type of illusion. *British Journal of Psychology*, **49**, 31–33.

Petermann, B. (1932). *The Gestalt Theory and the Problem of Configuration*. London: Kegan Paul, Trench & Trubner.

Petrinovich, L. (1979). Probabilistic functionalism: a conception of research method. *American Psychologist*, **34**, 373–390.

Piaget, J. (1967). *Six Psychological Studies*. New York: Random House.

Pirenne, M.H. (1970). *Optics Painting and Photography*. Cambridge: Cambridge University Press.

Pittenger, J.B. and Shaw, R.E. (1975). Perception of relative and absolute age in facial photographs. *Perception and Psychopysics*, **18**, 137–143.

Pittenger, J.B., Shaw, R.E. and Mark, L.S. (1979). Perceptual information for the age level of faces as a higher-order invariance of growth. *Journal of Experimental Psychology: Human Perception and Performance*, **5**, 137–143.

Popper, K.R. (1960). *Conjectures and Refutations: the Growth of Scientific Knowledge*. London: Routledge & Kegan Paul.

Porter, P.B. (1954). Find the hidden man. *American Journal of Psychology*, **67**, 550–551.

Poulton, E.C. (1968). The new psychophysics: six models for magnitude estimation. *Psychological Bulletin*, **69**, 1–19.

— Pradham, P.L. and Hoffman, P.J. (1963). Effect of spacing and range of stimuli on magnitude estimation judgements. *Journal of Experimental Psychology*, **66**, 533–541.

Quine, W.V. and Ullian, J.S. (1970). *The Web of Belief*. New York: Random House.

Reed, E. (1982) Descartes' corporeal ideas hypothesis and the origin of scientific psychology. *Review of Metaphysics*, **35**, 731–752.

Reed, E. and Jones, R. (eds) (1982). *Reasons for Realism. Selected Essays of James J. Gibson*. Hillsdale, New Jersey: Lawrence Erlbaum Associates.

Reed, E.S. (1987). James Gibson's ecological approach to cognition. In Costall, A. and Still, A. (eds), *Cognitive Psychology in Question*. Brighton: Harvester Press.

Restle, F. (1979). Coding theory of the perception of motion configuration. *Psychological Review*, **86**, 1–24.

Rogers, S. and Costall, A. (1983). On the horizon: picture perception and Gibson's concept of information. *Leonardo*, **16**, 180–182.

Rosenblatt, F. (1959). Two theorems of statistical separabilty. In *Mechanisation of Thought Processes: Proceedings of a symposium held at the National Physical Laboratory, November 1958*, Vol 1. London: H.M. Stationery Office.

Rubin, E. (1915). *Synsoplevede Figurer*. Copenhagen: Glyndendalska.

Rumelhart, D.E. and McClelland, J.L. (1986). *Parallel Distributed Processing*. Cambridge, Mass.: M.I.T. Press.

Rumelhart, D.E., Hinton, G.E. and McClelland, J.L. (1986). A general framework for Parallel Distributed Processing. In Rumelhart, D.E. and McClelland, J.L. (eds), *Parallel Distributed Processing*. Cambridge, Mass.: M.I.T. Press.

Rushton, W.A. (1964). Colour blindness and cone pigments. *American Journal of Optometry and Archives of the American Academy of Optometry*, **41**, 265–282.

Russell, J. (1984). *Explaining Mental Life*. London: Macmillan.

Sanford, R.H. (1936). The effects of abstinence from food upon imaginal processes: a preliminary experiment. *Journal of Psychology*, **2**, 129–136.

Sedgwick, H.A. (1980). The geometry of spatial layout in pictorial representation. Chapter 2 in M.Hagen (ed.), *The Perception of Pictures*, Vol 1. New York: Academic Press.

Sekuler, R. and Blake, R. (1985). *Perception*. New York: A.A. Knopf.

Selfridge, O.G. (1959). Pandemonium: a paradigm for learning. In *The Mechanisms of Thought Processes*. London: H.M. Stationery Office.

Selfridge, O.G. and Neisser, U. (1960). Pattern recognition by machine. *Scientific American*, **203**, 60–68.

von Senden, M. (1960). *Space and sight*. London: Methuen.

Shannon, C.E. (1948). A mathematical theory of communication. *Bell Systems Technical Journal*, **27**, 379–425.

Shaw, R. and Bransford, J. (eds) (1977). *Perceiving, Acting, and Knowing: toward an ecological psychology*. Hillsdale, New Jersey: Lawrence Erlbaum Associates.

Shaw, R.E., McIntyre, M. and Mace, W. (1974). The role of symmetry in event perception. In MacLeod, R. and Pick, H.(eds), *Perception: Essays in honour of James J. Gibson*. Ithaca, New York: Cornell University Press.

Shaw, R.E., Turvey, M.T. and Mace, W. (1981). Ecological psychology: the consequences of a commitment to realism. In W. Weiner and D.Palermo (eds), *Cognition and the Symbolic Process*. (Vol 2). Hillsdale, New Jersey: Lawrence Earlbaum Associates.

Shimojo, S. and Nakajima, Y. (1981). Adaptation to the reversal of binocular depth cues: effects of wearing left-right reversing spectacles on stereoscopic depth perception. *Perception*, **10**, 391–402.

Simon, H.A. and Newell, A. (1958). Heuristic problem solving: the advance in operations research. *Operations Research*, **6**, 6.

Skowbo, D., Timney, B.N., Gentry, T.A. and Morant, R.B. (1975). McCollough effects: experimental findings and theoretical accounts. *Psychological Bulletin*, **82**, 497–510.

Slater, A. and Morison, V. (1985). Shape constancy and slant perception at birth. *Perception*, **14**, 337–344.

Sommer, R. (1959). The new look on the witness stand. *The Canadian Psychologist*, **8**, 94–99.

Spence, K.W. (1956). *Behavior Theory and Conditioning*. New Haven: Yale University Press.

Sperry, R.W. (1951). Mechanisms of neural maturation. In S.S.Stevens (ed.), *Handbook of Experimental Psychology*. New York: Wiley.

Sperry, R.W. and Miner, W. (1955). Pattern perception following insertion of mica plates into visual cortex. *Journal of Comparative and Physiological Psychology*, **48**, 463–469.

Sperry, R.W., Miner, W. and Meyers, R.E. (1955). Visual pattern perception following subpial string and tantalum wire implantations in the visual cortex. *Journal of Comparative and Physiological Psychology*, **48**, 50–58.

Staniland, A. (1966). *Patterns of Redundancy*. Cambridge: Cambridge University Press.

Stevens, K.A. (1978). Computation of locally parallel structure. *Biological Cybernetics*, **29**, 19–28.

Stevens, S.S. (1957). On the psychophysical law. *Psychological Review*, **64**, 153–181.

Stevens, S.S. (1959). Cross-modal validation of subjective scales for loudness, vibration, and electric shock. *Journal of Experimental Psychology*, **57**, 201–209.

Stevens, S.S. (1961). The psychophysics of sensory function. In W.A. Rosenblith (ed.), *Sensory Communication* New York: Wiley.

Stevens, S.S. (1962). The surprising simplicity of sensory metrics. *American Psychologist*, **17**, 29–39.

Stevens, S.S. and Galanter, E.H. (1957). Ratio scales and category scales for a dozen perceptual continua. *Journal of Experimental Psychology*, **54**, 377–411.

Stevens, S.S., Morgan, C.T. and Volkmann, J. (1941). Theory of the neural quantum in the discrimination of loudness and pitch. *American Journal of Psychology*, **54**, 315–335.

Stratton, G. (1897). Vision without inversion of the retinal image. *Psychological Review*, **4**, 341–360.

Sutherland, N.S. (1957). Visual discrimination of shape by octopus. *British Journal of Psychology*, **48**, 55–70.

Svaetichin, G. (1956). Spectral response curves from single cones. *Acta Physiologica Scandinavica Supplementum*, **134**, 17–46.

Svaetichin, G. and MacNichol, E.F. (1958). Retinal mechanisms for achromatic vision. *Annals of the New York Academy of Sciences*, **74**, 385–404.

Swets, J.A. (ed) (1964). *Signal Detection and Recognition by Human Observers*. New York: Wiley.

Swets, J.A. (1973). The receiver operating characteristic in psychology. *Science*, **182**, 990–1000.

Tanner, W.P. and Swets, J.A. (1954). A decision-making theory of visual detection. *Psychological Review*, **61**, 401–409.

Tanner, W.P., Swets, J.A. and Green, D.M. (1956). Some general properties of the hearing mechanism. *University of Michigan Electronic Defence Group Technical Report* No. 30.

Thompson, R.F. (1967). *Foundations of Physiological Psychology*. New York: Harper and Row.

Thorpe, W.H. and Zangwill, O.L. (eds) (1961). *Current Problems in Animal Behaviour*. Cambridge: Cambridge University Press.

Tinbergen, N. (1951). *The Study of Instinct*. London: Oxford University Press.

Titchener, E.B. (1901). *Experimental Psychology: a Manual of Laboratory Practice*. New York: Macmillan.

Todd, J.T., Mark, L.S., Shaw, R.E. and Pittenger, J.B. (1980). The perception of human growth. *Scientific American*, **242** (2), 132–144.

Treisman, M. (1964). What do sensory scales measure? *Quarterly Journal of Experimental Psychology*, **16**, 383–385.

Turvey, M.T. (1977). Contrasting orientations to the theory of visual information processing. *Psychological Review*, **84**, 67–88.

Uhr, L. (1963). Pattern recognition computers as models for form perception. *Psychological Bulletin*, **60**, 40–73.

Ullman, S. (1979). *The Interpretation of Visual Motion*. Cambridge, Mass.: M.I.T. Press.

Ullman, S. (1980). Against Direct Perception. *The Behavioural and Brain Sciences*, **3** (whole issue).

Valvo, A. (1971). *Sight Restoration After Long-Term Blindness: the Problems and Behavior Patterns of Visual Rehabilitation*. New York: American Foundation for the Blind.

Wald, A. (1950). *Statistical Decision Functions*. New York: Wiley.

Walls, G.L. (1942). *The Vertebrate Eye and its Adaptive Radiation*. Birmingham, Michigan: Cranbrook Institute of Science.

Weber, E. (1846). Der Tastsinn und das Gemeingefühl. In E.Wagner (ed.), *Handwörterbuch der Physiologie*, **3**, 481–588.

Wells, G.L., Lindsay, R.C.L. and Ferguson, T.J. (1979). Accuracy, confidence and juror perceptions in eyewitness identification. *Journal of Applied Psychology*, **64**, 440–448.

Wertheimer, M. (1912). Experimental studies on the seeing of motion. Reprinted in T. Shipley (1961). *Classics in Psychology*. New York: Philosophical Library.

Wertheimer, M.(1923). Untersuchungen zur Lehre von der Gestalt, 2, *Psychologische Forschung*, **4**, 301–350. (Republished in Ellis, W.D. (ed) (1938). *A Source Book of Gestalt Psychology*. London: Routledge & Kegan Paul.)

— Winograd, T. amd Flores, F. (1986) *Understanding Computers and Cognition*. Norwood, New Jersey: Ablex Publishing Co.

Woodworth, R.S. and Schlosberg, H. (1955). *Experimental Psychology*. (3rd edition). London: Methuen.

Wulff, F. (1922). Über die Veränderung von Vorstellungen (Gedächtnis und Gestalt). *Psychologische Forschung*, **1**, 333–373.

# Author index

# Subject index